No Alternative

Book Forty-four
Louann Atkins Temple Women & Culture Series
Books about women and families, and their changing role in society

No Alternative

Childbirth, Citizenship, and
Indigenous Culture in Mexico

ROSALYNN A. VEGA

University of Texas Press ◆ *Austin*

The Louann Atkins Temple Women & Culture Series is supported by Allison, Doug, Taylor, and Andy Bacon; Margaret, Lawrence, Will, John, and Annie Temple; Larry Temple; the Temple-Inland Foundation; and the National Endowment for the Humanities.

Requests for permission to reproduce material from this work should be sent to:
    Permissions
    University of Texas Press
    P.O. Box 7819
    Austin, TX 78713-7819
    utpress.utexas.edu/rp-form

♾ The paper used in this book meets the minimum requirements of ANSI/NISO Z39.48-1992 (R1997) (Permanence of Paper).

Library of Congress Cataloging-in-Publication Data
Names: Vega, Rosalynn A., author.
Title: No alternative : childbirth, citizenship, and indigenous culture in Mexico / Rosalynn A. Vega.
Description: First edition. | Austin : University of Texas Press, 2018. | Includes bibliographical references and index.
Identifiers: LCCN 2017049902
    ISBN 978-1-4773-1676-4 (cloth : alk. paper)
    ISBN 978-1-4773-1677-1 (pbk. : alk. paper)
    ISBN 978-1-4773-1678-8 (library e-book)
    ISBN 978-1-4773-1679-5 (non-library e-book)
Subjects: LCSH: Childbirth—Social aspects—Mexico. | Maternal health services—Mexico. | Women—Mexico—Social conditions. | Indigenous women—Mexico—Social conditions. | Discrimination in medical care—Mexico. | Birth customs—Mexico. | Natural childbirth—Mexico. | Midwives—Mexico.
Classification: LCC RG518.M6 V44 2018 | DDC 362.198200972—dc23
LC record available at https://lccn.loc.gov/2017049902

doi:10.7560/316764

For Rikin, the person who makes my every day extraordinary.

For our parents, whose immense love and sacrifice paved the way.

Contents

List of Illustrations

Acknowledgments

I am grateful to mentors at UC Berkeley and UC San Francisco for shaping me as a scholar and guiding me through the early stages of writing this book. Throughout my graduate career, Charles L. Briggs urged me to challenge established frames of reference, deconstruct binaries, and begin "as if I know nothing." With his encouragement, I embraced "border thinking" (thus traversing disciplinary, sub-disciplinary, and geospatial boundaries) and engaged in binational production of discourse with both US and Mexican scholars. My present ethnographic writing was cultivated and galvanized by Nancy Scheper-Hughes. Her close accompaniment throughout the writing process inspired me to weave stories in a way that provocatively advances the goals of public anthropology, boldly intervenes in ongoing theoretical debates, and does justice to my informants. Charis Thompson provided me with interdisciplinary perspectives on intersectionality, thus signaling spaces in my work for deeper critique of interpenetrating class, race, and gender inequalities. Ian Whitmarsh has helped me think about how a plurality of ethnic identities is transformed into a science of race, as well as how biologic race is contested by practices around nation, state, and family. I am also thankful to my "writing partner" during this time, James Battle, for being a consistent source of motivation and inspiration.

I am also indebted to my colleagues and friends in Mexico, without whom this book would never have been completed. Eduardo Menéndez at the Center for Superior Research and Studies in Social Anthropology (CIESAS) served as a generous and stimulating mentor during my time as a visiting scholar in the Permanent Seminar in Medical Anthropology (SEPAM). By inviting me to teach courses in the medical school and health sciences graduate program at the National Autonomous University of

Mexico (UNAM), Alfredo Paulo Maya and Roberto Campos welcomed me into a vibrant scholarly community that assisted me in matching the content of my theory with the content of my ethnography. Ongoing dialogue throughout the writing process with members of the health sciences graduate program at UNAM has been a formative influence for this present work.

At the University of Texas Rio Grande Valley, I appreciate the support, guidance, and mentorship of Margaret Graham and Margaret Dorsey. In addition, I revised the manuscript for this book with the moral support of Marci McMahon and Marisa Palacios-Knox as we wrote in silent solidarity.

I am profoundly grateful to the funding agencies and fellowships that allowed me to pursue doctoral research: the Jacob K. Javits Fellowship, UC Regents Fellowship, UC Human Rights Center, UC Global Health Institute, UC Institute for Mexico and the United States, UC Berkeley School of Public Health (specifically Dan and Susan Lindheim as stewards of the Roselyn Lindheim Award), and the Ford Foundation.

I have also enjoyed wonderful editorial guidance from the University of Texas Press. Casey Kittrell has supported my scholarship and this book project since the early stages of writing. This book was strengthened by the close reading of two expert readers. Their insight helped to improve the manuscript and develop its fullest potential.

Finally, I am blessed to have such a loving family that has supported me through many different endeavors. Thank you for making my life so full. I am forever grateful to the two extraordinary women who raised me, Tuen Wong and King Chun Wong—I strive to follow their examples of selflessness, love, honesty, and dedication. I am inspired by my father, Vincent Vega, his journey in life, and our journey together. Being the older sister of two brilliant, talented, and thoughtful siblings, Jason and Esther, fills me with pride—their passions and interests reflect the love of both their mother and father. I am privileged to have the friendship of Kim Hartson, whom I love as a sister and admire for her intellect, beauty, strength, and grace. I am so fortunate to have my mama and papa, Ramesh and Ranjana Shah—their total embrace has brought so much joy to my life, and I am thankful to them for giving me my greatest gift. Last, but definitely not least, I am filled with gladness because Rikin Shah, my husband, partner in all things, favorite person, safe place, and best friend is always by my side. Thank you for your immeasurable love, and for sharing life with me.

No Alternative

Introduction

I traveled to Tepoztlán—an artsy community composed of affluent Mexicans and American expatriates. There, I spent the day with Yanira García. Although this was our first meeting, I already knew a bit about this traditional midwife from an American-made documentary on her work. At the time the documentary was filmed in 2005, Yanira was attending birthing mothers at a feverish pace. Both Mexican and foreign women traveled to Cuernavaca to give birth in her thriving home clinic. After the documentary, however, Yanira became the target of kidnapping threats. Shaken to her core, she and her husband abandoned Cuernavaca overnight. Initially, Yanira moved to Veracruz, hoping to take over the clientele of Adeli Hirsch, a midwife also under threat who had fled to Brazil, but Yanira ended up opting for a lower-profile lifestyle and a slower-paced practice in Tepoztlán. Her workload has fallen from forty to ten births per month.

I wondered about how Yanira's increased celebrity within transnational humanized-birth forums caused interactions to shift between Yanira and members of her hometown. I gently inquired about the specific circumstances causing her to abandon her successful, well-known Cuernavacan clinic, but Yanira told me that the occurrences were too painful for her to talk about. Instead, she told me about how she became a midwife and about the unique position she holds within the transnational humanized-birth community.

Yanira's mother, two aunts, a grandmother, and two great-grandmothers were all midwives and *curanderas* (traditional medicine healers). Her Nahua grandmother married a Spaniard and was trilingual in Nahuatl, Spanish, and Latin; however, Yanira is monolingual in Spanish. Yanira began assisting her mother and grandmother when she was seven and started attending births on her own when she was fourteen.

Figure 0.1. Yanira and a Spanish apprentice

Yanira was first exposed to the transnational humanized-birth community when she met Jan Tritten, founder and editor in chief of *Midwifery Today,* at a midwifery conference. The impression she made on Jan Tritten provided the impetus for her eventual celebrity. Subsequently, she met the editor of an Italian midwifery journal and accepted an invitation to speak about traditional Mexican midwifery in Italy. As her reputation spread and her birthing clinic grew, Yanira began receiving apprentices from around the world—from Austria, Denmark, Norway, Italy, Spain, Brazil, Costa Rica, the United States, and Israel. She has organized an "exchange" with these apprentices and has traveled to their countries to speak about her work. Her next speaking engagement is in Moscow. She explained to me that *Midwifery Today* invites "the most traditional" midwives to speak internationally, all expenses paid.

Yanira is a special case in Mexico since she, along with a few others across the entire country, has constructed an identity that employs place-based knowledge as currency within transnational circles. Yanira's celebrity depends on the balance of two contradictory elements: despite her mono-national origins, she has become transnational, and despite becoming transnational, she continues to be perceived as mono-national. The paradoxical way in which Yanira is perceived and interpellated reveals the non-binary nature of nationality. As I delved deeper into my fieldwork, tracing humanized-birth-oriented social networks in order to interview and observe all the "usual suspects," I began wondering if Yanira's paradoxical position is engendered by the transnational humanized-birth community's fetishization of indigeneity—a fascination that allows for several indigenous women to serve as representatives of traditional Mexican midwifery at international conferences but does not permit merging of "traditional" and "professional" midwifery.

When I asked Yanira what a "traditional birth" means to her, she responded, *"parto respetado"* (a respected birth). Her response interested me because I had never heard a traditional midwife use this term. In the context of my ethnographic research, *"parto respetado"* unfolded as a multivalent descriptor that signals birth that is respected and respectful, and that evidences the respectability of its practitioners. *Parto respetado* is a term used by Mexican, Latin American, and Spanish obstetricians who participate in the humanized-birth movement. Yanira's use of this specific term signals her exposure to the lexicon of a particular niche within Latin American and Spanish obstetrics.

Nonetheless, I asked her to clarify what she meant. She explained that she respects the woman's choices, encourages women to move around during the birth, practices delayed cutting of the umbilical cord, and prepares a birth-inducing drink using chocolate, cinnamon, and *zopatle,* a traditional medicinal plant. During the course of my research, I have observed that delayed cord cutting is highly valued among humanized-birth practitioners. Likewise, chocolate, cinnamon, and *zopatle* is a well-known "folk remedy" that has achieved international "cult status" among those interested in traditional Mexican midwifery. She uses massage techniques such as *la sobada* and *la manteada* as necessary. During prenatal consultations, she inquires about the mother's diet and previous births, evaluates blood pressure, and tests urine samples for protein levels and infections. Although Yanira describes her midwifery techniques as "nothing extraordinary," the amount of attention they have drawn from a global audience certainly is.

Yanira's case piqued my interest since she was selected for being one of the "most traditional" midwives in Mexico; however, she does not speak Nahuatl and practices popularized "traditional" methods. During the course of my research, I had many opportunities to observe midwives who primarily or exclusively speak indigenous languages and whose repertoires are composed of remedies and techniques unknown in transnational circles, yet these midwives are not present at humanized-birth conferences or Mexican Midwifery Association meetings. However, the delicate balance upon which Yanira's paradoxical identity rests has not gone undisturbed. Her increased mobility provoked violent reactions in her community, resulting in a type of exodus. Ironically, Yanira's mobility in humanized-birth circles dictates and limits where she can live, resulting in immobility in everyday life.

I also interviewed Lucía Fernández, an obstetric nurse living in Mexico City and one of Yanira's former apprentices. She first met Yanira at an international conference organized by Adeli and attended by Jan Tritten of *Midwifery Today*; Robbie Davis-Floyd, author of *Birth as an American Rite of Passage*; and a number of Brazilian midwifery advocates. Lucía explained to me that at the time she was curious about midwifery, but as the mother of two, she could not travel too far from home or commit to apprenticing every day. She apprenticed under Yanira twice a week for more than a year.

Lucía emphasized how generous and open Yanira had been toward her apprentices. Yanira accepted everyone who wanted to learn, allowing her students to sleep and eat in her home free of charge. However, as the mother of five boys, Yanira had to begin assigning apprenticeship dates to her various students so there would not be too many people in her house at the same time.

When it was her turn, Lucía spent two weeks apprenticing in Yanira's home, together with another woman from Brazil. It was common then for Yanira to have more than one birthing mother at a time in her clinic. One day, three women were in labor simultaneously. Yanira decided that she and her two apprentices would each attend a birth, and Lucía's first thought was, "Me? How?" She had never attended a birth before. The mother she attended was giving birth to her sixth child, and the birth progressed smoothly, without any complications. When the woman's water broke, Lucía was bathed in amniotic fluid and was "baptized" as a midwife.

When Lucía considered she had "learned a bit" from Yanira, she joined forces with another obstetric nurse from the Center for Maternal and Infant Research, Birth Studies Group. Lucía is not comfortable attending births alone but does enjoy partnering with another obstetric nurse. She has attended nearly eighty births over the last seven years. In addition, she gives perinatal education workshops at the National Autonomous University of Mexico, Panamerican University, and the National Institute of Cardiology. Most of her time, however, is dedicated to leading the Mexican Midwifery Association, as president. She started the association using funds from the MacArthur Foundation with the goal of reducing maternal mortality.

Although Lucía has limited experience attending births in comparison to my other informants, as the former apprentice of Yanira, she is able to leverage her proximity to "traditional" and "indigenous" birthing practices in a way that Yanira cannot. Lucía's influential position as president of the Mexican Midwifery Association helps to illuminate pathways to power and prestige within the humanized-birth movement in Mexico. Yanira's unique and paradoxical position in the humanized-birth community results in ongoing invitations to transnational meetings, but it was also the impetus for the violent backlash that caused her to flee her hometown. Mayra Gómez, another indigenous informant complained to me that her inclusion in a Midwifery Alliance of North America conference in Canada had been solely based on her physical appearance—during the conference she was fetishized as a living "poster" of indigeneity. Thus, whereas Yanira serves as a representative of "traditional midwifery" at international midwifery conferences, Lucía's trajectory demonstrates that unfettered cultural capital is derived not from being Yanira, but rather, from being *near to* Yanira.

Lucía does not fulfill what may easily be assumed as requisite for the post of president of the Mexican Midwifery Association—she is neither a professional nor a traditional midwife, nor does she possess extensive experience attending births. Nonetheless, she has played a key role in perpetuating and deepening the juridical divide between "traditional" and "professional" midwives. I attended a Mexican Midwifery Association meeting in Mexico City and observed that most of the board was composed of obstetric nurses and transnational birth attendants (women who are either foreign-born or foreign-trained). The association hopes to administer certification exams and create a professional guild in an effort to lend legitimacy to the work of (particular) midwives across Mexico. However, according to the rules established by the directive board (a board that includes obstetric nurses and "professional midwives," but does not include "traditional midwives"), only midwives who have completed an academic course of study, in Mexico or elsewhere, are eligible for admittance into the guild. "Traditional midwives" shall be excluded until they become "professional midwives" by undergoing an academic course of study—a path that is unlikely for indigenous midwives who practice midwifery out of their rural homes while also raising families.

Although Lucía was a key player in determining that traditional indigenous midwives would be excluded from the professional guild until completing an academic course of study, one could also argue that Lucía has not completed an academic professional midwifery program and therefore should be excluded from the guild. Lucía's qualification for her post is based on her hospital-based training as an obstetric nurse (suggesting continued biomedical hegemony despite positioning of humanized birth as resistance to patriarchal biopower and medicalized birth). The underlying logic that buttresses Lucía's position as president also evidences how deeply the simultaneous commodification of indigeneity and exclusion of indigenous people are embedded within the humanized-birth movement.

"Humanized" and "Traditional" Births

Covering twenty-eight months of in-depth, multi-sited research across Mexico, from October 2010 to November 2013, this book analyzes the physical and social mobility of some individuals, and the relative immobility of others, through the lens of natural-birth practices across Mexico. In this book, I focus primarily on two contrasting types of birth. When "studying up" (conducting ethnographic research within spheres of affluence, see Nader 1972), the alternative births described in this book were most commonly called *partos humanizados* by parents, obstetricians, and professional midwives. On the other hand, the midwife-assisted births of indigenous women in rural contexts were referred to as *partos tradicionales*. In referring to these births as "humanized" and "traditional," I am simply using the terms I encountered in the field.

Likewise, the women I refer to as "professional midwives" self-identify with this term and are classified as such by their clients, and some (with important exceptions) have undergone formal training and licensure. With respect to "traditional midwives," I am again adopting the terms these practitioners use for themselves. Indigenous midwives most often self-identify as *parteras tradicionales,* with a small minority referring to themselves as *parteras empíricas* ("empirical," or experience-based, midwives). Although all of these terms were the ones offered to me by informants, they also come from the realm of policy. *Parteras profesionales* and *parteras tradicionales/parteras empíricas* are the terms used by the Mexican Secretariat of Health and by other governmental bodies such as the Mexican Institute of Social Security (IMSS). Midwives may use these terms to describe themselves as a result of their engagement with government agencies for training, certification, hospital privileges, and so on. I am by no means assigning a value judgment to either type of birth attendant, nor am I arguing that traditional midwifery practices are anchored in the past, while professional midwifery practices represent greater modernity (see Bauman and Briggs 2003).

The term "humanized birth" (*parto humanizado*) is usually used in Mexico and elsewhere in Latin America to describe birth that purposefully resists medicalization and technocratic practices (see Davis-Floyd 2004 [1992]). In this text, the terms "humanized birth," "gentle birth," and "tranquil birth" are used interchangeably to signal a movement that aims to "empower" women and eliminate obstetric violence. (To what degree and for whom these goals are met will be critically examined throughout the book.) This movement is analogous to the home and water-birth movements in the United States, Canada, and Western Europe. Births are often attended by professional midwives (although some obstetricians have joined the movement) and accompanied by doulas (professional companions who provide physical, emotional, and informational support before, during, and after birth). In general, proponents of humanized birth criticize power inequality inherent in physician-patient relationships and denounce medicalized practices such as unnecessary cesarean sections, episiotomies, isolation of birthing mothers in hospital labor and delivery areas, labor induction (including the use of hormones such as Pitocin), and the repetitive insertion of medical personnel's fingers into women's vaginas to assess dilation.

However, some informants expressed a more nuanced definition of humanized birth, explaining that a highly medicalized birth can be considered "humanized" if the interventions were medically necessary and/or "chosen" by the birthing mother. At the same time, some Mexican obstetricians have railed against the terminology of humanized birth, asking if the birth they attend is, by default, "animalistic." Thus, some prefer the term "respected birth," since it highlights respect for birthing mothers' choices, which can be prioritized in both biomedicalized births and births attended by alternative birth attendants.

Likewise, traditional birth (home birth attended by a traditional midwife) represents an alternative to the biopolitical control of women's bodies for which medicalized, technocratic, hospital birth is often criticized (see Foucault 1990 [1978]). It is important to stress that I am not extending an essentialized notion of traditional birth—one of the aims of this book is to disrupt the traditional-modern binary. However, for many indigenous people across Mexico, certain birthing practices are widely referred to as "traditional." In a recently circulated letter, the Organization of Indigenous Doctors of the State of Chiapas (OMIECH) reiterated the sentiments of many of my indigenous informants when describing traditional birth as being threatened and worth defending.

The traditional births I observed involved indigenous midwives attending indigenous mothers either in the midwife's home-clinic or the home of the birthing mother. Since indigenous mothers often arrived with extended family in tow or were surrounded by family members in their home-birth environment, these births were sensitive to how complex gender- and generational-hierarchies unfold in specific local contexts. The births often included herbal remedies and massage techniques. Some traditional births recruited and incorporated biomedical techniques by applying traditional medicine logic to "modern" resources. For example, I observed a traditional midwife apply a postpartum IV to "replace vitamins"—in this instance, administering IV fluid was cast as a more direct method of providing blood tonic than postpartum soups and teas. Traditional birth is a medically pluralistic form, and thus, the IV was combined with a postpartum herbal bath. At times, the midwives provided their clients with their baby's placenta after the delivery. Payment schemes were often flexible in quantity, timing, and type, reflecting the socioeconomic realities in rural indigenous villages.

Although traditional birth is also an example of resistance to the hegemonic way of birthing, the women who have traditional births occupy a highly contrastive positionality within society when compared to their humanized counterparts. Their births are less about "choice" and more explicitly about resistance to biopower (see Foucault 1990 [1978]) and the Mexican Secretariat of Health mandate that *all* births take place in hospitals since *every* birth can potentially involve life-threatening complications. The Mexican government uses the conditionality of the cash-transfer program Oportunidades to incentivize recipients to adhere to the Secretariat of Health mandate, citing the reduction of maternal and infant mortality as the primary goal. These forms of "reproductive governance" (see Morgan and Roberts 2012) are differentially experienced and understood by poor and indigenous recipients of Oportunidades. As Vania Smith-Oka (2013) points out, some women reject traditional midwifery and actively seek out "modern" motherhood through medicalized birth. In this book, I focus on indigenous women for whom giving birth with a traditional midwife exemplifies their refusal to be racially discriminated against in government hospitals and socialized as "appropriate pregnant subjects" whose bodies are "sites of risk" (see Howes-Mischel 2009).

My research focused on the births of two socioeconomic extremes of Mexican society—what is missing from the story is the vast majority of Mexican women who make out their lives somewhere between these two distinct poles. Likewise, although there are no data to tell us what percentage of women have humanized and traditional births in Mexico, these two birthing strategies represent a small minority. The vast majority of births take place in hospitals and are highly medicalized, with cesarean section representing 45.8 percent of births in public Mexican Institute of Social Security hospitals[1] and approximately 70 percent of births in private hospitals.[2] In spite of these facts, I have chosen to study humanized and traditional births because of what they together reveal about the mutual imbrication of colonial legacies and transnational economies operating in the present day. My work is not about how the bulk of Mexican society gives birth, but rather about examining life and the process of bringing into life at the extremes of Mexican society in order to understand the unfolding of intersectional racialization and the limitations of the citizenship concept in a globalized, neoliberal world.

By contrasting racialized Oportunidades recipients with members of the "global professional class" (Kapoor 2004), I mean to tell a complex story in a complex way. Through examining these exceptional cases in conjunction, we can begin to see how citizenship is actively sought but not fully attainable for some, while being devalued for others who forgo government-provisioned services in favor of the cultural capital gleaned from the "conspicuous consumption" (see Veblen 2006 [1902]; also Ritzer 2001) of more socially valuable bodily practices. Referring to the work of Elizabeth Currid-Halkett (2017), I question the degree to which conspicuous consumption has become inconspicuous, while satisfying the goals of the emerging "aspirational" class. My story uses birth as a point of departure, thus seating theoretical arguments in ethnographic accounts describing both sensual and violent moments experienced through the flesh and authored with blood, births unfolding in both symbolically cleansing water and on life-producing dirt floors; however, the subject of my theoretical analysis reaches far beyond the object of ethnographic description: a critical rethinking of "race," citizenship, and the consumption of "culture."

The Mexican Context

My research moves from the realm of everyday reproductive practice to transnational organizations and policy making, and it evidences how women's bodies are often the locus where race, class, and gender oppression converge. I began my research at the Center for the Adolescents of San Miguel de Allende, or CASA, Professional Midwifery School—a nongovernmental organization (NGO) cofounded by an American woman and staffed by Mexican and American employees and volunteers. In 1996,

CASA opened a midwifery school that became the first accredited program for the technical education of professional midwives; its first generation of professional midwives graduated four years later. CASA's ongoing popularity is facilitated in large part by thousands of Canadian and American retirees living in San Miguel de Allende (San Miguel, for short), many of whom are CASA donors. CASA's formal recognition by the Mexican government suggests the successful exportation of the humanized-birth model and professional midwifery from the United States to Mexico. However, I ask what might be revealed if this "border crossing" were to be more closely examined. Under the rubric of "commensurability," how do concepts and medical technologies travel (see Pigg 2001); what are the disjunctures, deformations, and discontinuities of such travel (see Lakoff 2005); and most important, what are the productive and disruptive effects of this travel on the socioeconomic milieu and geopolitical landscape?

Because of professional midwifery's formal inclusion in the health sector, and CASA's insertion in the universal health system, even the poorest pregnant women in the state of Guanajuato have formal access to professional midwifery services and water birth at CASA Hospital. In practice, however, women using the public health-care system must request a referral for CASA's birthing services, and such referrals are rarely granted. Again, socioeconomically and geracially stratified birthing methods belie uncritical notions of free choice and equal access.

My work examines how CASA—in cooperation with the National Center for Gender Equity and Reproductive Health, the Pan American Health Organization, the World Health Organization, and a slew of American and Canadian donor corporations—foments its clients' sense of belonging through participation in a transnational and deterritorialized community of consumption. Here, I define "clients" as those who "buy into" the product that CASA offers—the humanized-birth model. These clients include those Davis-Floyd refers to as "postmodern midwives" (see Davis-Floyd 2007), pregnant women seeking professional midwife-assisted birth, volunteers, visitors, and donors. Their community-wide discourse is mired in human rights vocabulary and suggests empowerment while obscuring powerful, underlying forces related to neoliberal consumption. My research will ask how this discourse was made, who the authors are, and what may remain hidden in the process.

As CASA works to expand the reach of the humanized-birth model from the state of Guanajuato to the states of Veracruz, Chiapas, Oaxaca, and Guerrero as well,[3] the spread of this particular commodity across sharply disparate socioeconomic and georacial contexts calls attention to

Figure 0.2. Professional midwifery student teaches a group of traditional midwives using dolls as props

the question of citizenship. For example, whereas in San Miguel de Allende and in Mexico City, professional midwife-assisted home birth is a source of cultural capital and contributes to identity formation within a global meritocracy, in impoverished villages in Veracruz, traditional Nahua midwives risk imprisonment when they, against government instructions, secretly attend birthing mothers in their homes. These births are cast as the "wrong" type of home birth, since indigenous mothers and midwives *must* submit to the expertise of biomedical physicians. Meanwhile, these same traditional midwives, many of whom have practiced midwifery for decades, are "trained" in workshops offered by CASA professional midwifery students, medical students, and even social workers—many of whom have never attended a single childbirth alone.

During my ethnographic research, I observed the way indigenous midwives were "taught" how to correctly perform midwifery, threatened with incarceration if a maternal or infant mortality were to occur on their watch, and effectively rendered unpaid hospital referralists at the service of the state (see Carrillo 2002 and Pigg 1997, 2001). Thus, ethnography on the humanized midwifery movement in Mexico unmasks the violent

Figure 0.3. Traditional midwife with the baby and placenta model she has sewn by hand

contradictions embedded in neoliberal consumption and the relationship between restricted participation in communities of consumption and restricted access to citizenship.

Methods

I used multi-sited ethnography to create a cartography of midwifery and humanized birth in Mexico, thus identifying different "windows" through which recent shifts in birth practices and health care can be examined.[4] My ethnographic research began at CASA. However, after joining CASA students and administrators on a "field practice" trip to the Nahua High Mountains of Veracruz, I began to think about the issue of place-based differences and the importance geographical location plays in the reproductive care women receive. This required redefining my preconceived notion of an ethnographic field site. The field I identified was not a "site" per se, but rather a network of people.

I began with professional midwives in Mexico, a contained and connected group of women, and subsequently gained access to their clientele. Simultaneously, I approached different transnational humanized-birth leaders and interviewed them about their respective roles in the movement, both around the world, and specifically in Mexico. Using the snowball technique and through my attendance at multiple humanized-birth conferences, I recruited more couples and humanized-birth attendants, including physicians and obstetric nurses, to my study. Over the course of my fieldwork, I volunteered at two different transnational NGOs, gaining access to training workshops for indigenous traditional midwives. Having befriended a few indigenous midwives, and while staying as a guest in their homes during repeat visits to their villages, I witnessed their interactions with indigenous women and the traditional midwifery care they provide. Finally, I observed medical professionals and maternity patients in both private and public hospital settings and solicited interviews with physicians and policy makers.

This process led me to the Mexican states of Guanajuato, Guerrero, Jalisco, México, San Luis Potosí, Veracruz, Chiapas, Oaxaca, Quintana Roo, Morelia, Querétaro, Puebla, Michoacán, and Nuevo León; additionally, I traveled to California for interviews, and to Brazil for brief participant observation in what turned out to be "traditional Mexican midwifery" popular education tourism.[5] Although the geographic breadth of this "field" is enormous, the specific people I traveled to meet, observe, and interview were very concrete and are conscientiously members of a cohesive transnational community. All the individuals in my study have acquaintances, and often great friends, among the other individuals in my study.

Interviews were semi-structured and lasted from fifteen minutes to three hours, with the average being approximately forty-five minutes. I tailored my questions to the interviewees' positionality within the humanized-birth movement (whether the interviewee[s] was/were a mother, a couple, a humanized-birth attendant [professional midwife, obstetrician, obstetric nurse], a traditional midwife, or a policy maker), but I usually included questions to help me understand the interviewees' positionality in society (education level, socioeconomic status, ethnicity, etc.). In addition, my questions generally followed these themes: his or her occupation, life history, perspectives on gender, the Mexican health system, positive and negative experiences with birth, and the shifting political climate regarding midwifery. By not overstructuring the interviews, I resisted scripting or leading the informants, allowing them to speak for themselves.

My data analysis is derived from detailed entries in my field diary, audio and video recordings from interviews, and digital ethnographic data gleaned from social media. Over the course of my research, I connected with many of my informants in person and via online platforms. I soon realized that the humanized-birth network is (media)ted by different websites such as Facebook, YouTube, and online blogs. As a result, digital sources of ethnographic data were included at the data analysis stage. Upon concluding my research, I engaged in an iterative process that used open coding to identify emergent themes and synthesize higher-order constructs. All the names that appear throughout this ethnography are pseudonyms, with the exception of humanized-birth public figures I encountered at humanized-birth events but who were not direct participants in my research.

The Emergence of Humanized Birth in Mexico: Inserting Race into Mexican Midwifery

A great deal of recent anthropological scholarship on "new midwifery" centers around how professional midwives in different countries are helping women reconnect with nature, teaching them to trust in their bodies, respecting women's choices,[6] confronting and defying hegemonic biomedical structures, and fighting for women's right to birth as naturally as possible.

In texts celebrating new midwifery, there is a tendency to position midwives as primary agents of change. Pregnant women and birthing mothers are the subjects who are transformed and "empowered," their lives changed forever by exposure to the midwifery model of birth. Empowerment is so central to the ideological underpinning of the humanized-birth movement that the 2014 World Week for Humanized Birth made its slogan, "*Parir es poder: empoderate*" ("To Give Birth Is to Be Empowered: Empower Yourself," my translation). I am critical of the notion of "empowerment," asking what it does and for whom. In the case of new midwifery in Mexico, transnational midwives are often framed as the women doing the empowering. Is hegemony really challenged if people in the Global South are "empowered" by ideas from the Global North? Does labeling some women as "empowered" and others "disempowered" (re)produce a false binary that obscures more about agency and dynamism than it reveals? Lastly, I am wary of how neoliberalism and the concept of individualism and choice inform the notion of "empowerment."

I problematize uncritical notions of free choice by drawing attention to how, for most Mexican women, choices are either nonexistent or prestructured. Women (especially indigenous and lower class) do not have options when giving birth in public hospitals. The very idea of "choice" emerges from a middle- and upper-class perspective—"choice" is a privilege of those capable of paying for private medical services. My argument is informed by Pierre Bourdieu's concept of habitus: class provides the conditions that determine tastes; however, the role of class in determining taste is concealed and the relationship between taste and education is repressed; thus, tastes seem "natural" and are used to legitimate the superiority of the wealthy (see Bourdieu 1984).

The disproportional inclusion of transnational birth attendants and stark exclusion of indigenous and traditional midwives I described at the outset of this introduction is reminiscent of Sheryl Nestel's 2006 study of how race inequalities are reproduced among the midwifery profession when professional midwives, employing a rhetoric of universal womanhood, fail to engage critically with their own (white, upper-middle class) positionality. Nestel's work is the counterhistory of the reemergence of midwifery, but she fails to critically examine race politics among recipients of midwifery care and within the humanized-birth transnational community. *My work is the counterhistory to the counterhistory:* it not only examines how race inequalities are reproduced but asks how novel claims related to race are waged on a global stage through consumption of transnational (ethno)medicine. Although the logic of my argument is similar (and the direction of my argument is opposite) to Elizabeth Roberts'

(2012b) description of how Ecuadorian women pride C-section scars that evidence their participation in private medicine and assisted whiteness, I emphasize how distinct racialized identities are constructed relationally and operationalized transnationally.

Theorizing Intersectional Racialization Processes

This book is about multiple, contingent *intersectional racialization processes* (see Crenshaw et al. 1995, Crenshaw 2014, Bridges 2011; also, De Genova 2005). I merge Kimberlé Crenshaw's concept of "intersectionality" with Khiara Bridges' perspective on pregnancy as a "site of racialization" and "race as a process." In so doing, I draw attention to the ongoing, interfacing processes that lead to the material (re)realization of racial inequality.

However, my perspective differs from Bridges', since for her, in order to "get to" questions of race, she first had to "go through" issues of class: "The analytic of race had to be folded into an analytic that began with class" (Bridges 2011:9). The experiences I encountered in the field imbued in me an understanding of racialization as a process through which multiple axes of inequality intersect simultaneously. When people meet for the first time, they engage in an immediate, predominantly unconscious, mental calculus that includes race *and* class, and ultimately maps race *onto* class, *and vice versa*. This mental calculus further incorporates phenotype, dress, education, language, nationality, and so on into racialized perceptions. Through ethnographic examples, I signal how one's intersectional positionality in society influences one's perception of oneself and others, and in turn how one is perceived by others. Thus, departing from Bridges, the multivalent ways in which women across Mexico use pregnancy as a site of racialization leads me to conclude that the physical body is only one of many complexly related signs of racial difference (albeit an important one). This book opens up a space within ongoing debates about intersectionality for considering how racialization processes are mapped onto the moral body.

Examples of intersectional racialization processes unfold through all the following chapters, and this concept serves as the central theoretical axis of the book. I offer the commodification of indigenous culture, differential access to citizenship-based resources, disparate degrees of social and physical mobility, and race- and class-specific expectations for motherhood as windows for examining how intersectional racialization processes are woven into the everyday fabric of social life.

Before developing this argument further, I must clarify a few themes that will emerge throughout the ethnography.

Thinking Race: Culture, Social Whitening, and Indigeneity

Throughout my ethnographic research, there were many times when informants lapsed into describing race-as-culture in which culture "can be appreciated as 'data about individual racial thoughts and fantasies' insofar as culture and race have begun to proceed to the same effect" (Bridges 2011:136). Although couples practicing humanized birth in Mexico are often urban, middle or upper class, fair skinned, well-traveled, and highly educated, they insist the practice does not correspond directly to social class. Repeatedly, I was told the determining factor was how cultured the couple is. During interviews, informants distinguished themselves and other members of the humanized-birth movement from the rest of society based upon their *"nivel cultural"* (cultural level) as opposed to socioeconomic class. In this way, culture was often used to obscure how intersectional racialization processes dialectically produce material repercussions, thus undergirding racial inequality.

My understandings of race and culture are quite distinct. I am not debating whether race is a biological given or a social construct (see Montoya 2011). Along with Bridges and Crenshaw, this ethnography goes beyond the notion of race as a social construct to ask about the processes of racialization that produce the powerful material repercussions of race-based differences, despite their lack of mooring in biology. My research critically examines the ongoing social processes undergirding "race," thus analyzing its origins and effects. I consider "culture" to be a reified object ready for consumption, not as a set of everyday beliefs and practices pertaining to a particular racial group. Throughout the book, I do not unquestioningly accept categorizations based on culture as accurate—in fact, I am attentive to how socioeconomic status allows for education and travel, and, thus, exposure to the humanized-birth movement as it unfolds in different countries around the world. Therefore, I ask if cultural capital is used to mask economic capital (see Bourdieu 1984).

Many of the aspirational couples in my study are fair-skinned, but their participation in the humanized-birth movement is also a process of "social whitening" on a global stage. My use of the term "social whitening" refers to the process through which individuals seek membership in a global meritocracy—a meritocracy that, due to a global history of imperialism and colonization, tends to be white or aspires to social whiteness (see Bashkow 2006). In this context, "white" does not strictly coincide with phenotype, but rather refers to a social category resulting from a dialectic process of perception and performance of an individual's positionality in society. This ongoing process is achieved to varying degrees, but never to completion.

Meanwhile, indigenous Mexican women and their traditional midwives are excluded (almost entirely) from this meritocratic community. My usage of the terms "indigenous women" and "indigenous people" refers to individuals who self-identify as indigenous, speak indigenous languages, and live in rural, indigenous regions. The indigenous people with whom I worked are from the following ethnic groups: Tlapaneco, Mixteco, Huasteco (Téenek), Nahua, Tzotzil, Tzeltal, Maya, and Purépecha.

In representing indigenous women as racialized mothers, I am not intending to reproduce universalizations that ignore the diversity of indigenous peoples across Mexico or reduce political-economic factors to a mere question of racial difference; however, I recognize that government programs and development discourse often do, employing similar strategies for dealing with reproductive health issues (mostly oriented around reducing maternal and infant mortality) across different indigenous populations (for example, see Cabral Soto et al. 2000). Also, I have deliberately selected processes of racialization as an analytical lens over "ethnicity" because, although important differences distinguish the various indigenous groups I describe, my overarching argument traces discriminatory politics in Mexico that contrast indigenous and mestizo individuals instead of distinguishing between different indigenous ethnicities.

Furthermore, although there is a celebration of "ancestral knowledge," the humanized-birth movement in Mexico—departing from the work of Marisol de la Cadena (2000) in Peru—is not about claiming and enacting "indigenous culture" while attempting to distance oneself from "Indianness" through *mestizaje* and the idea of *indigenous mestizos*. In Mexico, indigenous people are distinctly "Other," and this new midwifery is decidedly not the midwifery of the old indigenous hag (see Weismantel 2001). When "indigeneity" is invoked, it is in à la carte fashion. The object is fetishized, separated entirely from its cultural, socioeconomic, and geographical context, and repackaged for mass consumption.

During this process of commodification, "indigeneity," "nature," and "tradition" are collapsed onto one another. Similarly, very specific indigenous women—only several across the entire country, Yanira being one of them—routinely attend international new midwifery conferences and forums. At these events they perform their indigeneity, wearing indigenous

costume even if this is not their everyday attire, thus buttressing the uncritical claim that new midwifery is, in fact, a descendant of traditional
midwifery, and that humanized birth means "going back to nature" and
recognizing "our shared humanity." Throughout the book, I question the
notion of a single, reified way of being an indigenous person. I draw attention to the way in which the idea of a singular "indigeneity" is mobilized,
versus the multiplicity of how indigenous people live their lives. In addition, the notion of nature can be deployed as a reified category to satisfy
specific objectives. I am not essentializing "nature" as pure and valuable,
nor am I arguing that through humanized birth, women are returning to
a more natural and, therefore, more positive state. Such value judgments
lie beyond the purview of my analytical work. Instead, my critical perspective on how the notion of "going back to nature" is collapsed into the commodification of indigeneity problematizes the traditional-modern binary,
Euro-American ontologies of time, and the chronology of progress.

The Humanitarian Encounter

This book describes cosmopolitan spaces in which highly educated, cultured individuals are fervently spinning meanings about birth, and, con-
sequently, about race; and rural contexts in which indigenous women's
bodies, the objects of government and NGO interventions, are scripted by
racial discourse imposed from "above." I am not arguing that indigenous
women do not ascribe meanings to their own bodies; rather, I am observing that government bodies and NGO leaders inadvertently perpetuate
race-based inequalities when they fail to recognize the "target population"
as knowledgeable interlocutors and instead utilize racial frameworks for-
mulated from within a locus of power.

These contrasting spaces are geographically distinct and reflect deep
material inequalities; however, they are also mutually constituted by relationships of power—neither space would exist in its current form without the other. I take a relational perspective (see Menéndez 2010; Molina 2013). My argument is not that these different spaces are individually
bound in ways that diminish their effects on each other; rather, they represent disparate lived realities and signal differential access to power, and,
thus, the unequal production of discourse and representations on a global
stage (see Fassin 2010; Malkki 1996, 2010).

Despite the glorification of "traditional birth" methods within
humanized-birth circles, the traditional midwifery care that indigenous

birthing women receive is not celebrated—instead, it must be corrected, rescripted, controlled, and surveilled. Indigenous mothers and the traditional midwives who attend their births are agentive and resourceful decision-makers, while facing the challenges of intersecting forms of oppression.[7] Professional midwives and international NGOs participate in this process under the guise of *capacitaciones* (training workshops) meant to reduce maternal mortality (see Berry 2013 [2010]; Molina 2006), their involvement bolstered by "humanitarian reason" (Fassin 2012).

In these encounters, the issue of race comes to the surface. Racial difference is visually evident in a classroom of indigenous midwives taught by a nonindigenous Mexican health professional, or by a foreign professional midwife. It is discursively evident in interviews of Mexican midwives and of NGO staff when they provide opinions on violence and inequality within the NGO hierarchy, and, in particular, the roles and actions of American NGO founders. Whereas inclusion in a global "white" community is sought by the middle and upper classes, being the objects of humanitarian (white) intervention is often resented by the indigenous lower class. These humanitarian encounters bolster the claim that "[l]andscapes of healing are differently (re)produced for various segments of the global population" (Buzinde and Yarnal 2012:785).

Aspirationals: Colonial Legacies and Neoliberal Market Logics

Through humanized birth, participants distance themselves from the majority of Mexican society, which they characterize as entrapped in a political and educational system that limits intellectuality. In line with Currid-Halkett's 2017 theory of the aspirational class, these informants value education and New Age bodily practices as mechanisms for accruing cultural capital. Moreover, with the help of professional midwives representing a foreign or transnational identity, they insert themselves in a transnational, affluent, and cultured community. Many professional midwives in Mexico are either foreign nationals or foreign-trained.

Most of the aspirational couples who seek humanized birth hold advanced degrees in the sciences and humanities (as opposed to technical) fields and have read widely in English or French. Their commitment to the humanized-birth movement is based in their deep admiration of the work of French obstetricians such as Fréderic Leboyer and Michel Odent; English and American midwifery and "gentle birth" advocates such as Sheila Kitzinger, Ina May Gaskin, Barbara Harper, Thomas Verney, and Robbie Davis-Floyd; and New Age birth methods such as Mongan Method Hypnobirthing. During in-depth interviews, they opine that the truly rich are often mystified by hegemonic biomedicine; however, they, with the fervor of religious converts, vow to a sort of enlightenment with respect to birth, allowing them to see what others cannot. During interviews with informants, analogies to religious conversion and descriptions of how humanized birth has influenced their lives, reconfigured their identities, and transformed how they relate to others were common themes. This enlightenment connects them to a global community, primarily in the United States, Canada, England, France, Holland, Spain, Chile, Argentina, and Brazil, based on shared passion for humanized birth.

The global humanized-birth community affords many examples of "biosociality" (Rabinow 1996); however, this is only a point of departure for my story. The ways in which members of the humanized-birth movement recognize themselves and others involved as "empowered" actors and conscientious parents of superiorly nurtured children provokes me to question how people position themselves vis-à-vis transnational communities. At stake are the criteria upon which novel, value-laden, intersectionally racialized identities are forged. I point to how people and information travel transnationally, and in the case of humanized birth, how this travel often originates in the Global North. In essence, I am pointing to how neoliberal ideologies circulate in the South, and how consumerism mobilizes a rhetoric of "humanity" among the "cultured class" *while simultaneously reinforcing social inequality* by inadvertently infusing transnational movements with intersectional exclusionary logics.

Thus, this book asks, is the transnational humanized-birth movement unfolding in Mexico an example of Renato Rosaldo's "imperialist nostalgia" (Rosaldo 1989)? Can these trends be read as mourning for "what one has destroyed" and "the passing of traditional society"? More specifically, what does the simultaneous surveillance of indigenous midwifery practices and the "return" to "traditional" types of birth among nonindigenous members of the humanized-birth movement indicate about imperial/colonial legacies operating in Mexico in the present day?

Although I resist far-reaching and often totalizing terms like "neocolonialism," I am interested in how colonial histories merge with present-day market logics under a rubric of transnational bioconsumerism. I am signaling how an increasing number of high-mobility individuals and expatriates—while forging their lives within the realm of "cosmopolitanism" and major political formations of neoliberalism—access medical resources, cultural capital, monetary and ideological exchanges, social networks, and belonging outside the scope of citizenship to a particular nation or state.[8]

Instead of discarding citizenship, I draw attention to the multiplicity of citizenship in our neoliberal age. I ask how a robust transnational consumer modality operating in biologically oriented communities modifies the meanings of citizenship. I examine the ways in which people perceive themselves as biological beings, forge identities through specific biological practices, and wage claims based on these biologized identities. Thus, bioconsumerism becomes a powerful framework for [bio]socialities, health-seeking behaviors, and (social and physical) mobilities.

This positioning of my ethnographic research at the intersection between processes of intersectional racialization and consumption (see Veblen 2006 [1902]; also Ritzer 2001) in Mexico illuminates how participation in the humanized-birth movement is used as a form of cultural capital with which to wage claims about race, gender, and identity on a global stage. Thus, the ethnography considers medical migrations to be a "racialized therapeutic landscape" (see Deomampo 2016). The book grapples with the intersectional relations of power and the linkages between place, history, and health in sites of ethnomedical tourism.

Hyper-Self-Reflexivity and Embodied Ethnography

Given this book's critique of multivalent processes leading to the inadvertent reinscription of social inequality between disadvantaged and privileged informants, I am both methodologically and ethically committed to Spivakian hyper-self-reflexivity (Kapoor 2004). I will begin by "acknowledging complicity" (Spivak 1988b). Although I am a woman of "ethnic" heritage (I am of mixed Mexican, Nahua, Blackfoot, and Chinese descent), I am also highly educated and privileged, raised in the urban and suburban United States. I cannot claim to be a subaltern, "native" informant.

My commitment to hyper-self-reflexivity goes hand in hand with "embodied ethnography" research methods. The ethnographer uses her mind, body, and social experiences—her entire phenomenological experience—in the production of field data. Ethnography is the sensuous craft of the "mindful body" (Lock and Scheper-Hughes 1987). For these reasons, my critical analysis of field data led me to reflect at length on my own intersectional identity, and how my unique positionality shaped my research while my research shaped me. This type of "hyper-self-reflexive embodied ethnography" led me to develop a contextual and dialogical framework for understanding intersectional racialization processes. I suggest that this type of research be done in an iterative fashion, such that ethnography informs theory and theory informs ethnography. For example, my being aware of how my privilege posed a potential constraint for my research and a threat to my physical safety led me to attempt to "shed privilege" by adjusting to the socioeconomic standard of my research contexts. At the same time, I recognized that "shedding privilege" can never be fully achieved.

My work attempts to uncover "partial connections" (de la Cadena 2015) and bring multiple "situated knowledges" under the same lens, while heeding Donna Haraway's admonition: "There is a premium on establishing the capacity to see from the peripheries and the depths. But here there also lies a serious danger of romanticizing and/or appropriating the vision of the less powerful while claiming to see from their positions" (Haraway 2014:45). Thus, I readily recognize my "partial perspective" (see Haraway 2014) and admit that my potential as an ethnographer was limited—at times, it was difficult for me to get indigenous women, many of whom are suspicious of *xinolas* (city women) and/or monolingual in their indigenous tongue, to speak openly about their birth experiences. I often had to rely on a translator, which limited my access and changed the dynamic of interviews substantially.

For ethical reasons, I placed women's comfort and respect for their privacy during intimate moments over my desire for ethnographic material. This meant, depending on the circumstances, occasionally choosing not to be present at the moment of birth. I made a conscientious decision to place myself in a learning role when dealing with traditional midwives and never sought to teach them or correct them. Also, I purposefully limited my monthly budget to 5,000 Mexican pesos (at the time, approximately US$400—more than the monthly earnings of many of my impoverished informants, but much less than my middle- and upper-class informants) in order to "unlearn my own privilege" (Spivak 1988a:287, Spivak and Harasym 1990:9). In many senses, practicing hyper-self-reflexivity has been advantageous—I was able to interview informants and conduct participant observation at both ends of the socioeconomic spectrum (see Nader 1972).

Critique of How Development Discourse Reinscribes Inequality

In turning to Mexico, and specifically to impoverished and indigenous regions, as the site for my research, I was not seeking a "repository of ethnographic 'cultural difference'" (Spivak 1999:388), but rather hoping to illuminate a counter discourse to the pervasive story of development. Too often it has been assumed that interventions originating from the Global

North (professionalizing midwives, providing traditional midwives with training workshops from medical personnel, implementation of humanized-birth strategies) will produce positive results among the "target population" (reduced maternal and infant mortality among indigenous and impoverished populations).

My research has shown that humanized birth is generally accessed by women who are highly educated, well-traveled, fair-skinned, urban, cultured, and so on. Although I witnessed the important ways humanizedbirth strategies have improved their birth experiences, the humanization of birth and the reduction of maternal mortality are distinct projects. As I will demonstrate in this book, the respectful, knowledgeable, and attentive care offered by traditional midwives in contexts of scarce economic resources is generally not included under the rubric of "humanized birth" as part of services offered by professional midwives, obstetricians, and doulas; when this sort of care is included, it occupies the niche of "traditionality," turning the traditional midwives into needy recipients of expert knowledge from professional counterparts. As a result, the women who tend to seek out humanized births (i.e., home births and water births attended by gynecologists or professional midwives) are not the women at risk for maternal mortality, nor are their children at risk for infant mortality.

Thus, whereas Spivak argues against the retrieval of information from the Third World for First World purposes (in humanized-birth circles, this has usually meant collecting maternal mortality statistics and using them as evidence of the dire need for humanized birth), I am attempting to show how First World strategies can unexpectedly induce intersectional racialization processes that deepen inequality. In doing so, I am pushing against false notions of "women's solidarity" on a global scale, as I agree with Spivak that these notions obfuscate historical, cultural, and socioeconomic differences and colonial legacies.

Outline of the Book

The main body of the book contains five chapters, each engaging with the fields of medical anthropology and anthropology of reproduction in novel ways.

Chapter 1 points to how the humanized-birth movement inadvertently commodifies indigenous culture in symbolically cannibalistic ways. Members of the transnational humanized-birth community seek "natural" births that reference "traditional" and "indigenous" birthing methods. However, these methods are not adopted wholesale; rather, they are reimagined by the community and reconfigured by capitalist marketing. I critically examine the notion that natural-childbirth discourse reflects race and class biases and is based on middle-class rationalist economic ideology emphasizing control and informed consumer choice and requiring access to resources available only to privileged women (see Brubaker and Dillaway 2009).

Recent research in anthropology explores how bodies increasingly enter into global market exchanges. The body can be bought and sold, both whole or in parts, dead or alive, effectively severing the body from the self, tearing it from the social fabric and bringing it under the purview of market transactions in the form of sperm banks and international trafficking of kidneys, to name two examples. In Nancy Scheper-Hughes and Loïc Wacquant's volume (2006), commodification of the body results in alienation of the self, whereas I explore the idea that the commodification of others' (imagined) "selves" can lead to violence being unleashed on their bodies. My research points to how the accrual of cultural capital through the commodification of "others'" culture is intimately and often destructively achieved in our neoliberal, globalized world.

Chapter 2 problematizes uncritical notions of liberation by asking how humanized birth may contribute to a new regime of pressures and standards for modern-day "good parenting" among aspirationals (see Currid-Halkett 2017). Through ethnographic examples of women who struggle or "fail" to give birth naturally (see Crossley 2007), the book points to how humanized birth may inadvertently represent another way the burden of correctly producing future citizens falls upon women, even as it aims to liberate women from biomedical hegemony. Although biopower has often been characterized as the control of populations through "paternalistic" institutional and governmental surveillance, humanized-birth practices beg the question of how constraining expectations might operate through social networks. I incorporate digital ethnography to analyze how parents use birth to stake claims to moral superiority.

My ethnographic research in Mexico points to how couples seek inclusion in a global meritocracy by investing time, money, effort, and emotions into being "good parents," and the criteria for good parenting is largely defined by parenting trends in their social network (humanized birth, extended lactation, organic/holistic nutrition, Montessori and Waldorf education, extracurricular activities, and so forth). As couples increasingly consider parenthood and their ability to produce well-nurtured, well-educated, well-rounded, ethically conscious children to be a marker of their overall success, their relationships to their children are changing. The book aims to add complexity to ongoing debates considering children as commodities (Jordanova 1995).

Chapter 3 is a response to the need for "comparative research on the subjective experiences of pregnant and birthing women at multiple social locations and multiple contexts, as well the experience and perspectives of midwives and medical providers. The aim is to provide a more critical and meaningful analysis of the complicated intersections of ideology, politics, practice and bodily experience" (Brubaker and Dillaway 2009). In this book, examining multiple social locations and contexts is exactly what I will do. Further, my multi-sited fieldwork is based on an interdisciplinary conceptualization of place and space.[9]

This chapter demonstrates how different spaces (contested, geopolitical, transnational, gendered, and embodied) converge to create specific places. Specifically, it describes the deep social inequality in the picturesque city of San Miguel de Allende, known for its large, semipermanent population of American retirees, and suggests that this contested space provides fertile ground for an emergent model of care. It gives examples of how this model has spread through geopolitical and transnational spaces, and how it articulates with gendered space and embodied space in other local and institutional contexts.

In addition, this chapter provides contrasting ethnographic examples of how local San Miguelenses experience their hometown as an internal borderland that excludes them from "gringo" spaces (except as service workers), and how urban "outsiders" are excluded from "closed" indigenous communities in the Nahua High Mountains of Veracruz. In this way, the chapter signals how "othering" in Mexico is both highly contingent, and a matter of perspective. The chapter offers intersectional racialization processes as a way to think about the syncretic nature of racialized identities. Intersectional racialization processes point to the multiple variables that figure into immediate, unconscious mental calculi structuring encounters of difference—that is, race, class, education, and other forms of cultural capital are folded into one another to produce social constructions of intersectional racial identity that include and supersede phenotype.

Chapter 4 builds on Chapter 3 by examining how racial discrimination buttresses systemic violence within Mexican obstetrics, thus eliciting complicity from medical personnel, with the greatest violations being unleashed on racialized women's bodies. Whereas others have made distinctions between race and racialized biology,[10] my work is about the construction of social identities that allow for the intersectional manipulation of race. What is being racialized is not just the biological body or the national body, but also the moral body. Building upon the work of Latin Americanist anthropologists, this ethnography demonstrates that *raza* ("race") in Latin America is a complex social category that extends beyond race to include class, education, and "culture."[11]

Chapters 2 and 5 both explore how whitening is sought through private medical care by educated, urban women, but in Chapter 4, I provide ethnographic examples of how "reproductive governance" is applied to the supposedly hyper-fertile indigenous women (Morgan and Roberts 2012). In doing so, I critique the concept of "interculturality" and use conditional cash-transfer programs such as Oportunidades as a lens for examining complex and unequal relationships of power between indigenous women and the Mexican government. Poor indigenous women are recruited into Oportunidades, shaped into obedient mothers, and required to give birth in government hospitals. Again disproving notions of a singular indigeneity, some of these women eagerly seek biomedical attention while giving birth, whereas others resist mandates as they have experienced prior racial discrimination. My framing signals the inadequate attention of "interculturality" to political economic factors and questions the reification of cultures upon which "interculturality" is premised.

Chapter 5 builds upon prior chapters by examining how citizenship does not adequately encompass the way privileged women are proactively constructing whiter subjectivities (see Bashkow 2006) through New Age approaches to natural birth and participation in the humanized-birth transnational network. This chapter adds to ethnographies on reproduction that have analyzed divergences between foreign interests and local moral worlds[12] and studies problematizing notions of "globalization"[13] when it examines medical migration among the humanized-birth community in Mexico. The book examines the ease with which "(ethno)medically situated" humanized-birth practitioners' travel across borders and contribute to transnational discourse, while "socially situated" women are restricted from medical migrations.

Although my ethnographic research provides detailed examples of how humanized birth is reshaped and reconstituted in sites that bear stark contrast to the social and geographic locations where the humanized-birth model was originally produced (see Roberts and Scheper-Hughes 2011:3), I am more concerned with how political-economic terrains are not only traversed but are themselves transformed by medical migration. Medical migrations and tourism imply big economic stakes for sending and receiving countries, *and* transnational negotiations of citizenship and capital. That is, my work expands upon previous work on medical migration and medical tourism since these discourses often focus on the macroeconomic effects for countries where medical tourism unfolds, whereas my work explores how identities are forged and leveraged by travelers in a transnational, gendered, racialized economy (see Deomampo 2016).

The conclusion addresses the importance of place when planning health programs and interventions. Using the example of the professional midwifery model in Mexico, the book questions the extent to which health models can be successfully applied to different local contexts (see Tsing 2015). Essentially, I draw attention to the impossibility of cleanly extracting health models from one local context and implementing them in another.

The conclusion of the book also exemplifies how the conceptual lens of intersectional racialization processes developed throughout can be turned to other objects of medical anthropology inquiry. Essentially, I link medical migration in the contemporary era to an intersectionally stratified negotiation of social identities. Further, I discuss how ethnomedical practices challenge Euro-American ontologies of time through differential meanings ascribed to "modernity" and "traditionality" by individuals with divergent positionalities in society. At the same time, notions of "social whitening" play out through consumption of ethnomedicine on a global stage.

CHAPTER 1

Commodifying Indigeneity: Politics of Representation

On a bright and dusty summer morning in 2013, I boarded a second-class bus to Matehuala, where I made a connection to Estación Catorce. Before this trip, I had attended several training workshops for practitioners classified as traditional midwives. At each of these events, I was struck by visible manifestations of power inequality. The event in Estación Catorce was billed as an *encuentro* (an encounter, or a meeting of two cultures) between professional medical personnel and traditional midwives. It was sponsored by the Secretariat of Health's Office for Traditional Medicine and Intercultural Development (TMID) and was organized by an anthropologist—elements suggesting a forum for mutual exchange of ideas.

At the *encuentro*, nurses, physicians, anthropologists, and professional midwives gave PowerPoint presentations to traditional midwives—again, these professionals emerged as *the* source of expert knowledge. Many are interested in New Age therapies, and some even dedicated their presentations to the benefits of medicinal plants. While watching various professionals teach "traditional" remedies to the traditional midwives, I wondered if I was the only one struggling with the irony of the situation. I perused the agenda for the three-day event. Were the traditional midwives to have an opportunity to share *their* expert knowledge? The last two entries, at the end of the final day, were presentations by "traditional midwives." All other entries named the presenting professional and title of the presentation, but the "traditional midwives" were unnamed, and of their presentation topics were not given.

Looking around, I asked myself what was different about this *encuentro* compared to other workshops I had attended. As I scanned the crowd, I noticed a curious number of piercings and tattoos, foreigners with camping gear, and many people from Mexico City. At the entrance to the *en-*

Figure 1.1. Sofia

cuentro, beside the registration table, was a display of natural products for sale (shampoos, teas, marmalades, homeopathic remedies, and the like). These products and event publicity materials were branded with a cosmic-floral image in earthy tones, and the word "Nanahtli." According to the brand's website, "Nanahtli" speaks to women in the Nahuatl world, represents the resolve to restore and dignify the ancestral knowledge of "our people," and plants conSCIENCE-iousness.[1] Staffing the table was Sofia Gil, a young woman with chestnut-colored hair wearing a tank top and a long skirt (a friend of the anthropologists who organized the event). Traditional midwives were not involved in the production of any items being sold; however, one traditional midwife, Liliana López, was given the task of manning the table for a few hours when Sofia was away—the expression of boredom and lack of interest on her face provoked me to wonder about the *feeling* of dispossession. At the registration table was a sign-up sheet for those who wished to participate in a nocturnal "*temascal* ritual" (an indigenous healing practice, similar to a sweat lodge), for an extra fee.

That night, I searched the hotel where the traditional midwives and professional midwifery students were staying, looking for a few professional midwifery students, friends of mine from earlier research whom I had not seen since they set out to perform their year of social service in different government hospitals across Mexico. The hotel was bursting with guests, and numerous cots had been shoved into the rooms. After knocking on what seemed like an endless number of doors, I finally found the right room. The professional midwifery students I was searching for had gone to the *temascal;* their suitemates, traditional midwives, had stayed behind.

Curious about the disjuncture between how the *encuentro* had been promoted and its manifest reality, I traveled to the TMID office in Mexico

Figure 1.2. Liliana

City, where I interviewed two planners of government health programs. I asked them to explain the relationship between their published work on "interculturality" and what had unfolded at the *encuentro* they sponsored in Estación Catorce. They did not want to be associated with the event, explaining that though they had sponsored the *encuentro,* they had not been involved in its planning or execution. Both doctors whom I interviewed assured me that what I had witnessed is not representative of their work. They have planned and executed more than fifty highly successful Encounters for Mutual Enrichment Between Health Personnel and Traditional Midwives at which traditional midwifery knowledge was "rescued" from the ongoing threat of extinction. I asked when their next *encuentro* would take place, stating I would travel any distance to attend the type of event they described, as it would be very informative for my research. Then they told me that Encounters for Mutual Enrichment were no longer being planned.

Consuming the Indigenous "Other"

Mexican midwifery is "good to think with" because it enables us to explore the consumption of cultural *medical* practices and the idea of a traditional past in ways that are exploitative of the very people it claims to celebrate, embrace, and represent. Other anthropologists have deconstructed the complexity of biopiracy, but Mexican midwifery serves as an entryway for examining the multivalence of "ethnomedical piracy." Mexican midwifery provides a vantage point for analyzing the emerging global ethnomedical marketplace, thus building upon how others have thought about cultural marketplaces (see Chow 2002; Comaroff and Comaroff 2009; Clifford 2013). (Another vantage point is the commodification and sale of shamanism to Western consumers; for example, shamanic tours to the healing compound of João de Deus in the Brazilian Amazon.) Although indigenous people are often discursively produced as specific types of subjects through research on topics such as land use, casinos, psychological pathology, and drug addiction (to name a few), Mexican midwifery is a unique example of how indigeneity as an object of consumption is sought through reproductive health.

I observed how people who self-identify as indigenous leverage their own racialized identities in order to use the commodification of "indigeneity" to their favor; however, I also witnessed interactions that led me to think critically about the historical underpinnings at play when ethnomedicine is usurped by transnational humanized-birth practitioners. I consider midwifery in Mexico to be an example of "imperialist nostalgia": "Nostalgia for the colonized culture as it was 'traditionally.' . . . Imperialist nostalgia uses a pose of 'innocent yearning' both to capture people's imaginations and to conceal its complicity with often brutal domination" (Rosaldo 1989:107–108). I suggest that through the emergence of humanized birth, traditional ways of birthing are destroyed through power, then reinvented through privilege. What is striking about this example, however, is how reinvention of Mexican midwifery provides a pathway to cultural capital, status, and profit. Through midwifery, I explore how in Mexico, indigenous people are often politically and culturally excluded as ahistorical "Others," while their "culture" is consumed and marketed as an object of desire. Although I resist the notion of a homogeneous culture among all indigenous peoples, I am pointing to how such a notion is socially constructed and then commodified.

Moments like the *encuentro* in Estación Catorce reveal how subtle processes of intersectional racialization surrounding indigenous traditional midwives render them needy recipients of expert knowledge produced by foreigners and mestizo professionals working in urban settings. This type of racialization operates in one direction: throughout my extensive observations and many interviews, urban health-care professionals and foreign humanized-birth proponents rarely questioned how their lack of indigenous language skills and experiences in the contexts in which indigenous women live might hamper their ability to provide culturally appropriate training or care.

This type of racializing logic, paired with "humanitarian reason," justifies the power differential inherent in all the workshops and *encuentros* I have observed (see Fassin 2012). That is, those who approach encounters with "needy" populations from a position of privilege do so because they believe intervention is not only possible but necessary. In line with Fassin, I am less concerned with determining the bad faith of some and the good conscience of others—in fact, I consider it part of the anthropological enterprise to resist normative judgments long enough to pursue an analytical inquiry about the inadvertent consequences of well-intentioned interventions. What is lost when a rhetoric of compassion and suffering occurs in lieu of interests and justice, thus legitimizing actions by rendering them humanitarian? The ways traditional midwives are engaged and not engaged by "experts" serves as a poignant example of how humanitarian reason operates: interactions of this kind presuppose a relation of inequality, re-entrench political asymmetry, and reveal domination in the upsurge of compassion.

My ethnographic work not only points to the relationship of inequality operating in encounters between government health personnel and traditional midwives but also examines how "indigeneity," "traditionality," and "nature" are conflated and subsequently commodified/fetishized by nonindigenous "allies" for economic profit. In these settings, the image of "indigeneity" is juxtaposed or overlaid on items or "traditional experiences" for sale, but indigenous people do not profit from these transactions and often cannot even access the goods that make use of their image. Humanized birth in Mexico is unfolding with a rhetoric of shared humanity while using and commodifying, indeed, dismembering, and reassembling indigenous birthing practices and images for economic profit. The very terminology of humanized birth points to the ambition to unify how children are born through the indivisibility of humankind; however, the humanized-birth movement unfolds among socially stratified actors, where indigenous people are constantly assumed to be the needy recipients of humanitarian intervention. Thus, my work uncovers oppositional forces at work during training workshops like the one described above, and more generally in the humanized-birth movement in Mexico. On the one hand, I observed a discursive debate about "humanity" and "humanization of birth" that criticizes the biomedicalization of childbirth and celebrates "traditional" birth practices. On the other hand, I was struck by the commodification of "indigenous medicine" by which nonindigenous individuals consume "indigeneity" while indigenous people are not engaged as equals.

The consumption of indigeneity, however, cannot be attributed solely to a lack of critical reflexivity on the part of urban health professionals and humanized-birth proponents around the world. Rather, it is also the result of political strategies in Mexico. A great deal of political propaganda is being produced by the Mexican government around programs meant to provide indigenous populations with culturally appropriate services, but these programs are often underfunded, if not entirely defunded. For example, although the TMID office is responsible for planning programs related to "intercultural" development and traditional medicine, in-depth interviews with three employees revealed that it does not possess the funding to implement these programs.

"Interculturality" is a concept that informs policy in Mexico. It has been deployed by the Mexican Secretariat of Health in ways that juxtapose allopathic medical services with "traditional indigenous" services, instead of actually integrating them. Furthermore, I have observed on multiple occasions the consistent privileging of allopathic medicine over "traditional indigenous" services offered in disjointed, decontextualized forms. For example, patrons of "traditional indigenous" services are often

Figure 1.3. One example of artwork circulated through online networks by humanized-birth proponents (artist unknown)

charged a fee, whereas allopathic services in government hospitals are always free of charge (resulting in further commodification of "indigeneity" and an upsurge of "traditional medicine" tourism among nonindigenous people while indigenous individuals seek remedies elsewhere). "Interculturality" has done little to challenge hegemonic biomedicine, leaving relationships of domination-subordination intact.

Many individuals, both laypersons and Mexican medical anthropologists, would argue that funding for health programs in Mexico not only exists but is plentiful—however, within a context of pervasive corruption, funds are routinely diverted to individuals' pocketbooks instead of being used to develop programs. In a private exchange with an informant and government health worker, I asked about a specific politician, describing him as "the man who is extorting *Seguro Popular* (Mexico's universal health insurance) funds and leaving hospitals in his jurisdiction without medications." My informant responded, "I don't know who specifically you are talking about. We all do that! Even me."[2]

In Mexico's decentralized health-care system, individual state governments are responsible for implementing and funding programs. Even when programs are implemented, they usually lack permanence—lasting only until the next elections. Thus, images of indigenous people, "tradition," and "nature" lend value to consumer items and political propaganda produced by nonindigenous people in urban settings; however, these items for sale and "intercultural" programs often do not fulfill the purpose of fostering equitable interactions between indigenous and nonindigenous Mexicans. In a subversive turn, Alfredo Paulo Maya (co-coordinator at the time of the medical anthropology program at the National Autonomous University of Mexico [UNAM]) opined that although the purported goal of "interculturality" has not been met, its actual aims have been adroitly accomplished. During a seminar I gave on September 10, 2014, at the Center for Superior Research and Studies in Social Anthropology (CIESAS), Mexico City, he argued that "intercultural" programs are exculpation strategies whose true purpose (placating human rights groups by developing programs for which "*indios*" are purported beneficiaries) is routinely and satisfactorily met—thus the continuity of "interculturality" as a political goal over time.

The indigeneity of anonymous indigenous individuals in Mexico emerges onto a global scene through a process of rearticulation. As James Clifford points out, "*Indigènitude* is sustained through media-disseminated images, including a shared symbolic repertoire ('the sacred,' 'Mother Earth,' 'shamanism,' 'sovereignty,' the wisdom of 'elders,' stewardship of 'the land')" (Clifford 2013:16). In my research, images connoting a feminized indigeneity are circulated by humanized-birth proponents, paired with words like "we are the Mother Earth," descriptions of "the moon within" (referring to women's menstrual cycles), and details about "the ancient practice of vaginal steaming and womb saunas."

Using my ethnographic fieldwork experiences of humanized birth in Mexico, I engage in a debate about the commodification of indigeneity and systemic power. My work links the performance and commodification of ethnic identities to a new regime of cultural production and reception (see Chow 2002; Comaroff and Comaroff 2009). The romanticization of traditional midwifery demonstrates how capitalist globalization encourages differences so long as these differences do not upset the dominant political-economic order. Cultural traditions are preserved as simulacrum, performed in a theater of identities, while ethnicity is produced and commodified in a "global shopping" mall of identities. Along with Rey Chow and John and Jean Camaroff, I observed a realm where ethnicity-for-tourism, folklore as fakelore, and nostalgic "culture" belie neoliberal marketing. However, although I link the performance and commodification of ethnic identities to a new regime of cultural production and reception, I join Clifford in resisting descriptions that portray power as totalizing and opt instead for dialectical analysis of hegemonic forms and countercurrents. At stake is the issue of agency—people with their own dynamism.

My research explores how humanitarian discourse and processes of intersectional racialization lead to the commodification of "indigeneity" and the consumption of culture; at the same time, I underline the agentive dynamism of indigenous informants. I intervene on this debate by providing complex ethnographic examples that suggest that while unequal power structures are operating in the transnational humanized-birth movement, indigenous individuals are also agentive actors who appropriate cards in decks stacked against them.

Through ethnographic examples, I examine the evaluative work on the part of indigenous women to achieve what they consider to be better birth outcomes. My work documents the strategies these women employ when proactively seeking out citizenship-based health services or subversively evading racial discrimination in biomedical settings. These actions, based on logical responses to an unjust reality, provide dominant sectors of society with further evidence for labeling indigenous women as "backward," as child-endangering irresponsible mothers, in dire need of humanitarian interventions. Thus, I remain attentive to these women's limited access to citizenship-based resources and resist the notion of "insurgent citizenship," as it romanticizes material poverty and exclusionary processes by emphasizing the innovation of people with "differentiated" access to formal citizenship (see Holston 2009 [2007]).

Consuming Indigeneity: (Ethno)medical Tourism in Binational Health Policy

In October 2012, I traveled to Oaxaca City, Oaxaca, to participate in Binational Health Week, a weeklong policy forum that brought together public-health experts and officials from North America and Latin America, but primarily from California and the state of Oaxaca. The event drew representatives from academic institutions, such as the University of California–Berkeley School of Public Health and Mexico's National Council of Science and Technology (CONACYT); public-health providers such as Seguro Popular (Mexico's universal health-care coverage) and the Mexican Social Security Institute; and international health organizations such as the World Health Organization and the Pan American Health Organization. While attending the event, I received an invitation from the coordinator of migrant health care for the Oaxaca Secretariat of Health to join a group of eleven special guests, mostly Americans, on a day trip to Capulalpam de Méndez, a small indigenous village in the Northern Sierra. I eagerly accepted his invitation.

Capulálpam was named a "Pueblo Mágico" in 2008—a designation granted by the Mexico Tourism Board that aims to promote a series of towns across the country by acknowledging their natural beauty, cultural riches, or historical relevance. Upon researching this village online, I read:

The new designation and the healing center were expected to boost tourism. The center, now open, employs traditional healers who provide medicinal plant therapy, massages, *temascal,* and herbal baths. The center has an herbal pharmacy and offers basic training courses about a great variety of medicinal plants. The *temascal* is a type of sweat lodge that gives physical and spiritual purification using the four elements of fire, air, water, and earth to give relief from the stresses of daily life. Participants may reach a level of consciousness similar to that of meditation.[3]

When we arrived at the intercultural clinic, we were greeted by a Oaxaca State Secretariat of Health physician, Arturo Martínez. His opening remarks about the clinic prepared us for the ethnomedical tour on which we were about to embark. He explained that traditional medicine is opposed to allopathic biomedicine, which for him is synonymous with European medicine. He argued that Mexicans should strive to preserve traditional medicine, because doing so means defending a shared national heritage.

Immediately striking to me was how the clinic was constructed: although the clinic is described as "*inter*cultural," in actuality, the clinic is divided into two distinct structures, separated by a grassy area. One structure houses the public biomedical clinic, which offers free or near-free medical care (for example, a consultation with a biomedical physician costs ten pesos, or less than US$1). Inside the other structure is the traditional medicine clinic, which offers traditional healing treatments for a charge: a five-minute *limpia,* or spiritual cleansing, costs 50 pesos, or approximately US$4; entrance into the *temascal* is 170 pesos, or roughly US$14; and a belly massage to cure *empacho* is 50 pesos (*empacho* is an ethnomedical term that describes instances where food gets lodged somewhere along the digestive tract with detrimental effects for overall well-being). When I inquired about the degree to which biomedical physicians and traditional medicine healers work as a team to treat patients, I was told that the two types of care providers do not "interfere" with each other's patients or treatments, with one important exception: biomedical physicians act as gatekeepers, since they perform a physical examination and provide medical permission before patients may partake in the *temascal* ritual.

I listened to Arturo explain the importance of initiatives like this clinic for recuperating traditional and indigenous medical knowledge. He argued that most of this valuable knowledge has been lost due to traditional healers not passing down their wisdom to future generations. Although

Figure 1.4. Mealtime entertainment for binational policy forum attendees

"tradition" undergoes constant transformation and negotiation, my ethnographic encounters suggest that a great deal of traditional knowledge *is*
passed down from one generation to the next; however, this transmission
is not recognized by state officials because it occurs outside of the realm of
Michel Foucault's (1973) "medical gaze."

The visitors and I were then escorted into the laboratory and pharmacy in the traditional medicine clinic. In the laboratory, there were sev-
enteen clearly labeled boxes, each indicating to visitors the types of herbs
on display. During extended stays in the homes of midwives and *curanderas,* I learned about their traditional medicine practices through participant-observation. I joined key informants on shopping trips to buy supplies for creating traditional remedies, watched as they prepared teas and
gave massages, listened as they described their methods for making tinctures and balms, read their handwritten recipes, went on countryside
walks to gather fresh herbs, and was at times the recipient of their expert care. Having already performed substantial research among indigenous healers and midwives, I noticed that the quantities of herbs in the
laboratory were insufficient for producing remedies, prompting me to ask
myself if their primary purpose in the "traditional laboratory" was to be
seen, but not used.

I also noticed that a number of herbs commonly used by indigenous
healers were not represented among the specimens laid out on display—

Figure 1.5. Medicinal plants on display in the laboratory

sangregado, hierba del sapo, ajenjo, epazote, eucalipto. We were then ushered into the room where *limpias* are performed, and two types of herbs were laid out on the ground, but *pirul,* the herb most commonly used for *limpias,* was conspicuously absent. *Limpias* are rituals that rid individuals of harmful energies—burning incense, rubbing an uncooked egg on the individual's skin to draw out negativity, spitting *mezcal* in order to cover the afflicted with an antiseptic mist, and sweeping the patient's body with cleansing herbs are regular components of this ritual. As I wondered silently how traditional healing was carried out without basic herbal ingredients, I had a feeling that I was in a showroom. Were we being interpellated as consumers in a simulacrum of "traditional medicine"? We were then guided into the "pharmacy," where the members of the group began exuberantly purchasing herbal balms and shampoos.

During our visit, there were no patients at the clinic. While the rest of the group admired the installations, I stealthily escaped from the tour. I wondered what members of the community thought about the clinic. I walked to a wooden cabin nearby—the home of an indigenous family that also served as a snack bar (selling gum, sweets, potato chips, and soda) for local villagers. The snack bar attendant, María del Rosario González, and a customer were at the cabin when I arrived. I asked them why there were no patients at the clinic. They explained that although a doctor and a nurse are assigned to the clinic, the doctor is often away in the town of Ixtlán, and the nurse has been gone for several days attending a workshop. I asked María del Rosario if many people visit the clinic. She responded,

Figure 1.6. Herbal balms and shampoos for sale in the pharmacy

"*Sí vienen, mucha gente viene. Mucha gente vienen para el turismo.*" ("Yes, they come, a lot of people come. A lot of people come for tourism.")

María del Rosario went on to say that the traditional medicine clinic built by the Secretariat of Health is not necessary because, for many common ailments, villagers possess enough traditional knowledge to heal themselves with herbs in their own homes. "*Cada madre tiene su propia forma de curar sus nenes.*" ("Each mother has her own way of curing her babies.") Although her comments are perfectly aligned with Eduardo L. Menéndez's observations about *autoatención* (all the health-care seeking, decision-making, and healing that takes place in multitudinous settings beyond the clinic, events that often go unnoticed by health officials since they unfold prior to encounters with physicians and medical institutions, frequently rendering would-be encounters unnecessary [Menéndez 1983]), they contradict the Secretariat of Health representative's assertions that traditional medical knowledge has been lost and must be restored and preserved through government interventions that defend Mexico's national heritage. María del Rosario further explained that when her children have an ailment that she is unable to cure herself, she takes them to the *curandera* (the local traditional medicine midwife), who provides three treatments for 100 pesos (about US$8).

After leaving María del Rosario's snack shop, I walked a little farther down the path and ran into a young man, Francisco Rodriguez, and asked him about his experiences at the clinic. Francisco told me he had inquired about the midwifery services in the traditional medicine clinic before his wife's recent birth but was told the midwife was only present a few hours on specific mornings. When his wife went into labor, Francisco rushed to the clinic, only to find that neither the physician nor the midwife was present. He made arrangements to transport his wife to the hospital in Ixtlán as swiftly as possible, where she had a biomedicalized birth. After these brief conversations, I returned to the group at the intercultural clinic. As far as I could tell, my brief absence had gone unnoticed.

Experiences such as the ones I have just described provided an invaluable lens for critically analyzing social inequality. In my approach, I apply theories of cultural consumption to the object of my ethnographic inquiry: the reinvention and commodification of present-day Mexican midwifery. My ethnographic fieldwork documented how indigenous midwives are excluded and denied professional status while their "traditional" cultural practices are pirated, lionized, romanticized, and sold for profit by affluent urban Mexicans and by international practitioners in humanized-birth circles. What humanized-birth proponents describe as an international feminist liberation for educated women is based in the exploitation of cultural-intellectual property rights (traditional midwifery) and the reproduction of inequality in Mexico, as the indigenous practitioners of these birthing arts and practices are prevented from practicing them in Mexican hospitals. Although I have observed indigenous midwives defy government restrictions, challenge biomedical authority in hospital settings, and attempt to market their traditional knowledge by forming their own association and opening a shared clinical practice, these examples of resistance emerge within a context of power and political economy that, more often than not, capitalizes on images of indigeneity while obscuring the lives, experiences, and opinions of indigenous people. Furthermore, the diverse methods indigenous midwives use to attend births are not equitably included by members of the humanized-birth community under the rubric of humanized birth, since they are relegated to the realm of traditional medicine from which humanized birth draws, then improves and develops.

Portraying Indigeneity: Politics of Representation

The multiplicitous ways indigeneity is leveraged, commodified, and sold evinces its social salience around the globe. Although this naturalizes the racial category of "indigenous" and results in real political and material consequences for those it encompasses, the pan-racial group defined as "indigenous" does not exist except through opposition with colonizers. In this way, the desire that leads to the commodification of "indigenous" practices and goods for sale emerges from "the standpoint of those who did the encountering" (Tallbear 2013:5)

Despite persistent evidence of marginalization of indigenous peoples and examples of profit-seeking around constructed images of indigeneity, I am attentive to the dynamism of my indigenous informants—I am careful not to deny these friends their agency by portraying them *only* as victims. Thus, I am concerned not only with how indigeneity is portrayed by nonindigenous ethnomedicine enthusiasts, but how indigenous individuals portray their own ethnic identities. I suggest that though indigenous people have suffered from centuries-long structural violence, they have also devised strategies for leveraging their indigeneity and, at times, view their indigenous heritage as a source of pride. My perspective does not sanitize the effects of violence and long-standing exclusion, nor does it diminish the agency and dynamism of indigenous individuals; rather, I aim to cast indigenous informants as agentive, proactive people who experience their indigeneity both as a source of marginalization and also as a valuable resource.

Although I am pointing to "indigeneity" as something that is produced, circulated, and sold, I am not arguing that there is one, singular "indigenous culture" that encapsulates all indigenous people. I recognize there are many ways of being indigenous; simultaneously, I point to how "indigeneity" and "indigenous culture" are constructed as objects of consumption, thus erasing diversity among indigenous peoples. Through ethnographic research, I documented how "indigeneity" becomes a consumer item, especially through "indigenous" medicine. As noted earlier, my use of the terms "indigenous women" and "indigenous people" refers to individuals who self-identify as indigenous, speak indigenous languages, or live in rural, indigenous regions. Also, as I have previously mentioned, the indigenous people with whom I worked are from the following ethnic groups: Tlapaneco, Mixteco, Huasteco (Téenek), Nahua, Tzotzil, Tzeltal, Maya, and Purépecha.

My ethnographic observations across these ethnic groups have allowed me to delve into the complex politics of representation of indigeneity. In addition to constructed representations of traditional and indigenous medicine that unfolded when I visited the intercultural clinic in Oaxaca, I have, on different occasions throughout my ethnographic research, observed how indigenous individuals perform their "indigeneity" for foreigners and transnationals. At times, it seemed that indigenous informants enjoyed ritualized representations of their indigeneity—that their indigeneity was a source of pride and a resource to be strategically employed to achieve desired outcomes. Other times, indigeneity seemed to be a liability, and indigenous informants made concerted efforts to portray themselves as "modern" individuals who practice Western techniques. Finally, in some instances, indigenous informants felt used for their indigenous appearance, fetishized as an image of indigeneity, and coerced into acting and speaking according to the interests of nonindigenous others.

During summer 2011, I volunteered and performed participant observation at the Center for the Adolescents of San Miguel de Allende (CASA). In July, I was invited by Sagrario Villareal, general director at the time, to participate in field practice in Veracruz—a two-week trip wherein professional midwifery students gave workshops to traditional midwives in government hospitals and subsequently joined them in their homes to continue the "exchange" of knowledge. Although the purpose of the field practice is to engage in bilateral exchange of knowledge, I observed a mostly unilateral flow of knowledge from "knowing" professional mid-wifery students (most of whom were only beginning to attend births or were totally lacking in experience) and "unknowing" traditional midwives.

I accompanied a professional midwifery student, Francisca, to the Na-hua village of Zacatochin, where we observed Doña Eugenia Navarro, a well-respected traditional midwife. This tiny village in the mountains is the farthest I have been from the conveniences of urban life. Zacatochin is perched high above the clouds, leading to a feeling of isolation from the nearest town, which is located a forty-five-minute windy drive down the mountain. Water is pumped once a week to a public spout in the center of the village, and on this day, women dressed in the traditional blouse and *bata* (a large piece of black wool cloth that is worn as a skirt, tied at the waist with colorful silk cloth) gather to wash laundry. Nahua women and their families travel long distances, as far as from the other side of the Orizaba volcano, to give birth with Doña Eugenia—her use of tradi-tional herbs commingled with biomedical techniques like application of an IV drip appeals to women who want the "modern" comforts of giving birth with someone possessing biomedical knowledge, the safety of labor-ing with the support of a woman who has learned generations of tradi-tional healing techniques, and the security of knowing they will not be discriminated against or mistreated while delivering their baby.

Doña Eugenia is an example of "hybridity"—someone who enters and exits modernity with ease (García Canclini 2009 [1990]). I will eventually deconstruct the "traditionality"-"modernity" binary, thus problematizing the idea of hybrid subjects who move between the two temporal frame-works. Also, I am attentive to the ways in which "hybridity" has been used only to describe "subalterns" and to the concerns some scholars have about this concept being inherently racist. However, for the time being, I am referring to Néstor García Canclini (2009 [1990]) to begin to trouble the idea that traditional midwives are antiquated subjects whose practices are necessarily rooted in the past. Doña Eugenia's work throws into ques-tion portrayals of "traditionality" and traditional midwives as frozen in some prior time, exempt from transformative processes that occur in "the outside world."

One night, I observed Doña Eugenia attend two simultaneous births. A twenty-year-old, María Elena, was giving birth to her first child in the living room of Doña Eugenia's home-clinic, while a second woman, Juana Sánchez, was birthing in Doña Eugenia's bedroom. I witnessed the entire evolution of María Elena's birth: María Elena's arrival with a horde of family members in tow, Doña Eugenia's direction of the extended family to the patio while only María Elena's husband accompanied her during the birth, the moment Doña Eugenia examined the shape of María Elena's belly and predicted a female child, the second when the baby girl emerged from her mother's vagina, wailing and filling her strong lungs with oxygen for the first time, the minutes when Doña Eugenia massaged the mother's belly to encourage the placenta to detach from the uterine wall, and the wordless entrusting of the plastic-bagged placenta to María Elena so she could bury it close to her home.

I did not witness Juana's birth, as she was uncomfortable with my presence and I respected her wishes. Since only a curtain covers the passageway to Doña Eugenia's bedroom, I heard the birthing while waiting outside. Later, I asked Doña Eugenia to describe the birth, and she did so with an air of formality, as if presenting a case at medical grand rounds before an attending physician. I wondered as she spoke, did I represent an authority figure in her eyes? Here is Doña Eugenia's spoken report of July 9, 2011:

> During the night she hardly had any pain, only the mucus plug. It was very slow and I thought they would have to go to the hospital. After, she started to have more pain, and at five in the morning I checked her dilation and she was at two centimeters. I told her it would be better for us to go to the hospital, but she said no—she wanted to wait a little longer. I conceded since they have a truck and I knew we could still go to the hospital later. At eight in the morning she started to have regular contractions, her water broke, and she bled a little—all normal signs her cervix was opening. At 8:50 I performed a vaginal exam, and it was definitive we were going to stay; she was completely dilated. At 9:06 a baby girl was born. I moved the [umbilical cord] a tiny bit, encouraging the placenta to come out, and the placenta came out on its own. The bleeding was normal; she bled a little. I suctioned [the baby's] phlegm immediately. The baby has good coloring, good movements, very active movements. The baby cried. After, I was orienting [the mother], encouraging her and stimulating her to breastfeed. Then, the mother and child stayed together. I dried her vaginal area, changed her sheets, and placed the baby girl with her mother. The mother is content, happy, conversing, and laughing. She is content because she didn't go to the hospital, and since the beginning she said she didn't want to go to the hospital. . . . She is around thirty-four years old and says this will be her last child.

The spoken report Doña Eugenia gave is striking because of the performative element that was evident to me even as it was occurring. Doña Eugenia systematically demonstrated she had done everything as instructed in workshops: she monitored Juana's dilation and bleeding, ensured there was viable transport to the hospital, successfully prevented hemorrhage, cleared the baby's airway, checked the baby's well-being, helped the mother with breastfeeding, was careful not to separate mother and child—and all this in a hygienic environment!

Her use of the medical-case presentation method is evidence of her experience working in biomedical contexts, thus disrupting definitions of what it means to be "traditional" versus biomedical and humanized. Furthermore, the "objectivity" of the case-presentation format serves multiple purposes: by presenting the births in this way, Doña Eugenia frames herself as a medically appropriate birth attendant, while also implying that her intention was to refer the birth to the hospital. In doing so, Doña Eugenia portrayed herself as both capable of independently attending birth and obedient to government mandates. However, what is missing from her report is just as operative as the important details she chooses to include. At the very end of the report, Doña Eugenia acknowledges that Juana never wanted to go to the hospital, before pausing and briefly reflecting on what to say next. She quickly concludes by saying that Juana is about thirty-four years old. Doña Eugenia (accidentally?) admitted that Juana did not plan to go to the hospital and that Doña Eugenia permitted Juana's will to be fulfilled—against the stipulations placed on mothers by Oportunidades. This birth is recorded in the official registers as having occurred in Juana's home, without the help of a birth attendant. Indigenous women in the region must give birth in the government hospital or else lose their conditional cash transfers.

Juana has a wizened face and quite a few white hairs, leading me to suspect she is in her forties, but Doña Eugenia told me she is "around thirty-four," because medical guidelines stipulate that births in women thirty-five and older are high risk and must be referred to the hospital. Midwives are ordered not to attend the births of women thirty-five and over since these women are at additional risk for maternal mortality. Doña Eugenia's assertion that Juana is "around thirty-four" is significant, since she is again ameliorating the disobedience to government mandates that could be associated with her involvement in Juana's birth. I can only speculate about Juana's exact age, but what interests me more is the context within which women weigh reproductive decisions, sometimes leading them to make choices that are deemed "risky" and "dangerous" by the biomedical system and the Mexican government.

I returned for two more summers, in 2012 and 2013. Along with my visits, I began forming a friendship with Doña Eugenia through letters and

Figure 1.7. Doña Eugenia

phone calls. She began to see me as her apprentice, and over time I earned her trust. After many intimate conversations, I asked Doña Eugenia to sit for a formal, video-recorded interview. I explained to her that this footage could potentially be edited into an ethnographic film and used to demonstrate the work of traditional midwives to American anthropology students and conference attendees. She acquiesced, on one condition: that I not start the video camera until she had finished dressing herself in her traditional indigenous attire, put on her best jewelry, and combed her hair. I agreed. Doña Eugenia is among the few women in the village who does not wear indigenous attire every day. I gazed curiously at her slow and deliberate movements while she searched among several plastic bags, until she finally selected the traditional blouse she wanted to wear while being filmed. She folded the pleats in her *bata* and straightened out the lace and ribbons on her blouse ever so carefully, in a methodical, almost ritualistic fashion. It struck me that although different informants make concerted efforts to portray themselves in ways that meet disparate goals, the politics of representation at play in this scene are not too far afield from a doctor putting on the emblematic white coat.

Doña Eugenia's purposefulness caused me to reflect on Clifford's assertion that "media images can lapse into self-stereotyping. And they express a transformative renewal of attachments to culture and place. It is difficult to know, sometimes even for participants, how much of the performance of identity reflects deep belief, how much a tactical presentation of self" (Clifford 2013:16). Why was it so important for Doña Eugenia to be seen by imagined foreigners in indigenous clothing when she wears Western clothing—long-sleeve sweaters, button-down shirts, long denim skirts—in her everyday life? Was this ritual production for foreign consumption? On the other hand, considering that many indigenous women in her village *do* wear traditional clothing every day, what does it mean for Doña Eugenia to wear Western clothing in most situations, and especially when going on shopping trips into town and during interactions with midwifery patients and staff at the village clinic? Moments like these have led me to believe that "presentations of self in everyday life" (see Goffman 1959; Hendrickson 1995) are based on a syncretic and situational sense of identity/identities.

Leveraging Syncretic Identities

Don Israel Pérez self-identifies as a "traditional doctor" and "midhusband" (*médico tradicional y partero*). He is one of the few men who attend births in the High Mountains of Veracruz, but his gender has not limited his clientele. He is well-regarded for his extensive knowledge of herbal remedies and leads an indigenous organization of traditional doctors. He and other members of the organization have formed a rotation for running the or-

Figure 1.8. Center for the Development of Traditional Indigenous Medicine

ganization's secluded clinic in the mountains—each participating traditional doctor works at the clinic one day a week.

I first heard about the traditional medicine clinic that Don Israel leads when I was staying with Doña Agustina Martín during my first visit to Zacatochin. Doña Agustina is an empirically trained traditional midwife who, when compared to Doña Eugenia and Don Israel, has not received many biomedically oriented trainings and certifications led by government workers in clinical settings. Doña Agustina holds Don Israel in high regard and considers him to be the most knowledgeable traditional doctor in the region. On one misty afternoon, she took me on an excursion to visit his clinic. I sat with her sons in the bed of their old truck while her husband drove, and whenever we encountered a hill, her sons would jump out to push the truck up the incline. At the clinic, I observed that the "laboratory" for preparing herbal remedies was bare, the traditionally designed *temascal* had fallen into disuse, and though two traditional massage therapists (*sobadoras*) were present, the clinic had no clients. Since Don Israel was absent from the clinic during our visit, we ventured to his house a few days later, traveling by collective taxi (a type of carpool that allows passengers to pay a reduced fare) and bus before hitchhiking and walking on foot.

Figure 1.9. *Temascal*

When we arrived, Don Israel graciously invited us into his home. The outside structure is made of wooden boards, but once inside, you see that his family living space surrounds an inner courtyard. At the center of his courtyard is a porta-potty—a more convenient alternative to the outhouses on stilts that are common in the region. (This is an example of how traditional medicine practitioners make use of "modern" apparatuses in their everyday lives, again disrupting notions that representatives of "tradition" conduct their lives in a time register distinct from those living in metropolises.) When I explained to him that I was eager to learn about his practice of traditional medicine, his eyes lit up. He told me about the many trainings and certifications he has received, and his collaborations with the government health sector, researchers at the state university, and chemical-supply companies. As he spoke, he showed me certificates, photos of moments when he had been recognized, and book publications for which he had shared his knowledge. During the entire visit, Doña Agustina's admiration of Don Israel's talents was apparent. I wanted to know more about Don Israel's interactions with the different "knowledge-producing" bodies he described, so I made a commitment to return and continue our conversation on a different visit.

The relationship between Doña Agustina and Doña Eugenia is also

Figure 1.10. Don Israel

characterized by respect, but with an undertone of rivalry, since these two are close neighbors and attend overlapping clientele. On one occasion, Doña Agustina was openly critical to me about Doña Eugenia, saying that the ability to attend a birth is a gift from God that should not be exploited for financial gain. Doña Eugenia charges many times Doña Agustina's fee for attending a birth—in part because she considers it her responsibility as a midwife to teach couples to value each child they bring into the world, because she feels she should be compensated for her time and work, and because of the high demand for her services. Over time, Doña Eugenia has built a home-clinic out of "expensive" materials (cement and glass-paned windows) with areas for several women to give birth at a time, plus a patio area that functions as a waiting room. Her home-clinic stands alongside the wooden shack where she used to live, where Doña Eugenia still has her kitchen, outhouse, and bathing area; and that structure in turn is attached to the store where she sells snacks and soda pop. Doña Agustina considers Doña Eugenia to be "enterprising"—her family manages with a more meager budget, derived mostly from her sons' and husband's carpentry.

I returned to the region where Don Israel and Doña Eugenia live several times over the course of my fieldwork. My relationship with both deepened with time, despite neither of them being able to receive phone calls in their homes. I wrote them both letters that, because of irregular postal service in the Mexican countryside, often took weeks or months to arrive. When they went shopping in the nearest town, they would take advantage

Figure 1.11. Doña Agustina giving a *"sobada"* (traditional massage)

of the rare opportunity to call me. As soon as I received their phone calls, I would return the call to the number from which they had dialed, thus assuming responsibility for the cost of the call. Both asked me to purchase things for them that they cannot buy in their area—Doña Eugenia asked me to bring her a pair of gold earrings, and Don Israel requested a digital camera. On one occasion, Don Israel and I traveled together to Mexico City to buy materials for making herbal remedies. Over the years, we gave each other many gifts: for example, Doña Eugenia gave me one of her *batas* and I gave her an embroidered satin blouse from San Miguel. On my trips to Veracruz, I would usually stay the majority of the time with Doña Eugenia and her family in Zacatochin, and upon my departure, she would cry and I would comfort her by telling her that I would return soon for another visit.

My experiences with Don Israel and Doña Eugenia point to the mutual imbrication of agentive representations of self and commodification of culture. Don Israel was proud of the many certifications and trainings he had received. And having been recognized in governmental, biomedical, and university settings led to his enjoying a higher regard among clients and fellow traditional medicine practitioners and birth attendants.

However, despite his track record of ongoing recognition, Don Israel has stopped attending births because he is wary of the consequences that would befall him in the case of a negative birth outcome. He follows the guidelines he has been taught in the trainings, which dictate that he refer birthing mothers to the government hospital. He pondered aloud in my presence about an apparent increase in ethnomedical tourism. Commenting on poorly designed *temascals* reflecting a lack of understanding about traditional medicine and the therapeutical mechanism that facilitates healing, Don Israel asked why his authentically constructed *temascal* lacked visitors. How could he attract more visitors? He considered putting up a sign on the road directing people to the *temascal* and offering courses on herbalism to the general public in the hope that this would attract more visitors to the clinic.

Although he is no longer attending births and his clinic is underfrequented, Don Israel leverages his identity as a regional leader of traditional medicine in a way that is generally satisfying to him. It could be argued that he is an example of someone who uses politics of representation mostly in his favor. However, the opposite argument could also be made: I witnessed moments when Don Israel was treated rudely by nonindigenous individuals. When we went shopping in Mexico City, he asked the clerk for a clarification about the difference in concentration between two types of oils and their appropriate uses. The shop clerk sighed loudly and was curt with him, and he reacted to her scolding tone by gazing down at the floor, placing his chin in his hand. I wondered about this interaction: Throughout the day I noticed how unfamiliar Don Israel was with the metropolitan surroundings. Was the shop clerk's harsh response related to Don Israel being a rural, indigenous, elderly man? Had racial discrimination come into play? When we emerged from the shop, I made a remark about the shop clerk's rude behavior. He responded, "People who act like that are just unhappy. We should pray for their happiness."

As time passed and I began asking Don Israel for more details about his interactions with university researchers, chemical-supply companies, and the Mexican government, I began asking myself if he was unknowingly being taken advantage of. Although his group of traditional doctors shared their knowledge with the Mexican Institute of Social Security, which subsequently published an extensive herbal manual, his name does not appear in the publication, nor does he receive royalties for the book. Moreover, he has shared his knowledge of *sangregado, Santa María,* and a few other herbs common to traditional medicine with the researchers at the state university, who in turn are partnering with a chemical-supply company to commercialize the herb and develop balms, tinctures, shampoos, and soaps. When I interviewed him about this project, he explained that the researchers were engaging in legal patent procedures involving the notary public and the Public Ministry.

A year later, I returned to visit him. In the interim, his wife's leg had to be amputated because of advanced diabetes, and he had been hospitalized as the result of debilitating leg cramps. The couple was unable to pay mounting debt from hospital bills, and they were sporadically going hungry. We went to town and after we sat down together to enjoy a meal, I ordered an extra roasted chicken for his family. Don Israel asserted that he only shared his traditional medicine knowledge with university researchers to protect himself from being exploited. As an academic, I know that not everything that is researched in academic settings is solely motivated by "the pursuit of knowledge." Although Don Israel derives a positive sense of self-worth when he is consulted and asked to share his knowledge on traditional medicine, I am concerned about biopiracy and wonder about the economic profit that may be resulting for the individuals with whom he shares his knowledge. By simultaneously pointing to the pride that Don Israel derives from sharing his traditional medicine practices, and also the potential exploitation and biopiracy of his ethnomedical knowledge, I am problematizing the binary nature upon which oppos-

Figure 1.12. Having a cup of hot chocolate in the kitchen before bedtime

ing notions of victims and agents are premised. Binary representations are insufficient for the complex reality of how individuals' cultural pride is infused with potential exploitation, and how entrepreneurship unfolds on the edge of uncertainty.

Doña Eugenia's case is perhaps less extreme. She seeks recognition mostly from within her own community and from the staff members at the IMSS clinic in her village. She does not derive a sense of pride from accumulating certificates. In the past she was employed by the local government as a community health worker, but she was underpaid and soon realized that the work limited her from dedicating herself fully to the more rewarding task of midwifery. For similar reasons, Doña Eugenia declined participating in Don Israel's indigenous organization of traditional doctors. She explained to him that with so many pregnant and birthing mothers under her watch, she simply did not have time to travel away from her home. These decisions demonstrate how much Doña Eugenia values her skills as a midwife and how protective she is of her indigenous knowledge. However, Doña Eugenia's relative success depends on a delicate balance: her harmonious relationship with the village physician who turns a blind eye to her midwifery practice, her recognition among local mothers but

Figure 1.13. After a baptism at which Doña Eugenia was *"la madrina"* (godmother)

"invisibility" to government officials, and continued luck with respect to birth outcomes. Although Doña Eugenia is a very skillful midwife, all it would take is one negative birth outcome for this delicate balance to come crashing down. She is very aware of the risks she faces and conscientiously manages how she is perceived (or not perceived) by others, but she is constantly teetering on the edge of uncertainty. How long will it last?

When I asked Doña Eugenia for a formal interview, she exuded a sense of pride as she performed her "indigeneity" for imagined nonindigenous spectators; however, other of my informants have been forced to enact their "indigenous" identity in a way that causes them to feel used and silenced. For example, Mayra, the only indigenous student at the Center for the Adolescents of San Miguel de Allende (CASA) Professional Midwifery School at the time, was asked to join two CASA directors on a trip to Canada for the Midwifery Association of North America annual meeting. Upon returning from Canada, Mayra came to my house for lunch and shared with me her impressions of the trip. As she began speaking, I was surprised by her lack of excitement, as I had assumed that she would be bursting with enthusiasm after her first international travel experience. While I prepared fish and red rice, she described to me how every time someone spoke to her at the conference, the two directors were immediately at her side, demanding to know the details of the interchange. "What did they ask you? What did you say?" She felt like she was being treated as an object of constant surveillance. Sitting on a stool at my kitchen counter, Mayra pondered aloud about the school administration's choice to take her on the trip out of all the girls in her graduating class. Then it dawned on her that she represented something of value, and that this value lies in her indigeneity. The school directors told her not to say anything to anyone—the person designated to speak was Evelyn, an attractive American woman with blue eyes and auburn hair, a certified midwife, a Brown University graduate, and CASA's clinical director. Mayra suggested that her strikingly indigenous physical appearance was what interested the other midwives at the conference—not her perspective or her experiences. She complained that in Canada, she felt like "a poster"—an image at whom others are meant to ogle—and living, breathing, fleshy evidence that CASA's model targets indigenous women. As a living image, she was meant to be seen but not heard, and her every word incited fear and anxiety from her school directors, as if at any moment she would commit an error, thus tearing apart the image they were so carefully crafting.

Desire and the Cathedral of Consumption

My multi-sited ethnographic fieldwork on the humanized-birth movement sought to trace the emergence of a global "cathedral of consumption," buttressed by the reenchantment of a transnational community by the most natural of physiological acts: nonmedicalized birth (see Ritzer 2001). How does a bodily practice as foundational to humanity as eating and having sex become alienated from our physiological repertoire, only to then be commodified and reintroduced into society as a fetish that deepens unequal power relations between the "haves" and the "have nots"?

What ethnographic research on the humanized-birth movement offers is a way of thinking about inequality embedded in the consumption of biological and medical goods, and divergent identities that emerge based upon the "conspicuousness" or absence of consumption (see Veblen 2006 [1902]). I am signaling the collective amnesia that permits commodity fetishism and inequity to operate within the realm of health-care provision (see Billig 1999). Furthermore, I am drawing attention to the *adverted gaze* that makes the exploitation of others—for example, the ethnomedical piracy that unfolds within the humanized-birth movement—not only possible but also real. What the humanized-birth movement unfolding in Mexico affords is an example of how gender-racialized indigenous others can be excluded and dispossessed in the name of humanization, and the subtle processes that allow for this increased marginalization to occur. If individuals were to gaze directly at the fetishized commodity—the origins of images of indigeneity and the effects of ethnomedical piracy on indigenous people—the façade upon which the very life of the fetishized commodity is premised would come crashing down. The questions linger: How much effort is involved in maintaining an adverted gaze? How much intention is embedded in inattention? How much should individuals be held morally accountable for the direct and indirect consequences of gazing elsewhere?

With these questions, I am broadening the scope of an ongoing debate in medical anthropology about the commodification of the human body. Nancy Scheper-Hughes and Loïc Wacquant explore how bodies increasingly enter into global market exchanges—they direct attention to the body-turned-merchandise. In subsequent chapters, I offer the concept of bioconsumer citizenship and the example of midwifery in Mexico in order to examine intersectional racialized identities-turned-merchandise, with real effects for the bodies of women. For Scheper-Hughes and Wacquant, commodification of the body results in alienation of the self, and the case of humanized birth in Mexico demonstrates how the commodification of others' (imagined) "selves" can lead to their increased exclusion and dispossession. Instead of exploring the political economy of the body under contemporary global capitalism, I turn to the transnational context of humanized birth to analyze the political economy of identities vis-à-vis the body.

CHAPTER 2

Humanized Birth:
Unforeseen Politics of Parenting

Intrigued by the question of racialized hierarchies among midwives, I began traveling to different states in 2013 to meet with foreign and foreign-trained midwives and collect their life stories. I traveled to nearby Mexico City to interview Paula Marin, a well-known professional midwife. Paula is an older woman with fair skin and white hair. Her poised movements and demeanor signal a life of privilege, beginning with her childhood and adolescence in Veracruz. She moved to Mexico City to study at the university, but she quickly fell in love and married, dedicating herself to homemaking and raising children instead of completing her studies. After a traumatic, highly medicalized birth experience, she familiarized herself with the prophylactic method and became a firm believer that women can have natural, vaginal births. Her conviction impelled her to teach prenatal education courses to "empower" women for fifteen years, but after seeing how this "empowerment" vanished as soon as women arrived at the hospital and submitted to biomedical authority, she became increasingly dissatisfied with her work. From Paula's perspective, (masculine) biopower is exercised over women's bodies within a patriarchal medical system, but my participant-observation draws attention to how humanized-birth social networks (premised on standards to maximize the benefits of natural birth for mother and child) are an unintentional mechanism through which women, spurred on by feminist ideals, exact burdensome social expectations on each other.

Paula decided to return to her studies, completed a master's degree, and worked at a private foreign-language school. She began reading about humanized birth and was deeply moved by the work of Sheila Kitzinger, anthropologist and natural-childbirth activist in the United Kingdom, and when she and her husband moved to London for his work, she was able to meet Kitzinger and discuss her traumatic birth experiences. Paula then spent time observing births with midwives in many countries, among them England, Austria, Holland, and Ireland. Upon returning to Mexico, she was determined to become a midwife. She met a midwife-anthropologist in the state of Morelos, in Tepoztlán, a town known for a large population of resident foreigners, who connected her to Olivia Olson, an American midwife who was attending water births for American and transnational couples living in Mexico. Paula is a transnational figure whose accrued cultural capital positions her as a conduit for clients to a humanized-birth community of consumption originating in the Global North.

Paula and a group of prenatal educators, along with one obstetric nurse and one acupuncturist, began taking classes from Olivia before traveling to El Paso, Texas, to acquire clinical training. (Later, Olivia Olson also gave classes to Doña Isabela, CASA's first and longest-lasting clinical director, thus playing a foundational role in the midwifery school.) Upon returning to Mexico, Paula led a civil association, traveling to different conferences around the world, lobbying for home birth, and obtaining funds from Japan International Cooperation Agency, Mexico's Secretariat of Social Development, and the MacArthur Foundation. The name selected for the association means "midwives" in Nahua and is meant to draw attention to how, in Paula's words, "professional midwifery is the recipient [of knowledge] from traditional midwifery." For the last eleven years, Paula has dedicated herself to attending births, and the association she led is no longer registered. Throughout my fieldwork, I observed how encounters between traditional midwives and professional midwives positioned professional midwives as experts and traditional midwives as knowledge recipients, even when these encounters were framed as opportunities for mutual exchange. The dispersal of Paula's civil association throws into question the plausibility and sustainability of positive, equitable engagements between mobile humanized-birth practitioners and their immobile, indigenous counterparts. She explained that the midwives of her association "passed the baton" on to other associations in Mexico, Brazil, and the Caribbean. These associations form a Latin American network, and though their connectedness points to the transnationalization of humanized birth, it does not diminish the "solitary contractuality" (Urry 2007:156, referring to Augé 1995:94) defining how disparate groups interact in Mexico.

Our interview was cut short when two couples, potential clients, arrived at Paula's home, seeking information regarding the services she offers. I was happy to sit and observe as the exchange took place between Paula and these two couples. Paula's domestic worker had shown the two couples into the library while Paula and I were talking in the garden. Paula entered the study and exclaimed, "Here I am, the one who is called 'midwife.'" One of the couples had a rather bohemian style, and the other couple displayed all the trappings of affluence. Paula explained that although she is certified in the United States, her certification is not valid in Mexico, so if there are any complications with the birth, they have to switch to Plan B at a small clinic where a "technical, medical team" composed of a surgeon, an obstetrician, and an anesthesiologist would administer an epidural and perform a cesarean.

Then the moment came for Paula to tell the couples exactly how much her services cost. She recommends prenatal consultations every month until the twenty-second week, then twice a month, and weekly during the third trimester. She charges 600 pesos (about US$50) per consultation. She always attends births with a fellow midwife, and they charge 19,000 pesos (about US$1,520), to be split between them for each birth. Paula also works as a team with a homeopath and a biodynamics practitioner. Thus, the base price for prenatal care and birth with Paula is about 31,600 pesos (about US$2,530), plus charges for homeopathic treatments and biodynamic sessions. Considering that minimum wage in Mexico was 67 pesos (about US$5.40)per day at the time of this research, birth with Paula represents 1.3 years of earnings at minimum wage. The cultural capital of her US training overshadowed her lack of certification in Mexico for the affluent couples she serves. Whereas Paula makes the most of lucrative opportunities afforded by humanized birth despite her lack of certification, the traditional indigenous midwives who participated in her extinct association did not enjoy similar opportunities. Paula's heightened mobility, fair skin, and high socioeconomic standing form a nexus that stands in stark contrast to the comparatively immobile, indigenous, impoverished midwives she no longer engages.

Definitions of "Humanized Birth"

"Humanized birth" (*parto humanizado*) is usually used in Mexico and elsewhere in Latin America to describe birth that purposefully resists medicalization and technocratic practices (see Davis-Floyd 2004 [1992]). This movement is preceded by the home and water-birth movements in the United States, Canada, and Western Europe. Births are often attended by professional midwives (although some obstetricians have joined the movement) who are accompanied by doulas. Generally, proponents of humanized birth criticize power inequality inherent in physician-patient relationships and denounce medicalized practices such as unnecessary cesarean sections, episiotomies, isolation of birthing mothers in hospital labor and delivery areas, labor induction, the use of hormones such as Pitocin, and repetitive insertion of medical personnel's fingers into women's vaginas to assess dilation.

However, some informants expressed a more nuanced definition of humanized birth, explaining that a highly medicalized birth can be considered "humanized" if the interventions were medically necessary and/or if the interventions were chosen by the birthing mother. Given socioeconomic and race-based disparities across Mexico, I question uncritical notions of "free choice." I analyze not only the limited agency of indigenous "others" within transnational, consumption-oriented, humanized-birth circles, but also how the very definition of what constitutes a humanized birth limits participants' choices even while celebrating "choice" as a central tenet of humanized-birth ideology.

According to a presentation in 2012 given by Dr. Alejandro Almaguer, director of the Office for Traditional Medicine and Intercultural Development within the Mexican Secretariat of Health, the goal of humanized birth is "that women, their children, and their families live the experience as a special and pleasant moment, in conditions of human dignity, in which the woman is the protagonist of her birth." Within the national offices of the Secretariat of Health, humanized birth is considered a "traditional" and "intercultural" matter; however, I will problematize the assumption that humanized birth is synonymous with "traditional" and "intercultural" practices in later parts of the book. Doctor Almaguer identifies the essential elements of this birth model to be: a vertical birth position, psychoaffective accompaniment throughout labor, massage, skin-to-skin contact between newborn and mother, breastfeeding immediately after the birth, de-medicalization of the birth to the extent possible, prevention of the abuse and overutilization of technology, and above all, the respect of women and their decision-making.[1]

Similarly, the website of a humanized-birth organization in Oaxaca explains, "[T]he humanized attention of birth is rooted in the value placed on the affective-emotional world of the people involved, and in the desires and needs of its protagonists: mother, father, infant daughter or son. It is based in the freedom and right of mothers and of couples to make decisions about where, how, and with whom to give birth, in one of the most important moments of their life." The principles of humanized birth are: respect of human and reproductive rights; respect of culture, rituals, and ancestral knowledge; and a vision of birth as a physiological, transcendent, intimate, and personal occurrence. Humanized birth is directed autonomously and freely by the woman, in an atmosphere of love, respect, and security; and involves no routine interventions into the natural process. Humanized-birth ideology prioritizes personalized connection between the couple and the team of professional attendants; respect of her privacy, dignity, and confidentiality; protection of the immediate bonding between mother and newborn child; and vision of the mother as protagonist of her labor and birth. This type of birth is envisioned as a form of culturally compatible care and interculturality, which implies respect for her traditions, language, and other cultural factors.

These are "official" and formalized definitions of "humanized birth," but the most illustrative way to describe how humanized birth is conceived in practice is through the words of its practitioners. I audited a course offered by Doña Isabela, a traditional midwife and clinical director of the CASA Professional Midwifery School. She explained to professional midwifery students that humanized birth involves making the birthing mother as comfortable as possible by orchestrating a harmonious environment for her to give birth in, and liberating her from misinformation about "correct" birthing. Women are socialized to think they must give birth lying on their backs, but it is the professional midwife's job to encourage the birthing mother to eat, ambulate, and adopt comfortable positions throughout the labor process. Doña Isabela taught students to use massage, aromatherapy, the music of the woman's choice, and, depending on the woman's religious beliefs, prayer and chanting to help the woman feel totally at ease during the birth.

According to a humanized-birth obstetrician and a doula, who were guest lecturers at CASA, humanized-birth attendants must strive to mediate biomedical hypervigilance that often provokes couples to become unwarrantedly anxious about "abnormalities" that are really just normal variation in pregnancy and fetal development. Additionally, humanized-birth practitioners help couples connect emotionally with their unborn babies by guiding interaction with the fetus throughout pregnancy. The goal of humanized-birth practitioners is to help couples "give birth conscientiously" and to lead them into conscientious parenthood. Another guest lecturer, an obstetrician from Querétaro, taught professional midwifery students to resist "masculine desires" for quickness and medical intervention, to respect the natural physiology of birth, and to view birth as an intimate and unique moment within a woman's sex life. The goal of the humanized-birth practitioner is to make the woman feel supported and empowered, while also preserving the integrity of the phenomenological experience of the child being born.

An obstetric nurse who attends humanized births in Mexico City emphasized the importance of knowing each individual mother personally, using her name when speaking to her, coaching her on breathing techniques during the labor, looking into her eyes, and being present without distractions during her birth. After the birth, obstetric nurses consider it part of their job to help mothers adapt to breastfeeding and make sure that the new family is doing well. Likewise, a young obstetrician and apprentice of humanized birth in Guadalajara told me, "The key is the relationship we build with patients. They are more like family than patients. We don't even use that term." He expressed that what is "humanized" about humanized birth is the relationship based on love and respect between the couple giving birth and the person who attends their birth.

A humanized-birth advocate in San Luis Potosí emphasized the importance of tranquility during birth at a workshop for expectant parents. She explained that the requirements for a tranquil birth are patience, no unnecessary interventions, the privacy of a private hospital, a quiet environment, absolutely no talk of pain from anyone present, constant accompaniment by whomever the woman chooses, freedom of movement, not being connected to monitors, freedom to eat and drink, and only a minimum number of required physical examinations throughout the labor process.

In Monterrey, I heard a contrasting perspective from a midwifery apprentice at a transnational NGO. Whereas the humanized-birth advocate in San Luis described stringent requirements for achieving a humanized birth, the midwifery apprentice explained that the priority is not that the birth take place at home or that the baby be born vaginally; rather, the priority is that the woman's embodied knowledge and the role of the baby as protagonist be prioritized throughout the birth. If the woman becomes too exhausted during the labor and wishes to switch to a medicalized birth or even a cesarean, this is still a humanized birth because the woman's decisions were respected. Although this midwife identified similar goals for humanized birth as some of the perspectives above (home birth, water birth, the active involvement of partners and doulas, the presence of family members and especially siblings of the baby being born, the absence of excessive pain and screaming, delayed cutting of the umbilical cord by a family member), the primary criterion was that the birth be controlled by the mother and baby.

For a transnational midwife who gives "traditional Mexican midwifery" workshops in Brazil, a humanized birth is the marriage of emotional and physiological, spiritual and corporal, and soul and body. Humanized-birth practitioners are advocates of women, life, babies, and families. These advocates lead the movement from many posts around the world, resulting in the globalization of humanized birth. Similarly, a Colombian nurse midwife living and practicing in Guadalajara works to help couples transition from thinking about birth as a physiological act to a transcendental act that will leave a mark on the future of both woman and child. For her, birth is something that affects future generations because the way people are born is predictive of individuals' emotional well-being and how they will treat others in society. The words and work of both of these midwives signal the transnationalization of the humanized-birth movement and the emergence of a globalized rhetoric for describing this type of birth.

When I interviewed the dean of a prestigious private medical school in Mexico City, he emphasized the dearth of scientific literature being produced in Mexico about humanized birth when compared to such countries as Brazil. (At the same time, the MacArthur Foundation is working to apply ideas authored in Brazil to the Mexican context through engagement with the Mexican government and advocacy for the reduction of maternal mortality and Millenium Development Goals.)[2] In his opinion, adopting humanized-birth practices is a strategy for bringing Mexico to the table of progress along with other developing countries. The challenge facing obstetricians who wish to attend humanized births in hospital settings is "the struggle against the routine of traditional care." In his perspective, "traditional care" refers to medicalized birth, and progress is aligned with an ethos of limited interventions bolstered by scientific evidence. Over the course of three decades, he has stopped performing routine episiotomies and no longer has nurses shave women's pubic hair and administer enemas, since "normal birth with interventionism has not demonstrated better maternal and perinatal results than natural birth."

Over the course of my fieldwork, other physicians rejected the terminology of "humanized birth," arguing that it implicitly suggests that medicalized births are "dehumanized" and "animalistic." They preferred more neutral terms such as *"parto respetado"* (respected birth), *"parto elegido"* (chosen birth), and *"parto natural"* (natural birth), as these terms highlight respect for birthing mothers' choices, which can be prioritized in both medicalized births and births attended by physicians. Furthermore, physicians agreed again and again that the "interventionism" instituted in public hospitals runs counter to the conditions necessary for humanized birth. For this reason, these physicians echoed that humanized birth belongs to the realm of private practice.

Figure 2.1.
The lobby of the private hospital dedicated to the integration of natural and holistic healing

At a private hospital that boasts a cesarean rate that is less than half that of the national average and focuses on the integration of natural healing, I inquired about the types of services the hospital offers because of its unique emphasis on holistic medicine, ecological living, and alternative-birth methods. (At the time of my participant-observation, this hospital reported an approximate cesarean-section rate of 20 percent. Although this figure is higher than the World Health Organization's recommended 10 to 15 percent, it is less than half of the Mexican national averages in both public and private sectors. Cesarean section represents 45.8 percent of births in public Mexican Institute of Social Security hospitals and approximately 70 percent of births in private hospitals.)[3] Birth-related services offered by the hospital are psychoprophylactic workshops, art therapy for older siblings of the new baby, homeopathic kits for pregnant mothers, and doula services. Obstetricians at the hospital do not routinely shave women's pubic hair, apply rectal enemas, insert IVs, ask mothers to fast, perform episiotomies, or use synthetic oxytocin. One of the chief officers of the hospital told me that the hospital was designed to look like a top-notch hotel, not a hospital, and all the food served to "guests" (as patients are euphemistically referred to) is organic.

The hospital presents all new parents with a commemorative gift: "handprints" and "footprints" of their newborn carved into a wood plaque by indigenous artisans (yet another example of the commodification of indigeneity within the humanized-birth movement). The hospital has also compiled a reading list of English-language texts on natural and alternative birth—evidence that the humanized movement traces its origins to the Global North and that the hospital's patients are bi- and multilingual transnational bioconsumers. The hospital implements nonhorizontal birthing positions, immediate skin-to-skin bonding between mother and child, and 100 percent lactation (there are no baby bottles in the hospital). Throughout this chapter, I suggest that this all-or-nothing approach inadvertently sets women up for failure, since not all mothers and infants are able to breastfeed immediately after birth.

Marketing "Nature": The Expense of Humanized Birth

Despite the commercialization of biomedicine, medicalized birth is far less expensive than humanized birth. In Monterrey, I visited a center that offers obstetric care, prenatal yoga, healthy cooking classes, and nutrition counseling. The center operates out of a mansion in the most affluent neighborhood of the metropolis. The taxi driver who drove me to the center told me that driving a client to that area of Monterrey was a rare experience since it was more likely for its residents to travel by private helicopter than by taxi. This center plays an important role in the humanized-birth community in Mexico and transnationally, having organized and hosted international conferences featuring American and French experts on humanized birth. One afternoon, I interviewed Elizabeth Smith, the center's founder, a woman of British heritage who travels constantly between Mexico and the home she has with her husband in California. She spoke at length about how biomedicine is undergirded by the pharmaceutical industry. As a cancer survivor who rejected biomedical interventions and instead adopted a holistic diet, she opined that the well-being of patients can often be achieved through organic and holistic methods, but biomedicine fails to explore these possibilities as they are not as lucrative as pharmaceuticals. Throughout my fieldwork, however, I observed how humanized birth is paradoxically a lucrative source of income and status for professional humanized-birth practitioners.

Later that afternoon, I asked to speak with the obstetrician at the center—a leader of the "health revolution" who uses "best practices for both mother and child." The obstetrician responded that he could fit me in if I were to book a patient appointment and pay his 800-peso (about US$65) consultation fee (about two and a half weeks of a minimum-wage salary). He explained that granting me an interview would take up time he could have spent with a patient. However, if I were to book a patient appointment, I could use that allotted time to ask him whatever I wanted about his work. I declined his invitation to pay for an interview because doing so would have violated the procedures regarding compensation of informants outlined in my Internal Review Board permissions for research, and moreover, my most pressing questions about how humanized birth is marketed to patient-consumers at this center had already been answered. My intention behind interviewing this particular obstetrician was not primarily to document yet another practitioner's definition of humanized birth, but to discern where the center fell on the continuum between a universalizing "humanization" of birth and marginalizing commercialization of services. His stringent attachment to the fee-for-service paradigm belies notions that the humanized-birth movement serves as an alternative to the capitalist machinery of biomedicine.

Interestingly, when I interviewed the deans of the aforementioned prestigious private medical school in Mexico City, the perspective they expressed about humanized birth was ironically parallel to comments on biomedicine made by Emma Müller, one of my midwife informants. They spoke to me about how "humanized birth" was becoming a buzzword in Mexico, and how obstetricians were beginning to see their lack of involvement as a missed economic opportunity. Instead of allowing "alternative-birth attendants" to reap all the commercial gain, some were beginning to market humanized-birth practices based on scientific literature from Brazil, thus securing their participation in the boom.

When I returned home to San Miguel, I sat down for a formal interview with Dr. Daniel Tellez, a physician whom I had been observing for months at the General Hospital. He described his academic trajectory to me, which includes a degree in homeopathy. Although he is a proponent of minimal intervention, he frowned upon the commercialization of humanized birth, saying that the expense of a natural childbirth is fortunate for physicians and unfortunate for patients. He explained that in Mexico, patients often believe that expensive services are the best, so when a bodily practice like humanized birth becomes "trendy," it also becomes expensive. Shortly after my interview with Dr. Tellez, I spoke with Jaime Breilh, director of Health Sciences at the Universidad Andina Simón Bolívar in Quito, Ecuador, about my research. He succinctly described what I was observing in my fieldwork: "When ancestral knowledge is commercialized, it becomes a functionalist element and is no longer emancipatory." Not only does humanized birth fail to fulfill its inclusionary promise relating to the rhetoric of "humanity," but further, it often fails to truly liberate even those who are able to access its benefits through the pathway of consumption.

Unexpected Politics of Parenting: A New Moral Imperative

My research utilizes the humanized-birth movement in Mexico as a lens through which to analyze transnational trends in parenting. Couples from the global professional class (Sharpe 2003:618) often view parenthood as the "last stop" in creating a successful life. That is, upper-middle- and upper-class couples aim to follow a life trajectory that includes higher education, professional development, marriage, home ownership, and *parenthood*. The criteria for good parenting are largely defined by parenting trends in a transnational social network originating in the Global North (examples are humanized birth, extended lactation, organic/holistic nutrition, Montessori and Waldorf education, extracurricular activities, and so forth). As couples increasingly consider parenthood and their ability to produce certain types of future bioconsumers as a marker of their overall success, their relationships to their children are changing, often resulting in greater demands on the parents' time and economic resources.

This chapter describes how parents and families form social networks oriented around a particular type of birth. Although humanized birth has so often been described as a pathway to feminist liberation and resistance to (masculine) biomedical hegemony, I problematize uncritical notions of liberation by asking how humanized birth may be the first step within a new regime of pressures and "requirements" presented by modern-day "good parenting." Through examples of women who struggle or "fail" to give birth naturally, my ethnography signals how humanized birth inadvertently represents another way the burden of correctly producing future bioconsumers falls upon women, even as it aims to liberate them from biomedical hegemony.

The Mexican women who participate in transnational humanized-birth social networks share notions of what constitutes good mothering and ideal birthing. Social bonds rest upon mutual understandings of what mothers must do to achieve the best possible birth; at the same time, mothers are bound both by the expectations of their fellow humanized-birth proponents, and by the very logic of how a humanized birth should progress. Humanized birth illuminates not only how the neoliberal meritocracy framing contemporary parenting concerns children's development post-birth, but how moral imperatives related to "proper parenting" push back into the womb. As the term "meritocracy" suggests, there is a fine, often vanishing line between elevating standards and provoking competition, shared passion and mutual obligation, defending rights and imposing ideology, challenging power and reinventing limitations.

Figure 2.2. Social networks: A gathering of families of children who have been born via humanized birth

Although humanized birth emerged out of resistance to biomedical hegemony and feminist desire to wrest the power over birth away from (male) doctors and place it back in the hands of birthing women, I point to the irony of humanized birth and ask how humanized-birth social networks may place a new set of social constraints and burdens on women. Humanized-birth circles are motivated by shared concern about biomedicalized birth and desire to improve birth outcomes for mother and child; however, they also incite a sense of obligation within women that can have harmful physical, psychological, and emotional effects. Although I eagerly recognize many instances when my informants reported feeling *empoderadas* (empowered), I am also signaling the murky edges of humanized-birth experiences and problematic moments in which exchanging biomedicalized birth for humanized birth may be replacing one form of tyranny for another. The ideology of humanized birth leads couples to make significant economic investments toward achieving their ideal birth and inspires mothers to agentively choose physical pain over anesthesia. These parents meet their socially influenced obligations to give children the best start in life through consumption and elected suffering.

In this chapter, I contribute a perspective that broadens the framing of current debates on "new midwifery." The existing literature primarily argues that professional midwives around the world are helping birthing mothers reconnect with women's natural abilities to give birth. In so doing, these midwives guide women toward greater trust of their bodies, defy and confront hegemonic biomedical structures, and argue that women have the right to choose a non-medicalized birth.

In this body of literature, mothers are described as transformed and "empowered" by their humanized-birth experiences. I, however, am wary of this use of "empowerment," since I argue that it is acritical of intersectional forms of hierarchy. I argue, based on my ethnographic observations, that the women who are the most readily "empowered" by humanized birth are those who have the least need when considering intersectional forms of discrimination. Those with the greatest need (women who suffer not only from gender discrimination but also from racial discrimination and grinding poverty) are the least likely to access humanized birth.

Thus, I signal how existing arguments for women's rights to choose the birth they prefer inadequately engage intersectional frameworks that structure women's ability to choose. I assert that the current approach to "choice" emerges from a middle- and upper-class perspective that fails to recognize the structural gap between indigenous and lower-class women giving birth in public hospitals and privileged women who pay for private medical services. My argument thus harks back to Bourdieu—class provides the conditions that determine tastes. I am cautious not to allow tastes to seem "natural" thus legitimating the superiority of the wealthy (see Bourdieu 1984).

Although my work employs humanized birth as its analytical object, the subject of this book extends far beyond birth. Parenting is a primary way that individuals accrue cultural capital within a transnational meritocracy, and as a result, individuals are incited to demonstrate good parenting before their children are even born. That is, the interpellation of individuals as parents originates in vitro and is perpetuated through social mechanisms that challenge anthropological notions of biopower.

Medical anthropologists have also developed an extensive literature on midwifery, positioning the midwifery model as a pathway to feminist liberation and resistance to (masculine) biomedical hegemony (see Davis-Floyd 2004 [1992]; Katz Rothman 2007; MacDonald 2008; and Simonds 2007, among others). In contrast, this chapter challenges notions of unrestricted liberation by pointing to how humanized birth may impose a new regime of standards for modern-day "good parents." Whereas biopower has often been characterized as the control of populations through "paternalistic" institutional and governmental surveillance, humanized-birth practices beg the question of how burdensome expectations propagate through social networks.

This chapter aims to add complexity to Ludmilla Jordanova's (1995) suggestion that anthropologists begin thinking seriously about children as commodities. I provide ethnographic examples that illustrate the complex intertwining of (1) how giving children the best upbringing increasingly entails material consumption among privileged families (commodities are consumed by parents for their children); (2) how children are parents' stake in a transnational neoliberal meritocracy (children are commodities that are consumed by parents); and (3) both commodities for children and children as commodities are bolstered by love, care, and sacrifice (see also Rotman Zelizer 1994; Hochschild 2012). In contrast to cross-cultural ethnographies of child rearing, I am probing a transnational neoliberal meritocracy that superimposes class-infused logic and globalized notions of gender on place-based practices to drive contemporary parenting trends. Thus, my work queries how meritocracy-fueled phenomena—examples are "helicopter moms" and "tiger moms"—unfold in places penetrated by deep disparities.

My work unfolds in conversation with Elizabeth Currid-Halkett's *The Sum of Small Things: A Theory of the Aspirational Class* (2017). Currid-Halkett applies a fresh perspective to Thorstein Veblen's 1899 *The Theory of the Leisure Class,* arguing that mass production and fast credit turned conspicuous consumption into a "mainstream" practice within reach of the middle class—thus, it ceased to be a marker for the elite. The "democratization" of conspicuous consumption, which has been heightened in recent years by online shopping, has led to the erosion of the leisure class and the rise of what she coins the "aspirational class." The shift away from an idle aristocracy to a self-made, meritocratic elite has resulted in a new group with a shared set of cultural practices and social norms, and a "more egalitarian" version of status. Currid-Halkett explains that aspirationals use knowledge and cultural capital "to make informed decisions around what to eat, how to treat the environment, and how to be better parents, more productive workers, and more informed consumers" (Currid-Halkett 2017:18).

Currid-Halkett's argument harks back to David Brooks' 2000 *Bobos in Paradise: The New Upper Class and How They Got There,* in which Brooks explains how nonmaterialistic values and economic wealth result in consumer habits that are still expensive but ultimately attempt to distance consumers from money by "transcending materialism." Currid-Halkett makes a slight distinction: aspirationals often lack the self-consciousness and financial means Brooks describes.

> They distance themselves from conventional material goods not because they are uncomfortable with wealth (bobos) but rather because material goods are no longer a clear signal of social position or a good conduit to reveal cultural capital or knowledge. Rich oligarchs and the middle class both can acquire "stuff," but, for the aspirational class, it is members' eagerness to acquire knowledge and to use this information to form socially and environmentally conscious values that set them apart from everyone else. (Currid-Halkett 2017:19)

Aspirationals tend to have a high level of education, buy organic food, breastfeed their babies, wear organic-cotton clothing, hire auxiliary staff, cultivate their children's growth, practice yoga and pilates, and, I add, participate in humanized birth.

The families I observed exhibit all the "aspirational" behaviors that Currid-Halkett describes. Many of these families also possess financial resources that allow them to live the expensive but "non-materialist" and "transcendent" lifestyles that Brooks observes. The humanized-birth movement encompasses not only parents' desire to achieve the best births possible through prenatal education and preparation, but also shared desire for information on conscientious child-rearing, sexuality during pregnancy (including orgasmic birth), nutritious meal preparation for pregnant mothers and their entire families, and prenatal yoga.

Moral Superiority: Birthing Self-Assured Children

On a chilly morning in December 2010, I hiked up the cobblestone road leading to the Center for the Adolescents of San Miguel de Allende for the very first time, stopping frequently to ask for directions. San Miguel is known for its large population of resident American and Canadian expatriates and is a popular destination for international and national tourists, but CASA is perched at the top of the Santa Julia hill in a working-class barrio. I was eager to visit CASA, because among its many programs was the only government-accredited midwifery school in the country and its maternity hospital represents a key site for the unfolding of humanized birth in Mexico. CASA's location suggests that the majority of its maternity patients are working-class Mexicans, but I soon discovered that its clientele was more transnational and from a broader, and more elite, socioeconomic range than I had expected.

When I finally arrived at CASA, I was struck by its charm: the beautiful cathedral-like dome, arched windows, warm yellow and burgundy hues, and pitter-patter of water in the courtyard fountain. As I walked down the hospital corridors, I saw a wooden sign on one of the birthing rooms exclaiming, "It's a Boy!" in Spanish. A staff member gave me a tour of its newly appointed water-birth facility and led me to a plaque proclaiming that, having undergone a workshop with Martha Lipton ("water birth educator, gentle-birth guardian, and celebrity" within humanized-birth circles), CASA has earned the designation of internationally certified water-birth center. A CASA pamphlet listed prices for different types of births. I noted the cost of water birth was nearly twice that of non-water birth.

A few months later, I was accompanying Magdalena Ruíz, one of the professional midwifery students, during her rotation in the CASA maternity hospital. She explained that the demographic of couples seeking water birth varies starkly from those seeking non-water birth: couples interested in water birth often travel great distances to give birth at CASA, are familiar with the humanized-birth movement and its European origins, are often transnational, possess a higher level of education, and can afford a more expensive birth.

Two years after Magdalena had graduated from CASA, I visited her and interviewed some of her home-birth clients. In contrast to the transnational couples that travel for midwifery services at CASA after reading about their unique model online, Magdalena has amassed her clientele purely by word of mouth. Her clients are professional and entrepreneurial Mexicans who live within the greater Guadalajara area, and a number of them are clustered in the city of Irapuato. Magdalena's clients connected me with other mothers from the same social circle who are also passionate about humanized birth. The women I interviewed formed friendships with each other by sharing tips and insights about humanized birth while waiting to pick up their children from school.

I sought out Yasmin Díaz, Magdalena's first client in the city of Irapuato. A couple of minutes after I rang the large copper bell hanging above Yasmin's front gate, Yasmin appeared and led me through the courtyard and into the well-appointed living room of her two-story home. She was more youthful than I had imagined, and I wondered how she and her husband had become so well established at such a young age. Over the course of our conversation, Yasmin explained that she and her husband own a textile manufacturing company specializing in the mass production of cloth dia-

Figure 2.3. Yasmin and her third son, born in water at a home birth. A staunch advocate of breastfeeding, Yasmin is wearing a shirt with the word "supply" across her chest while her son wears a matching shirt with the word "demand" across his chest.

pers. Their respective families are both from Irapuato, and her mother and grandmother live just a few houses away.

Yasmin is twenty-six years old and the mother of three children. Her first two sons were born via cesarean section when she was twenty-two and twenty-three years of age, respectively. Defying all odds, she gave birth to her third son in a home water birth.

During her first pregnancy, Yasmin had wanted to give birth naturally, but as the labor unfolded, her dilation subsided. Yasmin was in the hospital for two days, and despite rhythmic contractions, every time the hospital personnel checked the condition of her cervix, her dilation was at one centimeter. At that time, she had not yet informed herself by reading any humanized-birth literature or participating in psychoprophylactic birthing classes, so she relied solely on the obstetrician's guidance when deciding how to proceed. The obstetrician told her everything was fine but that at any moment fetal distress could occur. Yasmin explained, "Of course, when any mother hears the words 'fetal distress,' she'll do whatever the doctor recommends so that her child isn't injured." Yasmin was afraid of having a cesarean since she had never undergone surgery, and she recalled the anxiety she felt when the hospital staff shaved her pubic hair and applied an IV and started anesthesia. They jostled her, jerking the sliced-open flesh of her belly. When they had extracted her baby boy, they showed Yasmin her newborn, giving her only a few seconds to catch a glimpse of her child before whisking him out of her sight.

Later, when she was in the recovery area and her baby boy was returned to her, they had already fed him formula. The baby was satisfied and did not seek colostrum from her breasts—Yasmin was a stranger to the biochemical process of birth, and although she desired ever so greatly to nourish the baby with her own milk, breastfeeding was physiologically out of synch with the surgery she had just experienced. She told me, "It wasn't until two or three days later that I realized I had become a mother and had had a baby. When you give birth [vaginally], you close a cycle. In comparison, a cesarean leaves ugly traces [on a mother's psyche]."

A year and three months later she was pregnant again, and they told her, citing the possibility of uterine rupture, "Once a cesarean, always a cesarean." Her doctor instructed her, "Go think of a date [for the cesarean]."

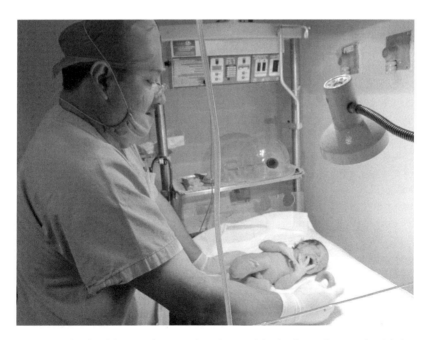

Figure 2.4. Pediatrician suctions newborn's mouth in the first minutes after birth

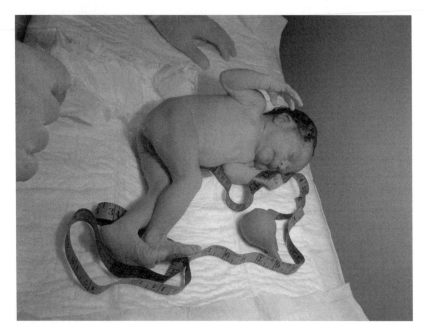

Figure 2.5. Newborn tangled in measuring tape after post-birth evaluation by pediatrician

They scheduled the surgery. Yasmin said her second cesarean was "terrible and frightful." In the operating room, the surgical team joked around among themselves while she was possessed by fear because the anesthesia had not properly taken effect. She was still moving her feet and feeling sensations in her body when they began cutting. She could hear her heartbeat throbbing loudly, drumming almost out of her chest, and she begged, "Please, don't open me." They gave her an inhalational anesthetic, covering her face with a mask and inducing her to sleep. When she awoke, she was still frantic. Her baby was no longer in her womb, and neither her husband nor the doctor was present. What had happened? She was overcome by desperation and physical pain. Her husband later told her their son was born limp and blue, like a dead rabbit. Yasmin believes the inhalational anesthetic had a noxious effect on her baby as well.

Upon discovering she was pregnant a third time, Yasmin was determined not to have another cesarean. "It is not possible that I cannot give birth vaginally!" she exclaimed. She told her obstetrician she wanted to have a vaginal delivery, but he responded, "Are you crazy? They only do that in the United States! And they are crazy because it cannot be done.

The women and doctors who pursue vaginal birth after a cesarean are crazy gringos." Yasmin asked herself, "Only crazy gringos can do it? I don't think so!" She decided to take psychoprophylactic classes, and the course-work helped her make a definitive decision: Yes, she told herself, I *can* give birth naturally.

Yasmin discussed her desire to give birth vaginally with Celia Hernández, a doula invested in humanized-birth practices. Celia gave Yasmin two options: a pro-birth obstetrician or professional midwives. The obstetrician told her that although Yasmin was at risk for uterine rupture, he was willing to see how the pregnancy progressed before making a decision. Yasmin's husband was comfortable with the obstetrician's plan. However, Yasmin wanted to meet with the professional midwives as well, but her husband was skeptical and anxious; his wife not only wanted a vaginal birth, but a vaginal birth at home, attended by midwives! Two weeks before the birth, they journeyed to Guadalajara to meet Magdalena and Antonia for the first time. An hour into the interview, her husband was convinced. Both Yasmin and her husband were moved by the careful explanations the two professional midwives provided for each of their questions. They were

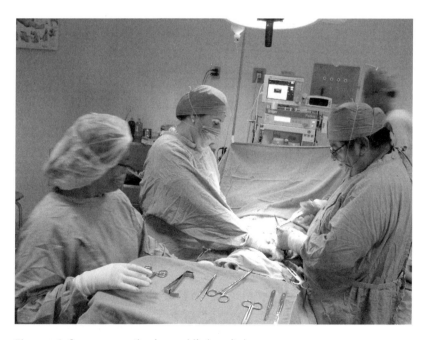

Figure 2.6. Cesarean section in a public hospital

struck by the difference between the physician's dismissive statement, "You don't need to know," and the midwives' close attention.

A week before the birth, the obstetrician told the couple that something was amiss with the fetus' position and prescribed medication that would induce contractions. By the time Yasmin left the doctor's office, she had already decided she wanted nothing to do with that obstetrician ever again. This time, she was not going to have an induced labor, painful synthetic oxytocin-driven contractions, or cesarean section.

Her third son was born after forty weeks of gestation. They placed a blowup birthing pool in the couple's bedroom on the second floor. It was December, but they took the chill off with space heaters. Yasmin was left feeling nothing but joy after her third birth, explaining that the experience transformed the way she and her husband both relate with their youngest son. Her husband was a participant in the water birth, not just a spectator as he had been in the hospital births of their other two sons. Yasmin asserts that her youngest son and children born through humanized birth are more loving and emotionally secure than other children and form closer connections with their fathers.

Yasmin expresses how grateful she is for what she has learned about her body and connecting with her fetus. She now knows that her body needs three days of labor to prepare for her delivery. She believes that if she had waited a third day during her first birth, her baby would have been born naturally and safely. "That is just how my body is." She recognizes, however, that natural birth is also about respecting the fetus' readiness to be born and communicating to the fetus when the right time has arrived. On the third day of her third delivery, while her mother and husband were knotted by anxiety, Yasmin went to bed by herself and whispered to her fetus: "Baby, you have to be born now." A few minutes later, her water broke.

The harmony she experienced during her water birth continued in the ensuing years and has culminated in her continued ability to breastfeed. Her third son benefited from a year and eight months of breastfeeding, whereas she only managed to give each of her other two sons six months of breastfeeding.

After the birth, Yasmin thought, "Wow! How beautiful! My life has changed!" It is now the couple's mission to inform other women of their options, and they use their cloth diaper business to facilitate their mission. In the eight months following Yasmin's water-birth experience, four other mothers followed suit, giving birth vaginally after having prior cesarean sections.

For Josefa Jiménez and Tomás Álvarez, the differences between their

Figure 2.7. From left to right: Josefa with Timoteo and Tobías, Tomás, and Celia (see her story, below)

two sons do not end with *how* the boys were born; rather, they are different *because* of the disparate circumstances surrounding their births. Tobías was born via cesarean section. He becomes angry, scared, or anxious when he hears a loud noise; for example, the vacuum cleaner, the washing machine, or a slamming door. In contrast, Timoteo, who is still a baby and was born in water, will only turn his head in curiosity to see what has made such a loud noise. Timoteo sleeps even in the noisiest environments, likes to sleep on both his mother and father's chest, and is soothed by the rhythm of their heartbeats. Timoteo is a tranquil baby, whereas Tobías seems to be perpetually decentered by his traumatic birth experience.

At the time of the interview, Tobías was almost four, and his innocence and inquisitive nature caused him to ask questions that provoked a deep emotional response in his parents: "Why did they snatch me from inside my mother when I was so happy being with her?" As the couple describes, children born via cesarean section are haunted by the unnaturalness of their surgical beginnings. In contrast, Josefa and Tomás' subsequent experience with professional midwives was "the birth of a human being."

What is remarkable about the many birth stories I heard during my ethnographic research is not only the way these women and couples emphasized resisting biomedical hegemony to achieve desired births, but also the striking moral dimension embedded in their recounting of events. At times, their retelling seemed akin to religious-conversion stories, as if through delivery they themselves had been delivered. Through psycho-prophylactic training and familiarization with transnational humanized-birth literature, these people prepared themselves for arduous labor and learned to place their faith in "nature," "tradition," and their innate capacity to give birth naturally over biomedical protocols. They cast cesarean birth as traumatizing, terrifying, and violating, while depicting humanized birth as beautiful and empowering.

Perhaps even more compelling is the way couples described humanized birth as the best method of bringing self-assured, well-adjusted, happy humans into the world. Even when labor lasts for days on end, couples asserted it is worth going through the pain of natural labor since the result is a healthier and more contented child. Basing their claims on the biochemical process that unfolds during an undisturbed childbirth (most notably, the secretion of oxytocin into the bloodstream, catalyzing the "letdown reflex" and facilitating the production of breast milk), these couples affirmed that humanized-birth practices correlate with easy, continued breastfeeding, thus strengthening their children's immune systems and reducing their likelihood of developing numerous diseases later in life. In essence, children born via humanized birth are described as the fortunate offspring of conscientious, caring, brave, and intelligent parents; their births link them to children also born in water, at home, and with the help of professional midwives in the United States and elsewhere in the Global North.

My argument is not a rebuttal of these couples' assertions, nor do I criticize their decisions. I agree wholeheartedly with the reduction of obstetric violence and unnecessary biomedicalization through safe, natural alternatives. However, stopping there would reduce the scope of my research (albeit valuable) advocacy around a woman's right to determine the conditions of her birthing. Instead, I am undertaking an analytic project; thus, the novelty of my research lies in the unveiling of multiple ironies embedded in humanized birth. I specifically draw attention to how humanized-birth ideology represents a new set of expectations to which women strive to conform and which they sometimes fail to fulfill.

A Community of Expectations: Digital Ethnography

The global humanized-birth community is bound by convictions and expectations about what elements should constitute an ideal birth. These expectations are shared during conversations people have while picking up children from school, in psychoprophylactic classes, in humanized-birth workshops (including birth photography!), during protests against obstetric violence, and through a thriving online community connected by Facebook and blog posts. "Aspirationals" are eager to share information with each other, and often the quickest and most accessible means is through digital multimedia. Many of my informants were quick to add me as friends in their social-media accounts, connecting me to the digital discourse surrounding humanized birth. Over the course of my ethnographic research, I realized how much of the humanized-birth movement's "biosociality" occurs online (see Rabinow 1996). An ethnography on humanized-birth social networks would be incomplete if it did not include illuminating data drawn from digital sources, since social media functions as a primary platform for the (re)production and (re)inscription of moral ideologies.[4]

When Mayra Calvette, one of the humanized-birth proponents I encountered in Brazil, was featured in *Vogue,* she posted a photo of her article on Facebook. The article's title translates to "Midwife Fashion" and describes how, after being born in a home birth before humanized birth was in fashion, she became the midwife of supermodel Gisele Bündchen and has helped dozens of women give birth naturally. No stranger to using diverse media to reach a broad audience, she traveled for nine months, discovering natural-birthing practices across the globe and recording her adventure in a film-length documentary. The video, *Parto Pelo Mundo,* was shared through a dedicated Facebook page and website, which was later used to disseminate announcements about her upcoming workshops. Mayra also created a personal website where she shares the birth stories of women she attends, her own birthing experience, and opinions on humanized-birth topics such as delayed umbilical cord cutting. These articles are accompanied by blog posts, a link to the direct services she offers, and information about workshops and courses she leads. Each page is visually designed to feature crisp, high-definition, people-centered photography.

Although the presentation of midwifery and Gisele Bündchen's midwife-assisted birth in *Vogue* suggests that humanized birth is the "vogue" option, other media outlets make value judgments regarding humanized birth more explicit. For example, an article by the British paper the *Telegraph* was shared and re-posted by Mexican and Brazilian humanized-birth proponents, who translated portions of the article into Spanish and Portuguese. The English title reads, "Busting the Smug Myth: Ladies, Home Births Really Are the VIP Labour Option." In response to this article, one of the midwives in my study commented, "[We are] a team at your total disposal, [ready] to spoil you in your house. It is for princesses . . . !!! Choose what is best for you!" The title of another article, published by Mexican news outlet *Publimetro,* translates to "Midwives Are Now VIP and They Are in Fashion."

Posts circulating shared beliefs and values regarding the superiority of humanized birth over medicalized birth can be read as demonstrating support and validation, but they can also inadvertently lead to community-level expectations for a "good birth." One midwife circulated a photo of a newborn baby, born through water birth, smiling and staring alertly into its parents' admiring eyes. The caption reads, "This baby came out smiling yesterday morning. He came out, reached his hand right up to his mama, smiled so big, then tipped his head back and grabbed for daddy. Not a dry eye in the room." These types of posts were later commented on by informants who expressed to me how babies born naturally are immediately more capable and develop quicker than babies born through medicalized births. At other times, links shared through Facebook directly assert the preeminence of humanized birth—for example, a link to a water-birth experience paired with the comment, "It is the best way to arrive to this world" (my translation). Another comment, referring to a study regarding the safety of water birth, reads, "And if home birth with midwives was not already the best that you can do for a natural birth, it turns out that water birth is even better!!!!" (my translation). These multiple assertions about the superiority of humanized birth and, specifically, water birth, point to a trend within a trend—not only is humanized birth vogue, water birth is the hottest humanized-birth practice of the moment!

Sometimes, comparisons of humanized birth and medicalized birth can turn contentious. In one blog post, a humanized-birth proponent specifically challenges her medicalized-birth counterparts, writing, "I have to make an aside for all of those women who decide to continue giving birth in the hospital. . . . *The hospital is the safest place to give birth,* you will say [emphasis in original]. Well, this would be true if within that safety, we didn't include the defenselessness to which we the crazy women [referring to humanized-birth proponents] find ourselves submitted to protocols that we haven't chosen, interventions we don't need, and verbal aggressions we don't deserve" (my translation). Social-media examples such as this one signal shared beliefs surrounding the value of women's resistance to medical practices that leave little space for women's choices.

However, other memes encountered in social media share opinions that could potentially lapse into judgments. For example, one meme depicting a water birth reads, "The only thing you need to be able to give birth is absolute confidence in yourself. This is the same thing you need to achieve anything" (my translation). This meme could easily be interpreted as casting judgment on women who are not able to achieve a natural birth sans medical intervention. Did those women lack confidence in themselves? Is the ability to achieve a natural birth aligned with one's ability to achieve other goals in life? Can this post be read as veiling privilege by failing to account for the enormous economic cost and georacial gradients of bioconsumption?

Another meme features a quote from Italian midwife Verena Schmid: "Each woman gives birth in the same way in which she lives her life. . . . If women were conscious of the immense strength that lives within them, not only would the birth scene change, but [so would] all of society" (my translation). Although this quote can be interpreted as providing inspiration to "change all of society," it can also be interpreted as placing the burden of shaping society's future solely on women's shoulders, and similarly to the former meme, criticizing those who lack "consciousness." What does this meme imply about women who give birth biomedically and how they live their lives?

This theme of placing the burden of properly shaping future generations on women's shoulders was reiterated many times during my participation in the humanized-birth online community. Much of the information circulated through Facebook and other forms of social media include the lifelong positive effects of humanized birth on the child, and, thus, the future of society. An article from Spain, circulated by an informant, can be summed up by its title: "The Way in Which We Are Born Affects Us for the Rest of Our Lives." The cover photo of a humanized-birth Facebook page emerging from Mexicali reads, "World Peace Begins Here." A documentary film "revealing the microscopic events during childbirth that could hold the key to the future of humanity" was shared in a post by a midwife with all the members of the Mexican Midwifery Association. The term "microbirth" places additional emphasis on women that these microscopic events must be carefully controlled and curated, urgently hailing the mother as the primary orchestrator, since the future of humanity is at stake.

The link between birth and interpersonal relationships is also located within the family. One YouTube video shared through Facebook highlighted a humanized-birth obstetrician's assertions that it is necessary for all members of the family to be present at the moment of birth in order to live in "total love." Furthermore, the time immediately after birth is referred to as "the sacred hour" (*la hora sagrada*) in the Facebook post of an

Argentinian article circulated by Mexican doulas. The title of a seminar offered by Michel Odent reiterates, "To Be Born in Love, Is to Live in Love."

On the other hand, the psychoemotional trauma and potential physical danger that a cesarean can have on infants is emphasized. One example is an article entitled, "Cesarean Delivery May Cause Epigenetic Changes in Babies' DNA." Emerging research on epigenetics suggests that a cesarean will not only have negative effects for a surgically born baby, it will have a noxious impact on the baby's DNA and will be inscribed in the genetics of future generations to come. The consequences of cesareans for offspring are replete with hashtags. For example, the newsfeed post for one article circulated on Facebook reads, "Does cesarean bring consequences for babies?" #Cesarean #Babies" (my translation).

The effect of the mother's reproductive labor extends beyond the birth itself since, as one Spanish post, circulated in Mexico, points out, "[Lactation] reduces the risk of diabetes in susceptible children" (my translation). Humanized-birth workshops are designed to follow this arc of reproductive labor, thus including content such as prenatal yoga and extending to postpartum topics such as "Respectful Child Rearing" (my translation). Other online materials shared through social media are directly instructive, for example, a blog post simply entitled, "Don't Reject Pain."

Over the course of my fieldwork, I began seeing social media as providing a platform for ethnographic understanding of how cultural capital can be sought by aspirationals through humanized-birth practices. Women's desire to achieve cultural capital through how they give birth is described in a poem posted on Facebook:

> Can I tell you a joke?
> The good girls from the village
> Go to get a cesarean in the state capital,
> The good girls in the state capital
> Go to get a cesarean in the nation's capital,
> The good girls of the nation
> Go to get a cesarean in the United States,
> The good girls of the United States
> Come to give birth in your birthing center,
> Here in the village.

This poem incorporates multiple criticisms, as indicated by the sarcastic phrasing, "the good girls." Although the poem is framed in terms of geographic concentric circles, it also refers to layers of cultural and economic capital. Women in the village are often mandated under the conditionality of Oportunidades to have a cesarean at crowded public hospitals in their state capital—for these women, natural birth is not an option. The poem then points to the metropolitan longings of women in "the state capital" who seek care in even larger cities, such as the nation's capital. The next layer echoes a criticism I heard from multiple humanized-birth practitioners and their "aspirational" clients—harking back to Brooks (2000), a critical gaze is cast on women who possess great economic capital and use these means to achieve a highly medicalized, "non-transcendent" international birth. Finally, the poem offers a critique on medical tourism, and the commodification of Mexico's "traditional ways of birthing."

Although this poem offers multiple layers of criticism, the different examples presented in this section can vary in interpretation from value judgments that women make about each other, to social expectations that shape birth-related desires, to the communications of women who hope to support one another through social(ly) media(ted) posts meant to empower. My goal is not to undermine the positive effects of online biosocial networks but, rather, to tease apart multiplicitous effects that may lead to an inadvertent sense of failure among women who are unable to meet humanized-birth expectations.

The Secret Tyranny of Humanized Birth: When Mothers Fail to Meet Expectations

In August 2013, I visited Dr. Horacio García,[5] a perinatologist, hospital administrator, and clinical professor at the National Autonomous University of Mexico, at his private clinic near the football stadium, Estadio Azteca, in Mexico City. His clinic is inconspicuously tucked into a small residential street, but once inside, I was struck by a plethora of photographs of healthy newborns intermixed with angel figurines, catholic relics, and *el Niño Jesus* (a Baby Jesus doll).

Dr. García's clinic features a roomy, light-filled water-birth suite on the second floor, with a sofa, regular queen-size bed, full bath, Jacuzzi, skylight, marble waterfall with an angel statue, and large windows providing views of the tree- and flower-filled garden. The suite was designed to maximize the comfort of the family and the ease of labor. A cord hangs above the Jacuzzi so the mother may suspend her weight and stretch her back while birthing. Wooden bars are fastened to the wall to facilitate prophylactic exercises that relax the pelvis in preparation for birth. Dr. García in-

Figure 2.8. The "bedroom" portion of the birthing suite at Dr. García's clinic

tentionally rejected a hospital bed in favor of a regular queen-size bed so that his clients would feel at home in the birthing suite, and to promote family bonding after the birth.

Although Dr. García's attention to detail signals his commitment to humanized birth, or as he prefers, "respected birth," his training in perinatology gives him a different perspective regarding pain and safety during childbirth than many of his doula and professional midwife counterparts. Dr. García is in favor of birth-preparation courses, but he emphasizes that if instructors teach pregnant women they can definitely achieve a vaginal birth using a set of relaxation techniques during labor, the results can be detrimental. On the one hand, Dr. García has been called to evaluate cases where the mother was in labor for over three days, but when he determined the situation was posing a risk to the child's health, the mother was intransigent—she was determined to give birth vaginally. On the other hand, Dr. García has had to intervene in cases where the mother is exhausted, in pain, and no longer wishes to continue with her humanized-birth plan, but others around her exert pressure on her to not give up.

In one instance, he was asked to consult on a home birth that was already at an advanced stage of labor. The birthing mother was begging for anesthesia, but her husband was insisting she not be given anesthesia since he was concerned about the effects anesthesia would have on his child. The woman's two doulas were coaching her to push through the pain. When Dr. García arrived, the birthing mother's cervix was dilated to eight centimeters. She grabbed his arm and exclaimed, "Operate me! I'm so tired! I've already had so much pain!" As Dr. García described, in this moment her emotional connection with the two doulas and her husband shattered. She looked into Dr. García's eyes and pleaded, "Doctor, don't leave me." Dr. García reassured her he would not leave her, but he explained that at such an advanced stage of labor, administering anesthesia was no longer an option. He continued accompanying the woman and forty-five minutes later, the baby was born.

Both circumstances—when mothers insist on vaginal birth even when they may be putting their child at risk, and when birth attendants and family members apply pressure to achieve a natural birth despite the mother's excessive pain and exhaustion—complicate uncritical notions of what humanized birth means for mothers and newborns. In both cases, humanized birth is cast as an accomplishment, while giving in to pain and accepting medical interventions is portrayed as failure on the mother's part. Beginning in earlier stages of pregnancy, women who subscribe to humanized birth take courses in meditation, self-hypnosis, breathing, and relaxation techniques in hopes that they will be able to harness their willpower, overcome physical pain, and give their child the best start in life—a birth free of synthetic drugs, hormones, obstetric violence, and traumatic memories that may leave lifelong emotional scars.

Dr. García is hypervigilant about the potential slippage between demedicalized empowerment and dogmatic endangerment. He explained to me that in Mexico, the prevailing cultural notion is that the more a woman suffers during childbirth, the more she must love her child. Dr. García contrasts himself with other obstetricians who practice humanized birth. He is critical of humanized obstetricians who are so resistant to performing medical interventions that they call upon him to intervene instead. In the case of a woman who had been in labor for three days and was fully dilated for over five hours but her contractions had stopped, Dr. García arrived at the request of his colleague and administered intravenous Pitocin to restart them. "I then withdrew from the birth as a hero." With his own patients, Dr. García explains that cesarean section is a final option—that way, if the birthing conditions are not favorable, he has saved the birthing mother the emotional distress of feeling she has failed.

The way in which natural birth has, for some women, become a marker of good mothering and failure to achieve vaginal delivery without medical intervention has been deemed a personal failure was evident in many of my interviews with parents. For example, one informant, Celia, recounts her reproductive history as a tale of trial and tribulation resulting from her physical inadequacy until she was finally able to overcome her limitations and reach empowerment. Celia has had five pregnancies. Her first was an ectopic pregnancy that resulted in the removal of a fallopian tube. Thereafter, she had difficulty becoming and staying pregnant. After several miscarriages, Celia and her husband, Javier Muñoz, finally gave up trying. Then Celia became pregnant with their daughter, Sandra. These combined events led Celia to think of maternity as a "*don.*" A don is a talent bestowed upon an individual by God; thus, Celia's difficult reproductive history has led her to believe that the ability to produce a child is a divine gift—some women have been blessed with the knack of producing children while others have not.

Sandra's birth was unexpected. After Celia's water broke, twelve hours passed without a single contraction. Her obstetric team administered oxytocin, but when it did not produce the desired effect, they later administered intravenous prostaglandins to induce the birth. When Celia finally began to have contractions, they were strong and painful. Celia demanded anesthesia "*a gritos*" (screaming at the top of her lungs), even though she had planned for a natural birth. The anesthesiologist took "an eternity" to arrive at Celia's bedside, and then took several more minutes to set up his epidural kit. He placed the epidural with difficulty and "scolded" Celia for being too fat. After that, Celia had regular contractions and Sandra was born an hour later. Even though Celia and Javier had advised the pediatrician before the birth that they wanted to keep Sandra with them for skin-to-skin contact and bonding, the medical team whisked Sandra off to evaluate her health as soon as she was born and to observe her in the nursery. Later, when the infant was finally returned to her mother, Celia was unsuccessful at breastfeeding because the nurses had already fed the baby formula.

Twenty months later, Celia became pregnant with Santiago. She describes her prenatal obstetrician as very "pro-cesarean." He told her she would require a cesarean because she had gained too much weight. Later, he told the couple the baby had a double nuchal cord and the birth would have to be via cesarean section. When they talked to the obstetrician about their birth plan, he insisted that an intravenous drip would be necessary but agreed to many of the other humanized-birth practices they requested. However, when Celia was forty-one weeks pregnant, he told them if the baby was not born in a matter of days, he would have to induce the birth. The couple became very anxious. At 11:00 a.m., at forty-one weeks and two days gestation, Celia began having contractions and had normal bleeding. She took a bath to ease the pain. She heard the daily "Ave María" on the radio signaling twelve noon and transitioned to the bedroom. She could not lie down because of extreme pain in her lower back. Upon arriving at the hospital, her cervix was already eight centimeters dilated. The obstetric team took her to the labor and delivery room on a gurney, despite her wish to continue walking. They instructed her to lie down even though the lithotomy position (back flat, legs spread, feet in stirrups) caused her great pain. Later, they allowed her to sit up, and the pain subsided.

The attending obstetrician at the time of the birth was a woman. She said to Celia, "If you want a natural birth, you must cooperate." This prompted Celia to become quiet and introspective and to concentrate her energy. When Santiago was born, they passed him to Celia immediately, but moments later they whisked him away. Unlike her experience after Sandra's birth, the pediatrician took only five minutes to evaluate Santiago's health and return him to Celia. Although Celia was never able to achieve exclusive breastfeeding with Sandra, she accomplished it easily with Santiago because she had overcome her distrust in her own body.

After the birth, Celia felt like "superwoman" because she had persevered throughout the experience and "everything turned out well." When she told her closest female friends about her birth experience, they exclaimed, "You are super wild! You are a carnivore!" Celia said, "Everyone had this attitude of 'Wow!' when I told them." The carnal language that Celia's friends used to describe her birth is derived from humanized-birth rhetoric emanating from France; and was circulated and reiterated on Facebook when an unassisted Mexican home birth was applauded as "mammalian . . . this is how women should be able to give birth." Specifically, the "primal health" rhetoric is disseminated to auditoriums of aspirationals by Michel Odent; for example, in a certificate-granting program in San Miguel de Allende.

Santiago's birth was the impetus for Celia to study prenatal education, and with Javier's financial and moral support, she earned her certificate and became a prenatal educator. Celia opines that information about birthing options is empowering because it can attenuate women's fears, and because obstetricians are unable to unilaterally dictate the terms of the birth to couples that are well informed. "Yes, it is painful, of course. But I decided, and I chose."

Celia's telling of her reproductive history highlights the complexity of humanized birth as it unfolds in the lives of Mexican women. On the one hand, Celia's story is an example of how humanized birth can lead to empowerment and feminist liberation. On the other hand, her account is peppered with comments signaling her own inadequacies prior to her successful birthing without medical interventions. By casting maternity as a "*don*," Celia explains her ectopic pregnancy and subsequent miscarriages as resulting from her deficient knack for motherhood. Celia identifies her faulty willpower and inability to overcome physical pain when she describes how she requested anesthesia and abandoned her plan of no intervention during Sandra's birth.

Underscoring the circuitous relationship between how physicians place the mandate of correct motherhood through self-discipline on pregnant women's shoulders and how women internalize these obligations, Celia mentions her excessive weight gain during both pregnancies as the reason for the anesthesiologist's difficulty placing the epidural and for the obstetrician's insistence that Santiago required delivery via cesarean section. Instead of pointing to the synthetic hormones she received during labor or the missed opportunity to initiate lactation immediately after the birth as causes for her difficulty breastfeeding Sandra, Celia situates the problem as resulting from her distrust in her own body—thus, her inability to breastfeed was a physiological shortcoming resulting from psychological misgivings. During her second birth, the solace she found in the "Ave María" counters celebrations of La Malinche as the original literate mother (see Haraway 1991; Moraga 1983) and instead points to the Madonna-like chosen suffering of "morally superior" mothers who give birth naturally.

Although Celia's reproductive history ends with victory and perhaps even the accrual of cultural capital through heightened recognition within her social network, I point to the multiple ways Celia has interpellated herself as an inadequate mother along her path to eventual success. Celia's telling of her reproductive history unveils unforeseen politics of parenting, and specifically, how the ideology of humanized birth—the idea that through conviction and preparation, birthing mothers can overcome the pain of labor to achieve a liberating and empowering natural-birth experience that will result in better health outcomes for both mother and child—can inadvertently lead to some women feeling a sense of disappointment and failure. Although humanized birth is hailed by feminist proponents as an alternative to (masculine) biomedical hegemony, it places a different, potentially noxious set of pressures on women. I am not dismissing the benefits of humanized birth for many women, but I am using a critical lens to signal that instead of a wholesale liberation, humanized birth once again obliges women to correctly produce future bioconsumers.

Humanized Babies and Cyborg Feminists?

Thinking of reproduction as a discursive field brings up questions of "authorship." Colonial legacies, racial discrimination, masculine dominance, and scientific ways of knowing are deeply embedded in the production of "truth" about human reproduction—potentially masking women's embodied knowledge. For example, Donna Haraway's work on the social construction of nature asks: Who are the agents creating representations of birth and reproduction, and to what end (see Haraway 1989)? Who has the power to define women's health?

Humanized birth is envisioned by its participants as inherently feminist since it inverts Sherry Ortner's (1972) identification of women's association with nature as the basis of their devaluation and instead casts "going back to nature" and the life-giving capabilities of female physiology as a source of empowerment and liberation. Whereas for Ortner, culturally constructed notions of nature buttress the universality of female subordination and seep into the underlying logic that assumes the inferiority of women, humanized-birth proponents have seized "nature" as a source of power and positive identification. However, my ethnographic work points to an inversion within this very inversion. This reinvention of nature is still dependent upon unequal power for its maintenance. I have already pointed to how the humanized-birth movement in Mexico inadvertently reinforces racialized logics rooted in colonial legacies and contemporary imbrication with the United States, and thus reflects desire for cultural capital based on "social whitening." Whereas Donna Haraway (1991) interpellates cyborg feminists to author narrative strategies that rewrite stories in which inequities of race, sex, and class are naturalized in "functioning systems of exploitation," my focus in this book is on the textual politics leading to persisting, unequalizing logics of class, gender, and sexuality, even through a movement that aims to position women as powerful agents by claiming "nature."

Haraway deems Michel Foucault's biopolitics "a flaccid premonition of cyborg politics" (Haraway 1991:150), but I wonder how, within the humanized-birth movement, the masculine biopower that proponents seek to resist has instead been replaced by social expectations that potentially restrain women. That is, what are the potential burdens of human-ized birth? Women have fled the hospital, escaped the "medical gaze," re-jected obstetric violence embedded in patriarchal biomedical systems, and recast the home as a space not of subordination, but of freedom. And yet, these very women are entangled in a social support system whose fabric is interwoven with definitions of what represents a correct and ideal birth. I challenge uncritical notions of women's liberation through humanized birth by pointing to how its social networks can lead to the subordina-tion of participants to a new regime of requirements for a glorified, moral-ized motherhood—an ideal that is only sometimes achieved and may thus result in feelings of failure and insufficiency. To what extent does a "ma-trix of women's dominations of each other" persist underneath battles to resist male-dominant capitalism and women's sexual appropriation "in a masculinist orgy of war" (Haraway 1991:154–155, referring to Sofia 1984)?

A movement among Mexican and Latin American women to move be-yond the textual politics of science and technology to something even more radical (*el recobrar el poder de las mujeres,* that is, taking back the power of women through ownership of nature, thus "seizing the tools to mark the world that marked them as [O]ther" [Haraway 1991:175]) would seem like a cyborg project of the twenty-first century. But human-ized birth does not satisfy Haraway's utopic vision of "a politics rooted in claims about fundamental changes in the nature of class, race, and gender in an emerging system of world order analogous in its novelty and scope to that created by industrial capitalism" (Haraway 1991:161). The moralized, feminized, "whitening" humanized birth that these feminists of color practice is not what Haraway imagined when she wrote that cyborgs are "suspicious of the reproductive matrix and of most birthing," (Haraway 1991:181), but I support Haraway's suggestion regarding the utility of sus-picion. Humanized birth points not only to how science and technology provide fresh sources of power, but how New Age, "traditional," and "ho-listic" therapies also require fresh sources of analysis and political action (see Haraway 1991 and Latour 197).

The New Age: New "Traditional" Identities and "Traditional" New Movements

The transnational humanized-birth movement points to the syncretic meanings and outcomes of New Age practices. A transnational reading of the New Age offers a series of consequential contradictions—that is, the

New Age is not just a philosophy, a way of life, or the passive intersection of an ecumenical global spirituality and "traditional" cultural forms. The New Age *does something*: it introduces the dual production of new "traditional" identities and the "traditionalization" of new movements (see de la Torre et al. 2013). The Latin American social scientists Renée de la Torre, Cristina Gutiérrez Zúñiga, and Nahayeilli Juárez Huet have critiqued European and American sociological approaches for advancing a globalizing argument that privileges the perspectives of cosmopolitan spirituality seekers. In contrast, they attend to both the circulation of teachers, symbols, rituals, knowledges, and concepts on the one hand; and on the other hand, the process of resignification, reinscription of what it means to be "ethnic," and reappropriation of the New Age by the masses. By signaling that the New Age is characterized by practitioners as a countercultural form of spirituality, an alternative to materialism and consumption, and a symbol of postmodernity and cosmopolitanism,[6] these scholars argue that the New Age engenders the dynamization of existing syncretisms into new hybrid cultures, and simultaneously, the essentialization of ethnic identities.

My contextual and dialogical perspective injects intersectional inequalities of race, class, and gender into de la Torre et al.'s emphasis on how multicultural, New Age encounters result in novel syncretisms that redefine social identities.[7] Although I engage the argument of de la Torre et al. regarding social identities, my ethnography in Mexico offers an alternative to their (2013) reading of the emergence of New Age practices in developed capitalist countries as an alternative to capitalist modernity among middle-class actors with access to art, science, and cosmopolitan culture. In the case of humanized birth in Mexico, participation by middle-class actors in transnational communities of consumption leads to the accrual of cultural capital. Whereas de la Torre et al. argue that the encounter between middle-class actors and indigenous and "popular" cosmovisions has resulted in cultural exchanges (in contrast to a globalized homogenization or the creation of a worldwide culture), my ethnographic fieldwork highlights the inequity inherent in these "exchanges," especially within the context of medical tourism (see Aguilar Ros 2008). At the same time, however, my critique is a kaleidoscopic departure from Molinié's (2013) denunciation of the hybridization of New Age practices as nothing more than a reshuffling of colonial forms of exploitation.

The humanized-birth movement in Mexico is a valuable example for rethinking the arguments presented in the literature on New Age practices. Transnational (ethno)medical tourism exploits the image of indigeneity when it usurps traditional medical practices and refashions them into hypermobile commodities. Furthermore, my research on humanized birth in Mexico clarifies the apparent contradiction between Molinié's argument and Aguilar Ros' (2013) conceptualization of the New Age as a postmodern, cosmopolitan, and countercultural alternative to materialism and consumption. The great irony lies in the fact that these parents view themselves as actively resisting materialism, but their very refusal of the corruption they diagnose in consumerism, nationalism, and late capitalism leads to the commodification of culture, heightened moralization and gradation of motherhood, reinscription of racial hierarchies, and (false) appropriation of indigenous notions of spirituality. The humanized-birth movement explicitly avoids direct references to consumption. That is to say, these mothers reject the most expensive baby carriages, nannying services, and similar markers of commodified or elite motherhood. Instead, they seek cloth wraps with which to bind their children to their bodies and promote mother-child bonding. Their cloth wraps, however, are not the woven shawls that indigenous women use; they are sold by specialized companies that use the Internet to market humanized-birth products as noncommodity commodities.

The subtlety of my argument lies in my sensitivity to the effects of intersecting forms of social inequality. In pursuing this approach, I problematize the assumption that New Age practices are adopted evenly among "the masses." My ethnographic examples add complexity to the interaction between New Age practices and contemporary construction of identities by pointing to the important effects of intersectional racialization processes. Thus, my work highlights the variability of social positions (and associated restrictions) from which individuals negotiate and portray their identities.

The ethnographic details in this chapter point to what the authorship of reproduction as a discursive field *does*, and what tensions it reveals or conceals. Research on reproduction is an important place to begin untangling the politics of representation and uncovering the relationship between gnoseological creativity and social and geopolitical power. I have argued that couples from the global professional class (Sharpe 2003:618) accrue cultural capital through participation in a "whitening" transnational meritocracy that dictates gendered parenting trends. What the term "meritocracy" obscures is the intersectional racialization logic upon which the criteria for "good parenting" is based. Cultural capital masks economic capital, naturalizing the idea that "good parents" *can* and *do* spend large sums of money on their children. Thus, the very notion of "meritocracy" perpetuates and reinscribes intersectional racialized inequality.

0.1. Yanira and a Spanish apprentice

0.2. Professional midwifery student teaches a group of traditional midwives using dolls as props

0.3. Traditional midwife with the baby and placenta model she has sewn by hand

1.1. Sofia

1.2. Liliana

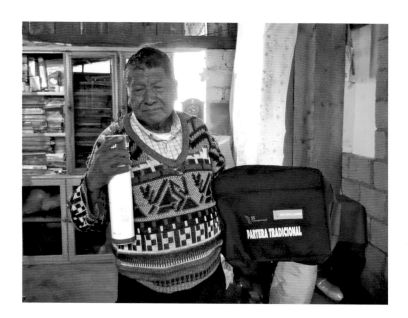

1.10. Don Israel

1.7. Doña Eugenia

1.11. Doña Agustina giving a *"sobada"* (traditional massage)

1.12. Having a cup of hot chocolate in the kitchen before bedtime

1.13. After a baptism at which Doña Eugenia was *"la madrina"* (godmother)

2.2. Social networks: A gathering of families whose children were born via humanized birth

2.7. From left to right: Josefa with Timoteo and Tobías, Tomás, and Celia

3.3. Flor and a fellow professional midwifery student with a baby whose birth
she attended

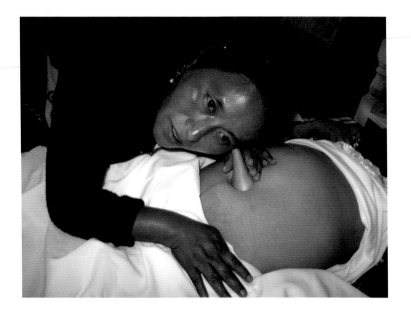

3.5. Doña Eugenia listening to fetal sounds

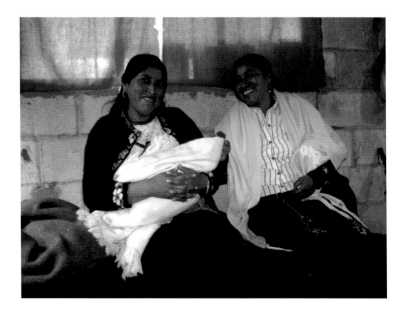

3.6. Doña Eugenia during a postnatal visit with a mother whose birth she attended

4.3. Medical personnel teaching workshop in Zongólica, Veracruz

4.4. Traditional midwives in attendance at the workshop

5.1. Dr. Maricelda with photos of the children whose births she has attended

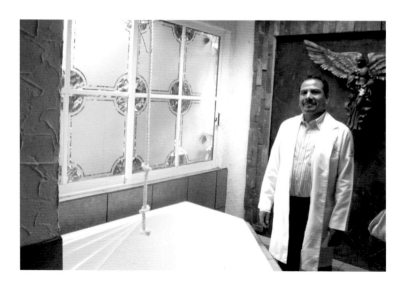

5.2. Dr. García's garden-view birthing suite with Jacuzzi, skylight, and fountain

5.3. Participants at the workshop on "Traditional Mexican Midwifery" (I am second from right)

5.4. Participants on a boat headed for a beach restaurant where the workshop was held that day

5.5. Using *rebozos* to manipulate the shape of the birth canal by applying pressure to the pelvis

5.6. Participants watching, filming, and photographing Adeli prepare herbal cosmetic balms

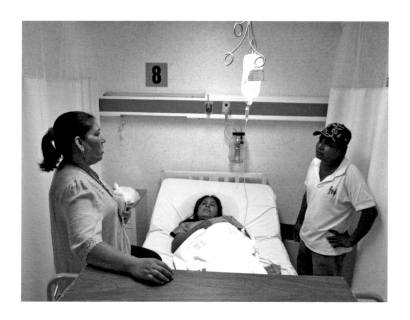

5.7. From left to right: Sagrario, María del Carmen, and Ignacio

5.8. Verónica's father-in-law talking to his son through the cell phone on the end of the wooden post

5.9. Verónica receives a prenatal exam from Sagrario and another professional midwife

5.12. The inside of María del Carmen and Ignacio's cabin; their children and family members

CHAPTER 3

Intersectionality:
A Contextual and Dialogical Framework

Anthropology is a scientific craft that involves extended participant-ob-servation with informants who, over the extended course of research, of-ten become close friends. In order to conduct fieldwork, anthropologists use their bodies as their primary research tool—research is a sensory ex-perience in which sights, sounds, smells, tastes, tactile sensations, and emotive responses all comprise the anthropologist's ethnographic expe-rience. The ethnographic enterprise has been considered "carnal" (Wac-quant 2005), and a form of "sensuous scholarship" (Stoller 1997:xv). Too often, the intimate ways in which the body becomes part and parcel to ethnographic data are left out of the analysis of results.

In *Fresh Fruit, Broken Bodies: Migrant Farmworkers in the United States* (2013), Seth Holmes, recipient of the 2016 Margaret Mead Award, enacts a truly embodied anthropology when he joins Triqui informants as they migrate across the Mexico-US border, and he subsequently dedicates his mind, body, and social experiences to the production of ethnographic notes as a farmworker. Holmes, referring to Maurice Merleau-Ponty (1996), calls for a phenomenological approach to ethnography in which the body is not something the ethnographer possesses or uses, but rather, that the body *is* the ethnographer and therefore the body produces field data. In this sense, the way in which we perform ethnography can enact Margaret Lock and Nancy Scheper-Hughes' concept of the "mindful body" (Lock and Scheper-Hughes 1987), thus deconstructing the (false) mind-body dichotomy.

In this section, I must acknowledge "the field notes offered by the body" (Holmes 2013:39) in order to offer thickness to my critical and hyper-self-reflexive ethnography of racializing processes in Mexico. Not only did my body determine which spaces I could access, but the years spent engaged in embodied ethnography molded me in ways that shaped how I was perceived by others. As I became increasingly embedded in my ethnographic field-site-turned-home and more and more affectively bound to informants-turned-friends, my body became legible to those around me in new ways, thus opening up further realms for embodied research.

By the time I returned to California in fall 2014 at the conclusion of my ethnographic research, my Mexican home and community had become so familiar to me that the transition "back home" felt strange. I had been speaking, thinking, and dreaming in Spanish for forty-three months, and word-finding in English was a challenge. I had not driven a car in several years. I was overwhelmed by a sense of novelty for everyday US things (bathtubs!); at the same time, I was homesick and filled with longing for the daily rhythm and the people I left behind. I miss the church bells, the rooster call, the Tuesday market, my favorite fruit stand, friends that I have no way of contacting until I next make the trek out to their remote locales, and, above all, my body *being in* that context that became mine.

My embodied anthropological research in Mexico was largely shaped by the familial context through which my research unfolded. During my ethnographic fieldwork, I spent time with my extended family, both consanguineal and affinal members. Although familial bonds gave me a sense of "belonging" in these households, I quickly found that my privilege could be a distinguishing, and essentially, distancing factor. If I was going to maintain positive relationships with family, I had to adjust my behavior.

At the outset of my graduate program, I was interested in structural violence and dire medical outcomes in Mexico, so I spent five months conducting preliminary fieldwork in La Costa Grande, Guerrero, where there is an epilepsy "epidemic." Genetic inheritance of epilepsy is relatively rare in Mexico, comparable to other nations, yet in this region of Mexico—located in the narcotrafficking corridor on the Pacific Coast—lack of infrastructure and contaminated water have led to neurologic parasites that cause epileptic seizures. This problem is so common that I liken its emergence to a local epidemic. I spent one afternoon asking local residents if they knew of neighbors who had experienced seizures, and using a snowball method, I interviewed fourteen epileptics within a one-kilometer radius.

Throughout my preliminary research in 2009, I stayed with my extended family. My experiences in this three-generation household were formative for how I conducted research in the following years. I quickly came to understand that, especially in rural contexts, gender hierarchies have maintained a rigidity that I was unaccustomed to, and to which I was expected to conform. I was a welcome guest, but family members made it clear to me what my role was as a woman in the household—they were not seeking any sort of "progressive influence" from me, and my attempting to catalyze change would have been received as an extreme form of hubris. As a woman of reproductive age, I was expected to demonstrate my deference to the men in the household, as well as my dependency on them for my physical safety and well-being. As time wore on, I came to realize that this dependency was hardly performative; over the course of my five-month stay, it became all too real.

The relatives I stayed with are mango farmers. They live in a four-room house (two bedrooms and two common spaces) on a 150-hectare plot of land. The house itself is modest. The front room has a cement floor, but the other rooms have dirt floors. The corrugated metal roof and brick walls lead to sweltering indoor temperatures during the summer months. There are no glass windowpanes or air-conditioning units in the village, so during the day, doors are left open to create a draft, and small fans are used to circulate air at night. The family was considered relatively wealthy because of their possession of land, and sufficient livestock for the family's consumption of meat, dairy, and eggs (a couple of dozen cattle, six pigs, a handful of hens, and a rooster). We had two *pilas* (above-ground, open-air water receptacles resembling large bathtubs) into which water was pumped weekly. There was an outhouse in the rear patio area that was divided into two sections—one side was for elimination, the other side for outdoor sponge bathing from a water barrel behind a drape.

In addition to selling mangos to the local *patrón,* the family derived income through the labor-intensive work of hand extracting *palapas,* the center vein of individual palm leaves, to be used in crafts (woven baskets, figurines, etc.). As a woman, the appropriate ways for me to contribute to this household were through cooking, washing clothes, and extracting *palapas* (for which I earned about US$1 a day). The men were responsible for working in the mango field and hunting. Gendered space was constantly maintained. Men did not enter the kitchen, and in the evenings, women did not linger in the patio where men created a circle of chairs and drank *chelas* (beer) into the early morning hours. Throughout each evening, my female relatives and I would remove bottle caps, deliver a fresh bucket of ice-cold beers, and swiftly take away empty bottles, but we did not become involved in the men's conversation. Only a few women in the village ventured into this masculine space—it was explained to me that they were sex workers, and that I should stay indoors to safeguard my reputation and purity. Notions of the outdoor patio areas as threatening to female purity extended to my needing to be accompanied at night by a male relative to use the outhouse. A male relative told me that some other men in the community lingered in the wooded area at night, waiting for an opportunity to prey on an unaccompanied woman, and that as a new addition to the community, I generated interest.

My extended family guarded me with heightened awareness, compared to the treatment of my other female relatives. For example, I sometimes experienced "cabin fever" and requested permission from the male head of the household to spend the afternoon at a grandparent's house. This request was met with a mild tone of annoyance, since someone would have to accompany me on the short walk down the dirt path. At the beginning of my stay, I did not fully understand the implications for my safety, and I took this to be solely because of how unaware I was of local customs, and how my body was ill-adjusted for the rural context.

My body was the focus of commentary and criticism of my ways, including male relatives questioning how my slender frame would ever produce healthy offspring. There were other ways my body did not "fit" the social context. Twice I was chided for wearing pants with a "revealing" fit—an opinion that confused me since my jeans were not immodest by US standards; meanwhile, women of similar age wore cropped midriff-revealing tops that I would not feel comfortable wearing. As I began realizing that my wardrobe was the source of both scrutiny and admiration, and that both induced social distance, I understood that one way to stop marking difference was to dress more like the people around me.

Embodiment of difference, however, was not just about body shape and wardrobe choices. I encountered the many ways in which "difference" was embodied—ways I could not seem to escape because they were corporally integrated into my being. I was heckled by female relatives about my inability to use my callous-free, sensitive fingers to flip tortillas cooking on the *comal,* the flat griddle they placed on top of a log fire. Even a small child can do this! In another instance, I recall how entertained my female relatives were by my constantly being targeted by blood-sucking tropical bugs while they sat unbothered as they extracted *palapas.* They teased me for having sweet American blood, commenting on excessive nutrition in the United States and saying that the bugs were tired of sucking their local blood but were drawn to the novel flavor pulsing through my veins. A close friend of mine began counting the scars on my back one day but stopped counting when she reached three hundred—these scars lasted for over a year, thus serving as a constant reminder of how the experiences of ethnography leave their mark on the body.

Later in my stay, however, I realized that my extended family displayed heightened care when looking after my safety because my privilege posed a threat to both me and them. At the time, I intended to study epilepsy in the region for my doctoral research, and further, I hoped that the region would be my second home for many years to come. I planned to build a house of my own. Like many women who try to manage their own construction projects, especially when the project is financed by the remittances of their migrant-worker partners, I was alone in overseeing the building process. Displaying extreme naïveté, and with my extended family's participation, I drafted blueprints of the structure, designing it to be a similar size to the one my relatives were living in, and enlisted the help of male relatives to hire local construction workers and buy building materials.

The house shared many characteristics with the other houses in the village, but it was distinct in two important ways that, at the time, I had neither the experience nor the foresight to critically examine. Firstly, the house included a *tinaco*—a plastic water tank installed on the roof that used gravity to deliver water to the kitchen and indoor bathroom. Secondly, the walls of the cement structure went up within a few short months. I mistakenly thought that since other houses in the region—as close as a mile away in the nearest town—began using this method of water delivery in prior years, it was fine for me to do so as well. Also, although I noticed the presence of many unfinished structures across rural Mexico—stalled at different stages of the construction processes—I did not appreciate the economic struggle of locals when it comes to the gradual, multiphased process of building a home. I began building the house with a great deal of pride and excitement, shoveling sand for the foundation in the mornings before temperatures rose and daydreaming about the red hammock I was going to install in the porch. I was later forced to examine the privileged assumptions that allowed me to overlook the distinguishing factors between my construction plans and other villagers.

By the end of my five-month stay, I understood that the larger houses in the region belonged to migrants who earned US dollars to build "lavish" houses in their hometowns, and that their display of relative success was met with both admiration and resentment. The latter often resulted in anonymous threats of violence. As a result, the homes of migrants (families and individuals who spent most of their time in the United States but made economic investments in their hometown through remittances and preparations for "one day" when they return home) were often protected by tall courtyard walls, barbed wire, and iron window grilles. I, too, became a target for anonymous threats. After we received phone calls describing the timing of my activities the day before and demanding

US$40,000, I was instructed never to answer the phone (to let male relatives answer the phone for me) and to remain indoors in order to reduce the likelihood of kidnapping. Eventually, the situation became too unsafe and unsustainable, and I was forced to leave the region and abandon my house, my plans for research, and my hopes for integrating myself into the village.

The next year, when I began my research on humanized birth across Mexico, my approach was deeply penetrated by my failures in Guerrero. I recognized that if I maintained even a portion of the privileged living standard I had in the United States, that would not only distance me from informants and preclude me from conducting effective ethnographic fieldwork, but more important, it would have negative effects on those around me. Thus, attempting to "unlearn privilege" as Spivak describes was not only a methodological choice, it was also a necessity from a perspective of physical safety, the well-being of my relationships, and the feasibility of my research (Spivak 1988a:287; also see Spivak and Harasym 1990:9).

My commitment to hyper-self-reflexivity shaped my research at multiple levels. The friendships I developed with both traditional and professional midwives endure to the time of this writing, and they have shaped me as a person. My husband and I chose to have our wedding ceremony in Tulum, Quintana Roo, and we limited our guest list to "fifty-percent or more blood relatives" and close friends—among them were former informants-turned-confidantes, reflecting how over the course of research, the exchange of confidence is mutual. I was deeply touched when one of my friends traveled across five Mexican state lines to attend our wedding.

The process of developing friendships in the field was at times facilitated by acts of reciprocity, including the exchange of gifts. In Guerrero, I had brought gifts to thank individual family members for hosting me, and in retrospect, I realize that I lacked sensitivity regarding the local economic scale and that I had created an uncomfortable situation because it was impossible for my extended family to reciprocate. Subsequently, I began giving gifts that were of appropriate value and could be reciprocated, and I felt I was making progress, not only as a researcher but also as a community member and friend, when these gift exchanges were initiated by others. In my post-fieldwork life back in the United States, these gifts from friends are placed throughout my home in spots where I can appreciate them—through these tangible items I feel the presence of friends around me, even in spite of physical distance.

Many of the gifts I received were articles of clothing. I would travel to Doña Eugenia's home every year in June. Doña Eugenia remarked to me that I was like a migratory bird, and that she knew it was summer when Rosalynn came to stay. At the end of each visit, we gave each other parting gifts, and Doña Eugenia shed a few tears because, she said, she was missing me already. On the last day of our first visit together, Doña Eugenia dressed me up in the traditional Nahua *bata* and blouse, admiring how beautiful I was in a way that was entirely reminiscent of Anne Fadiman's experience in *The Spirit Catches You and You Fall Down*. On the next trip, Doña Eugenia mentioned to me how much she liked an embroidered blouse I wore, so when I returned the next year, I brought an identical blouse for her to keep. She went to her wardrobe, searched through her different garments, picked one that was "my size" (the smallest one she owns), and gave it to me to keep. In this way, and across multiple gift exchanges with different friends, my blouse collection started growing.

My identity is shaped and defined by the relationships that are closest to my heart. I cannot speak for other anthropologists, but I imagine that this may be a common experience for anthropologists, not to mention for many people in general. Thus, over the course of my research in Mexico, these affective experiences were incorporated into my body. To give an analogy for how I became "more Mexican," my hair steadily grew during those years, and while I had not noticed the day-to-day change, by the end of my fieldwork, my black *trenzas* had become a part of me. *Trenzas*, two long braids, often appear in depictions of indigenous women and were mentioned by informants as a trait of traditional midwives. I had not intentionally grown out my hair to be like anyone else—rather, my appearance was increasingly unaltered throughout the fieldwork experience since aesthetic manipulations using hair dye, styling products, high heels, and cosmetics are impractical, given many of the geographical terrains and socioeconomic contexts of my ethnographic work. I did not make a concerted effort to mark difference, and I adapted to the available services and living standards in my field sites.

This analogy about *becoming*, however, does not adequately describe the nonvisible elements that led others to perceive me as Mexican. My experiences in Mexico were incorporated into my habitus and written on my body in ways that became legible to strangers when I returned to the United States. Prior to conducting fieldwork, I was often taken for a Pacific Islander or an East Indian. Post-fieldwork, on multiple different occasions, I was approached by Spanish-speaking individuals seeking my help with directions and translation. During these instances, I was silently engaged in everyday activities (i.e., walking down the street, riding the bus, entering a store) when I was approached and had not intentionally com-

municated my Mexican identity. In one instance, I was actually emphasizing my Asian heritage—I was speaking Toishanese while buying Chinese
herbs when a Spanish-speaking man requested in Spanish that I translate
for him.

These experiences led me to wonder how my "Mexican-ness" became
more pronounced over the course of my fieldwork. After returning to the
Bay Area to write my dissertation, I cut and styled my hair and, wary of
the cultural commodification I was critiquing, made sure to avoid wearing
ethnic Mexican clothing. (The blouses I received as gifts hang in my closet
and I visit them daily with a feeling of warmth for the friends who gave
them to me, but I do not wear them in the United States.) Since I am phe-
notypically the same as I was before I left for fieldwork, something about
my gestures and mannerisms must signal to others that I am a Spanish
speaker. My embodied experiences in Mexico not only define the contours
of my internal psycho-emotional landscape, but they are somehow percep-
tible to others who have similar embodied experiences. Without speaking,
there is something in them that recognizes that same something in me.

This realization led me to reevaluate my understanding of racializing
processes and to consider the extra-phenotypical factors that shape how
identities are perceived. Furthermore, I realized that identity is not only
about self-identification—rather, identities are constantly being negotiated between individuals who make perceptive judgments about each
other. With these things in mind, I point to how intersectionality unfolds
in ways that are at once contextual and dialogical. That is, even when a
single individual is in question, the ways that person's intersectional identity is interpreted depends on the context framing the encounter and the
person(s) doing the perceiving. This contextual and dialogical process constitutes the central theme of this chapter.

The Intersection of Race and Class

Emma is a Swiss woman who works as a midwife in Tulum, Quintana Roo.
Before moving to Mexico sixteen years ago, she studied naturopathy at a
university. She has eight children with her Mayan husband. Emma and her
family live near the crystalline waters of the Riviera Maya in a small but
touristy town that attracts visitors to the pyramids and resort-goers on
holiday. This was not always the case. Before living in Tulum, Emma and
her family lived in her husband's Mayan village for five years, but she was
never accepted by the villagers—her white skin, blonde hair, blue eyes,

height, and body shape were too much for them to look past. She wanted to practice midwifery in her husband's natal village, but the women did not want her to attend their births, saying that a white woman could not really know. As a result, Emma now attends the births of foreigners. Although she aimed to construct a "local" identity and integrate herself into the community, her European origins, phenotype, and multilingualism (which did not include native Mayan) led to her being racially identified as "Other." Moments of rejection render visible the syncretic nature of identity formation.

Despite being rejected by Mayan villagers, Emma's commitment to racial equity made a deep impression on me. As the mother of half-Mayan, half-Swiss children and the wife of a Mayan man, Emma is sensitive to racial inequality in Mexico. She described to me how her husband went to pick up their baby from the hospital on one occasion and was stopped by a police officer on the street and accused of stealing the baby. For him to be the father of a baby that fair, the policeman reasoned, the mother would have to be Caucasian, and that was just ludicrous! The police officer's assumption that "white" and "indigenous" do not mix points to reified notions of interethnic interaction (and its limits). Racialized categories upon which inclusion/exclusion are based persist despite centuries of biological and genetic admixture.

Emma seemed almost allergic to whatever privilege she might be granted based solely on her skin color. She told me how she is sometimes called a "professional midwife," and how she makes a point to correct the speaker by explaining that she has never had any formal training, and, thus, should not be grouped with professional midwives just because she has fair skin. In Quintana Roo where she lives, there is a large Mayan population, but in general, professionals and those who are in positions of power tend to be *güeros* (fair-skinned) and have Spanish surnames. For Emma, race and national origin are more salient categories than socioeconomic class. For example, she explained, when she showed a Louis Vuitton–carrying woman from Mexico City a video on water birth, the woman responded, "How nice! But I already scheduled my cesarean." According to Emma, the women who seek out humanized birth are either foreigners living in Mexico or Mexican intellectuals who can think beyond Mexico's "paternalistic culture" and "culture of fear." Although I understand the point Emma is trying to make, it is a key observation of this book that power is not necessarily exercised by men and exacted on women. I use humanized birth as a lens for examining "the matrix of women's dominations of each other" (Haraway 1991:155).

The importance lent to race versus class cannot be parsed as simply as in Emma's determination. An important part of my argument is that race is mapped onto class, and vice versa, through processes of racialization. Class can by no means be denied. When interviewing Carolina, a prenatal yoga instructor in the city of Monterrey, I asked her to describe the socioeconomic class of her clients and she responded with one word: "High." Her work is about "transcendence" through practicing yoga, and she explained that although there are a few "transcended" people who are "extracts from the lower classes," these people do not attend her classes. A midwifery student at the same health center described her clients as "middle-upper class, professional, educated, and informed." Two obstetric nurses in Mexico City insisted that although they attend births of women from varying socioeconomic backgrounds, all of the women they attend are well educated and well read. During that same series of interviews, a homeopath and midwife told me that her clients are middle-upper class, informed, and actively seeking alternative care.

After several years of living in Mexico, I realized that the disparity between those who form the powerful elite and those who struggle to make ends meet at the margins of Mexican society follows a color gradient. This gradient can be observed through media images: upon turning on the television any given evening, viewers can observe the difference between the fair-skinned actors and actresses on the screen and average men and women on the street. If a darker-skinned actor or actress appears in a telenovela, it is likely that he or she is playing the role of a servant. Whiteness continues to be an ideal in Mexico, but unlike some Asian and Middle Eastern countries where skin creams and sun protection are used to physically whiten skin, whiteness in Mexico emphasizes extra-phenotypical factors, almost masking the effort invested in individual portrayals of whiteness, and the sustained role of race and racism in everyday life.

However, given the ethnographic examples in this book, my point is not to deny class in favor of race, or vice versa, but rather to extend Kimberlé Crenshaw's concept of "intersectionality" when I explore the ways in which race makes class and class makes race. Intersectionality is a conceptual tool for understanding how different dimensions of inequality co-construct one another (Grzanka 2014). It is a way to think about the problem of sameness and difference in relation to power, a foundational logic of interlocking oppressions, and an examination of systemic domination that overlaps sexuality, race, gender, economic class, and so on (Grzanka 2014; Cohen 1997).

Intersecting dimensions of inequality are not additive. Crenshaw's analogy of the increased likelihood for injury from crossing traffic at an intersection elucidates how black women sometimes experience gender discrimination in a similar way to white women; other times they experience racial discrimination similarly to black men; and still other times they are discriminated against as black women—not the sum of racism and sexism, but something that supersedes these individual categories and cannot be described as a derivative of white women's or black men's lives. Crenshaw emphasizes gender discrimination against women who are already marginalized because of race and/or class, and she argues that though racialized women face some of the same obstacles that more elite women face, they also encounter obstacles that are unique to them.

My ethnographic research in Mexico builds upon Crenshaw's concept of intersectionality by pointing to how intersectionality unfolds contextually and dialogically. Racial judgments are made about self and others using complex, interlacing social and physiological criteria that depend on the context of the encounter and the individuals involved. Education, habitus, socioeconomic status, and cultural and social capital are all variables in the calculus of whiteness. Furthermore, racial identification of self and others is necessarily a syncretic process. It is through this multifaceted construction of self through contrast to others that acid remarks aimed at "them" were rarely explicitly racist, even as race persists as a primary axis of discrimination. In this chapter, I use ethnographic examples from contrasting geographic locations, San Miguel and the High Mountains of Veracruz, to provide texture in demonstrating how intersectionality unfolds and thus explore how "racism" operates through processes of differentiation.

The Exclusion of Racialized Locals in "Gringolandia"

After my initial enchantment in 2010 with San Miguel's cobblestone streets, vibrant-hued buildings, baroque cathedral, mariachis, and officers on horseback subsided, I began thinking more carefully about the unequal politics of transnationalism and identity embedded within my chosen ethnographic "field." I noticed that in San Miguel, the *rebozo*-cloaked women clutching mud-streaked babies while begging in the street all have indigenous features. Brown-skinned primary-school–age children wander in and out of local businesses during school hours, begging and demanding alms (employing the form of conjugation used for giving an order), their practiced "needy" expressions and aggressive tones elicit feelings of

Figure 3.1. Panoramic views of San Miguel de Allende (photo 1)

discomfort and guilt, effectively luring coins from the hands of many un-accustomed visitors and foreigners. Meanwhile, on weekends the town center is flooded with tourists and wedding guests from bigger cities—many of whom flock to the local Starbucks, converting the international coffee chain into a bustling and noisy hot spot. On Saturdays, the parish on the main square hosts a wedding every half hour—the beautiful fair-skinned women gather near the *zocalo* (the main square) to take photos in their elegant beaded gowns.

I spoke to Flor Romero, a CASA midwifery student at the time, and an informant who has evolved into an extraordinary friend. She told me that in San Miguel, there are invisible walls—spaces she cannot access—these are the unspoken rules of inclusion and exclusion for lower-class Mexican women. Having only begun to think about intersectional racialization processes, I didn't fully understand her meaning and initially I was incredulous. How could this be if I had never encountered any obstacles moving through numerous spaces in San Miguel?

As a brown-skinned woman, I was still thinking of racism in terms of phenotype instead of considering how intersectionality works to make judgments about individuals' positionality in society based on complex

Figure 3.2. Panoramic views of San Miguel de Allende (photo 2)

criteria that include *and* supersede phenotype. I could not understand how Flor, a woman who is significantly fairer than I am, would be discriminated against but I would not be. Having initiated my ethnographic fieldwork only several months before, I had not yet arrived at the hyper-self-reflexivity that anthropological work on inequality requires. I still did not understand how my affluence was written on my body—wrapped up in my tone of voice, exuded in my gestures, written in my face-forward gaze, and embedded in my everyday ways of engaging with others (see also Holmes 2013:36–37). Over time I was able to shed many of these visible markers that had up until then been invisible to me. At that point, I still had much to learn.

Flor looked me in the eyes and said, "Of course you've never been discriminated against! Because you are you, Rosalynn! I could never go into Starbucks." I challenged her. Could she demonstrate to me how this intersectional discrimination was operating at Starbucks? She proposed that we do an experiment: we would go to Starbucks and attempt to use the bathroom. I was to remain silent, submissively by her side. She explained that young people with fair skin and large pocketbooks are invited to loiter at Starbucks (sometimes without making a purchase), but lower-class Mexicans are interrogated and often barred from the premises. We would inevitably be turned away. We approached the Starbucks entrance nonchalantly, hoping to blend in with the constant flow of young iPhone-carrying patrons on this busy weekend and to cross the threshold into the courtyard. (Starbucks is located in a former hacienda that now houses a number of boutiques and art galleries. There is a bathroom in the courtyard for anyone visiting Starbucks or the neighboring stores. In actuality, these bathrooms are considered "public" to anyone who possesses the right amount of cultural capital—but not for everyone, I was about to find out.) The guard stopped us. Where were we going? Flor answered, "We had a coffee here this morning. We'd like to use the bathroom." He asked to see our receipt, stating that we could not come into the building without a sales receipt. She responded, "I threw it away after we left. I'm pregnant and the pressure of the baby on my bladder is causing me a bathroom emergency!" She patted her plump belly to emphasize her words. The guard was unmoved: "If you don't have a receipt you can't come in." Flor retorted, "If you don't let me in, I'm going to pee in my pants!" The guard responded, "Then pee in your pants. You can't come in."

It may seem that Flor was barred from the premises because of her lower-class standing and because she was identified as a racialized "Other," but this assumption can be problematized further. Throughout this chapter I present race in Mexico as a complex algorithm that orders social hierarchies based on criteria that extend far beyond biology, genetics, and phenotype to also include class, education, national identity, and other forms of cultural capital. I employ the concept of intersectionality when I analyze the multiple variables contributing to the immediate, often unconscious, mental calculus that occurs during quotidian encounters of difference. In this way, my perspective on intersectional racialization processes goes beyond "racial profiling" by discarding US racial politics as the frame of reference; taking transnational encounters as the lens for analysis, examining social interaction in "internal borderlands" such as San Miguel, where both colonial legacies and contemporary international relations are woven into the fabric of everyday life; and explicitly attending to the amalgam of nonbiologic elements that are folded into notions of "race."

About a year later, I spoke to my landlady, Pati Gutiérrez, about the intersectional racialization processes that were occurring around me. Pati had recently broken up with her common-law husband, with whom she had two children, because he had relapsed into alcoholism. I lived in a small room above their living quarters and paid about US$120 monthly in rent, utilities included. Over time, Pati and I became close friends, and she shared plenty of her heartaches with me. One evening, we were sit-

Figure 3.3. Flor and a fellow professional midwifery student, with a baby whose birth she attended

ting in the kitchen, chatting, when she told me that as a housekeeper it would behoove her to improve her conversation skills in English and thus be able to communicate with her American employers. When I offered to help her, Pati explained to me that she had already attempted to sign up in San Miguel for a language-exchange program at the Public Library, or Biblioteca Pública, which is actually an NGO funded by donations from foreigners. (The Municipal Library, which pales in comparison, is located around the corner and is unknown to the majority of Sanmiguelenses. The Public Library traces its origins to 1954, when Mrs. Helen Ware set out to provide access to educational and reading materials for Mexican children.) The language-exchange program pairs American retirees and expatriates with "local Sanmiguelenses" so that both can improve their speaking skills in the other's native language. Thus, Pati had gone to the Public Library one afternoon after cleaning house and asked to be placed on the wait list. The attendant at the desk gave her the "once over" and decided that she was unsuitable for the program. "I'm sorry—there are no available spots and you cannot be placed on the waiting list."

Having already pondered the invocation of humanitarianism during training workshops for traditional midwives that inadvertently reinforce racialized hierarchies and commodify indigenous cultures, and keeping in mind Haraway's 1991 approach to "textual politics," I wondered about the *visual politics* of NGO programs that seek exchange with the local community at the same time as they make certain community members appear and others disappear. Program participants-who-never-were, such as Pati, are invisible to foreign participants in the language-exchange program— language partners learn curated versions of "culture" by conversing with each other about personal experiences—therefore La Biblioteca Pública's native English-speakers will never know about Pati's desire to learn, the houses she cleans, or her home and children tucked away in a narrow hillside alley. I considered the irony of Pati's exclusion from the language-exchange program while "favela safaris" and other forms of touristic voyeurism of poverty and suffering emerge on the global stage. How are some forms of inequality hidden from privileged sojourners while others are revealed and even marketed?

After listening to her story, I wondered about the flexibility surrounding my own racial identity and how context could determine how I was perceived and therefore (mis)treated. It was obvious to me that Flor and Pati's perceived class had a lot to do with how they were being treated. But this was not the question. Rather, I was curious about how much the perception of race was also influencing the mental calculus that individuals used when they decided how to treat other individuals. I had learned that social class is operative during moments of encounter and exclusion, but how is race collapsed within social class (and vice versa) as a marker for social categorization?

I dressed myself in the clothing that, at this point in my research, had become a regular part of my daily wardrobe—an embroidered linen blouse, a long skirt, and sandals—and twisted my waist-length black hair into two braids. I had visited the Public Library on several occasions earlier during my ethnographic research, dressed casually in a T-shirt or cotton blouse and jeans. How would this slow transformation in my presentation of self alter the cordial treatment I had formerly experienced?

Upon entering the Biblioteca Pública, I chose a table in an area with about a dozen tables and no patrons. I pulled out my copy of Hannah Arendt's book *On Violence* and began underlining and writing in the margins. I acted as I had on prior occasions and carried on with work as usual. I could feel a library employee standing nearby staring at me, wondering what to do, but I feigned ignorance of his conundrum and continued reading. A minute later, an older Caucasian woman sat down a couple of tables away. The library employee spared no time in approaching her table and asked her, in English, if he could prepare her something to drink from the library's café. She said, "No, not now. I'm fine, thank you." He then approached my table and asked me hesitantly, in Spanish, if he could offer me anything. I responded, also in Spanish, "Not right now. Thank you." (By this stage in my fieldwork, my American accent was virtually undetectable, and I was often taken for a woman born and raised in Mexico.) He then responded, "In that case, I'm going to have to ask you to leave. This space is only for our patrons."

At that point, I could have spoken to him in perfect American English, forced him to acknowledge his racist presumption, and demanded he retract his statement. However, doing so would have been an exercise of privilege. My intention had not been to challenge existing racialized hierarchies, but to try to comprehend the mechanisms of inclusion/exclusion from which I had thus far been shielded. As my research progressed, a key strategy for my achieving ethnographic acuity was to learn to shed all visual markers of privilege, let my appearance go unaltered, and experience exclusion firsthand. My ethnographic methodology is bound to my theoretical commitment to intersectionality. According to Patrick Grzanka, scholars of "strong intersectionality" (as opposed to "weak intersectionality") engage in constant self-reflexivity, wielding the concept as an analytic tool that critiques power and privilege, and producing counter-hegemonic knowledge about marginalized and subjugated groups.

The total monthly budget for my two-person household, including rent, was approximately US$400—an amount that dictated what I was able to buy at the grocery store and caused me to travel by bus and on foot instead of taking taxis. As an ethnographer committed to my craft, it was crucial for me to maintain congruence within my embodied experience of having limited resources. Over time, this embodiment led to a decline in my physical health. I lost weight and developed mild anemia and vitamin deficiencies, and my cholesterol soared. I quickly learned about the pragmatic consequences of limited economic resources and malnutrition.

I recognize that "shedding privilege" can never be truly achieved. As academic researchers, many ethnographers choose to experience poverty and structural disadvantage, and this choice can be unmade at any moment. I possess cultural capital that, whether I choose to engage it or not, separates me from informants-turned-friends who cannot choose to live with privilege. If given the choice, of course, those living in poverty would not likely choose to live in poverty. Nonetheless, to gain the trust and respect of my lower-class Mexican informants, it was important that I live like them (see Holmes 2013:33 on how informants understood his project as meaning "[h]e wants to experience for himself how the poor suffer"). The close friendships I developed with informants were facilitated by my decision to live on their socioeconomic scale. I was no longer one of the *gringas* whose presumptive superiority informants criticized, but I became, rather, *una amiga*.

I chose subservience as a response to the library employee's discrimination, but the local Mexican population and Mexican employees at American-led NGOs show resentment over the racialization performed by these NGOs. Over the course of my research, I realized that it is not unusual for American founders at humanized-birth NGOs to be accused of extortion. Mexican employees and "beneficiaries" of NGO programs wonder about the apparent disproportion of their salaries and resources when compared to the lifestyles NGO founders lead. Throughout my research, I was often asked by individuals associated with the NGO how founders are able to engage in so much personal travel, leading a transnational life that includes a home in a US metropolis and an extravagant hacienda-style house in Mexico on a sprawling plot of land, among other properties. One NGO founder explained to me how hard he has worked his entire life in the world of public health, with sparse economic returns. His posture, phrasing, and tone of voice gave me the impression that ongoing criticism has led him to preemptively justify his actions. Upon moving to Mexico, he explained, he took the opportunity to design and build a beautiful home for the very first time. Unfortunately, the property he has amassed in Mexico has led to suspicion within the NGO he runs and has resulted in a nasty lawsuit from a spiteful, disgruntled ex-employee. Some of his friends, also leaders of NGOs that are meant to benefit the local Mexican community, have had similar experiences. When I interviewed him, he was contemplating filming interviews of himself and his friends and putting together a documentary about "the do-gooders," what moves them, and the challenges they face. During the same trip, I interviewed a few of his current employees, and they spoke to me at length about the personal kindness of the NGO founder and the importance of his advocacy efforts. Shortly thereafter, he and his wife both left Mexico, returning to their hometown in the United States. Since then, he has been supervising the NGO transnationally and is reinserting himself into the Mexican context. My intention is not to minimize the altruistic intentions of individuals engaged in humanitarian work; rather, I am pointing to tension resulting from inherent inequality embedded within humanitarian encounters (Fassin 2012).

From Race to Intersectional Racialization Processes

In Mexico, the category of *güero*, literally meaning "fair-skinned," can signal a phenotypic category but is often indicative of a social category, using socioeconomic status as a primary criterion for inclusion. For example, the term *"güero"* is used by shop owners to show respect for potential clients, even when the client is not fair-skinned. There is an underlying tone of subservience in this terminology, which can be traced back to Mexico's colonial past.

My work examines what I call "intersectional racialization processes": the dialectical, relational, and power-laden process resulting in the construction, negotiation, negation, and (re)production of racialized identities that are operationalized transnationally with political and economic effects. I am not only describing instances of racism; rather, I am pointing to how perceptions of race unfold in and through processes of intersectional racialization. That is, throughout this book, I resist the reification of race and instead use ethnographic observations to critically analyze processes of intersectional racialization. In doing so, I am applying an intersectional approach to ongoing conversations about racialized identities to which other Latin Americanist anthropologists—for example, Michael Montoya (2011), Marisol de la Cadena (2000), and Elizabeth Roberts (2012a and 2012b)—have greatly contributed.

I build upon de la Cadena's 2000 argument that "social whitening" can be achieved through education, employment, locale, dress, class, levels of *"decencia"* (decency), and sexual conduct by signaling that perceptions of race are shaped by the context framing the encounter between the perceiver and the perceived. Intersectional racialization processes can work in both directions—as with examples of "social whitening," the opposite can also occur. People who are fair-skinned and lacking indigenous heritage can be racialized, "socially darkened," and treated as inferiors because of their limited education and lower-class standing. However, intersectional racialization processes are never total—they are constantly occurring, but never reach completion (thus drawing attention to the ongoing effort individuals exert to influence how they are perceived by others). Others have written about biologized race and racialized biology,[1] but my work is about the construction of social identities that allow for manipulation and multiplicitous interpretations of race. What is being racialized is not the biological body or the national body, but the moral body.

The intersectional racialization processes I observed bring Crenshaw's concept of intersectionality to bear on Gayatri Spivak's notion of "class apartheid" (the class divisions within individual nations that lead people of the same "culture" to live divergent realities, and the elite global professional class that is so often blind to the "Third World subaltern" [Sharpe 2003:618]) and then builds upon both concepts by drawing attention to how the inter-embeddedness of race, class, and gender unfolds contextually and dialogically. When considering the instances of exclusion that women like Flor and Pati experience when attempting to access transnational spaces, these missed encounters beg the question of whether race is doing the work of class or whether class is doing the work of race. I will argue, "yes," and "yes." Racialization and class, as well as resulting categories such as education level and geographic location, are mutually imbricated and compounded in people's lives. People cannot experience their positionality in society through only one of these factors; rather, they necessarily structure their identity and their relationships with others through the quotidian intersection of these factors.

However, while describing intersectional racialization processes, I primarily examine the race axis of intersectional forms of oppression, thus noting that colonial legacies undergird inequality in Mexico. An extended consideration of racialization points our attention to how identities are shaped, perceived, and interpreted in postcolonial contexts. That is, by placing emphasis on racialization as an analytical lens, I am questioning how a history of colonialism shapes the contemporary transnational order (see Mignolo 2000).

CASA: Spearheading the Professionalization of Midwifery from the City of San Miguel

The humanized-birth movement in Mexico at once references state and national geopolitical boundaries, while referring to ideology, birth practices, policy, and proven results from abroad. The movement points to the effectiveness of midwifery in reducing maternal mortality in Malaysia and Sri Lanka, as well as the sustained low infant-mortality rates in Switzerland and Holland, where midwifery holds a privileged status and is widely respected as the best and safest way to give birth. It is important to remember that CASA's donor network is largely based in the United States, and a significant portion of its members (from cofounders to directors and even students) are transnationals.

CASA forms a network connecting 70,000 foreign donors and thousands of poor Mexican recipients. Furthermore, CASA is tied to many corporations in the United States through financial contributions—over 40 percent of its donations come from American corporations.[2] The community CASA forms through multiple forms of connectedness is "real" due to its financial impact, but it is "fictitious" in the sense that donors and recipients do not share a lived reality. CASA's mobility and CASA's positionality within San Miguel de Allende, a transnational site of circulation and unrelenting movement, make the professional midwifery model of care mobile—so much so that in September 2011, the Ministry of Public Health and Population in Haiti and the Mexican Subministry of Health Prevention and Promotion agreed to send two to four Haitian women to learn professional midwifery at CASA, in order to reproduce CASA's model in their home country.[3]

CASA is a physical and metaphysical space that forms connections between peoples and social groups that are not based upon propinquity. John Urry writes, "There are multiple forms of 'imagined presence' occurring through objects, people, information and images traveling, carrying connections across, and into, multiple other social spaces" (Urry 2007:47). This fluid community evidences that in addition to the corporeal travel of midwifery students and CASA administrators and affiliates, CASA is a site of physical movement of objects (money and other resources), imaginative travel through multiple print and visual media (for example, in pamphlets and solicitations for donations), and communicative travel through person-to-person messages (via e-mail, texts, letters, telephone, and fax). Although imaginative travel implies that the readers/viewers of print and visual media are imagining themselves in the distant location described or depicted in the media, communicative travel is a way to achieve copresence in the midst of absence through communicative propinquity (see Larsen, Urry, and Axhausen 2008). CASA is an "assembly of humans, objects, technologies and scripts that contingently produce[s] durability and stability of mobility" (Urry 2007:48).

On the subject of mobility, Urry writes, "Individuals thus exist beyond their private bodies, leaving traces of their selves in space . . . These changes involve novel, extensive and flickering combinations of presence *and* absence of peoples" (Urry 2007:15–16). The heightened mobility and perpetual travel of CASA employees and volunteers form a network across North America and the world, thus opening up the possibility for the spread of the professional midwifery model across spatial distance. Through these women, CASA has become a node that allows for an emerging ideology about birth and respect for women's bodies to propagate, spread, and fortify.

Transnational space disregards national borders. By pointing to transnational space, I am emphasizing the way the humanized-birth movement is informed and shaped by forces originating beyond Mexican borders. These forces have profound effects on the way individual women experience birth at the local level. CASA and its professional midwifery model could not exist without the city of San Miguel de Allende. San Miguel, to put it simply, is a perpetual "contact zone." However, I would like to depart from this oversimplification to provide a more nuanced explanation of how San Miguel provides a fertile (but not unproblematic) ground for the professional midwifery model of health provisioning.

San Miguel de Allende is characterized by a large, visible population of semipermanent resident American or Canadian retirees. (Increasingly, upper-class Mexican families and youth also flock to San Miguel on the weekends for a brief escape from their hometowns.) These senior Americans and Canadians live on a different economic and moral scale than the Mexican locals, and, thus, from the perspective of many Mexican locals, they enjoy the privileges of tourists on an ongoing basis. Urry, referring to Zygmunt Bauman, writes, "The tourists 'pay for their freedom; the right to disregard native concerns and feelings, the right to spin their own web of meanings . . . The world is the tourist's oyster . . . to be lived pleasurably and thus given meaning' (Bauman 1993:241). Both vagabonds and tourists move through other people's spaces, they involve the separation of physical closeness from any sense of moral proximity and they set standards for happiness" (Bauman 1993:243; Urry 2007:33).

Although Bauman's assessment is rather harsh, it is true that in San Miguel two distinct worlds exist: the world accessible to most American and Canadian long-term residents, and the world in which many Mexican locals struggle to survive. San Miguel is composed of two distinct phenomenological landscapes—two disparate realms of possibility—unfolding simultaneously. Stark economic disparities (most foreign long-term residents receive pensions or have savings in US dollars, whereas local Mexicans earn in pesos) have led to two distinct economies, making some experiences (like dining out at one of the "mid-range" restaurants) unreachable for many Mexican locals. In San Miguel, the service sector has swollen to meet the desires of thousands of American and Canadian retirees, and the percentage of Mexican families depending on near-minimum wage earnings is high.

At the time of my research, minimum wage across Mexico ranged from 61.38 to 64.76 pesos per day (approximately US$5.00). Dinner at a "mid-range" restaurant would easily cost 500–600 pesos per couple, or eight to nine days' wages. Rent for a studio apartment, equipped with American-style conveniences (furnished, with television, microwave, Wi-Fi, heating, and so forth) costs around US$700 per month, or what a local Mexican getting minimum wage would earn in 6.5 months. Entire neighborhoods and real estate developments, such as Los Frailes and Las Ventanas, are cost-prohibitive to Mexican locals—prices are hundreds of thousands of dollars, and often extend into the millions—more than Mexican locals getting minimum wage will earn in a lifetime.

On this note, Urry comments, "Such non-places are spaces: where people coexist or cohabit without living together; they 'create solitary contractuality'" (Urry 2007:156, referring to Augé 1995:94). In this chapter, I place Urry's solitary contractuality in conversation with Nicholas de Genova's "pluralization of urban space that identifies transnational processes as simultaneously capable of violent disjunctures and creative ferments, both of which are disproportionately felt among the poorest people" (De Genova 2005:123). San Miguel for sojourners is touted as "The Heart of Mexico" and holds the history of the Mexican Revolution. The highest accolade came in October 2013, when Condé Nast *Traveler* magazine Reader's Choice Awards identified San Miguel as the Number One city worldwide, citing "great atmosphere, excellent restaurants, culture and ambiance galore." However, San Miguel for Mexican locals is sometimes characterized by one word: "Gringolandia."

Over the course of my research, I have recognized the "reverse discrimination" my native-Sanmiguelense informants described (using the Spanish term *discriminación reversa*) as a result of San Miguel's fragmentation and the pressure of solitary contractuality (Augé 1995:94). San Miguel is divided into two parallel but mutually exclusive worlds—for many Mexican locals, San Miguel is not always experienced as an authentic place. Urry writes,

> Cities are becoming . . . less places of specific dwellingness and more organized in and through diverse mobilities and the regulation of those multiple mobilities. . . . These are the new global order, points of entry into a

world of apparent hypermobility, time-space compression *and* distancia-
tion, and the contested placing of people. (Urry 2007:148–149)

In San Miguel, services such as bars, cafés, restaurants, hotels, shopping centers, casinos, and gyms have emerged to impress and entertain
visitors and "foreign" residents. San Miguel memorializes movement and
circulation, but the idyllic resort town that foreigners enjoy eclipses the
difficult reality many Mexican locals face. Often, Mexican locals live in
the shadows of American and Canadian proximate strangers, and this experience has profound consequences for their individual psyches. I told
Sagrario, the general director of CASA, "I imagine that always seeing so
many services intended for Americans that locals will never be able to afford affects locals' self-esteem." Sagrario responded, "And we are so aware
of it!" Some argue that San Miguel has become so touristy that it caters almost entirely to foreigners and upper-class Mexican visitors, to the detriment of the Mexican people.

These frustrations are "back stage," as in Erving Goffman's term (1959),
while San Miguel is "on performance" on the global stage. Urry writes that
notions of certain tourist destinations are "not fixed and given but on the
move, traveling the world via the media, the internet and the World-Wide
Web, or packed away in suitcases of informal commercial importers, music
pirates and drug dealers. There is no given original paradise on these paradise islands" (Urry 2007:58). San Miguel is not an island but is considered
an enclave. Amid threats of kidnapping and narco trafficking in many regions across the Mexican landscape, San Miguel is touted as a safe place
for English-speaking retirees to stay and enjoy themselves for extended
periods of time.

From my perspective as a person who has resided in San Miguel for several years, San Miguel is eerily reminiscent of Jamaica Kincaid's Antigua
in *A Small Place*. The beauty of its cobblestone streets and colorful colonial buildings is undeniable. However, like the Antiguans of *A Small Place*,
Mexican Sanmiguelenses experience discrimination and corruption as
part of their everyday lives. Kincaid describes the colonial possession of
Antigua by Great Britain and how it resulted in the subservience of Antigua to England and English culture. Claudio Lomnitz-Adler (2005), L. de
Zavala (1976), and M. Suárez-Orozco and Mariela Páez (2009) all point
to the eclipse of European dominance and the simultaneous ascendancy
of the United States to the post of hegemonic world power as key to how
Latin American countries experience the United States.

In Mexico, fear of cultural degeneration in the face of ubiquitous US cultural influence is paired with the "sneaking admiration" of US-style modernity. David Fitzgerald (2009) points to the plethora of US styles, slogans, and media images that cross into Mexico and how US styles function as a sort of cultural capital—a marker of modernity. Not only are US styles imported into Mexico, but the United States also influences the way Mexican traditions are celebrated and represented—certain aspects of Mexican culture are stylized for foreign observers. In *Skulls to the Living, Bread to the Dead* (2006), Stanley Brandes discusses how the Day of the Dead has become a kind of cultural capital used to attract tourism and benefits the economic, political, and social well-being of towns and the national state. In San Miguel, this cultural capital is exercised constantly—a multitude of holidays lead to "traditional" parades, fireworks, and celebrations almost every week.

When Mexican president Felipe Calderón inaugurated Rosewood San Miguel, a landmark resort, in March 2011, the spectacularization of inauguration was for the benefit of potential tourists to San Miguel. There was the sense that the whole world was watching—and Mexican locals were watching, too, but their gaze was not of consequence since they could never hope to step inside the front doors of Rosewood San Miguel (except as receptionists, waiters, and housekeepers). Ironically enough, Rosewood San Miguel's philosophy is "a sense of place." For many Mexican locals, entire areas of San Miguel are characterized by a lurking, and not easily ignored, sense of placelessness. In the presence of so many luxuries that locals can never partake of, except from the position of service workers, locals feel *dis*placed. Although I purposefully resist Urry's notion of "nonplace" and the total lack of agency it implies, I emphasize that San Miguel is simultaneously a site of both belonging and dispossession.

Pleasant images of San Miguel can be like one-way reflective glass—sojourners may see diversion and relaxation in their own reflection without seeing the Mexican service workers on the other side of the glass, while Mexican locals watch sojourners' performance of being "leisured" through the glass without being able to cross to the other side or see themselves in these moments of enjoyment and ease. Urry argues that "the performances of place often cannot be realized or there are contested performances or 'emotional geographies' of place" (Urry 2007:261, referring to Bondi, Smith, Davidson 2005).

I suggest that in San Miguel, the emotional geography is a well-kept secret from expatriates and sojourners and is only momentarily revealed when specific violent acts against foreigners catch media attention. For example, San Miguel was abuzz after the murder of three elderly US citizens in late January and early February 2011. According to CBS News, "For decades the city of San Miguel de Allende, nestled along the mountainous region of Central Mexico, has attracted scores of Americans, Canadians and Europeans seeking to retire in the mild climate and tranquil, culturally rich region. But in just the past three weeks, the safe haven community—known for its low crime rates—has been shattered by the unsolved murders of three Americans."[4] More recently, in September 2013, a seventy-two-year-old Canadian woman was bludgeoned to death in her home,[5] causing many foreign women, especially those who live alone, to fear for their safety. It was as Urry said: "To be a tourist is to be on the front line in places of positive affect but places that can transmute within a split second into places of carnage" (Urry 2007:270).

The real San Miguel is fraught with inequality and suffering. As I've already mentioned, locals earn in pesos despite the "dollarization" of the local economy. Pointing to the weakened acquisitive power of many Mexicans' wages and increasing poverty, ex-presidential candidate Andrés Manuel López Obrador writes, "Currently, the earnings per person of 70 percent of Mexicans is less than 2,680 pesos monthly" (a mere US$215 monthly, see López Obrador 2010:95), and he explains that as a result, 41 percent of the economically active population do not earn enough to afford good nutrition (López Obrador 2010:97).

Many Mexican locals are *displaced* because it is difficult to impossible for them to find an affordable place to live in the pricey center of their own town. I remember once being invited to the home of a well-respected medical professional (an employee at San Miguel's Seguro Popular clinic by morning and a private clinician by night) in a *colonia* (small community) beyond the edges of town. This man was born and raised in San Miguel, and he trained at the National Autonomous University of Mexico. I had passed by a gleaming shopping plaza and several luxury resorts to get to his home, and when I finally found my way, I was standing on a dusty path in front of a fifteen-foot-wide cinderblock box. A few minutes further away from the town center, a good friend of mine, Frida Moreno, a restaurant kitchen worker and pet sitter, lives in a small structure without electricity.

I do not mean to overemphasize the deep social inequalities that separate sojourners from Mexican locals. Also, my intention is not to deny locals their agency. In pointing to the emotional geography of San Miguel, I demonstrate the disruptive features of foreign and local juxtaposition, while also alluding to the productive possibilities of these encounters. San Miguel, a place where "traditionality" and ultramodernity intermingle, is

fertile ground for the production and revision of ideology, especially related to birth and respect for women's bodies. San Miguel, as a contact
zone, makes the production of emergent health models possible—if only
through donations of American and Canadian dollars.

However, I also point to the careful and constant negotiation of CASA's
work in San Miguel, specifically because of the deeply penetrating divide
between people of white and brown skin. Sagrario told me that the American founder's primary role is to fund-raise, since she is the only one who
can. Sagrario commented, "If our founder were not an American, but a
Mexican woman, our donors would say, 'Oh, that's a nice organization,'
forget about us and never donate a single dollar. We could not exist without [her]." Perhaps her judgment is too black and white (or should I say,
too white and brown), but the frustration she expresses points to important lapses in communication between Mexican locals and foreign donors.

The Exclusion of Urban Outsiders in the
Nahua High Mountains of Veracruz

In San Miguel, processes of racialization (and dollarization) distinguish
Mexican locals from American and Canadian retirees, but in the High
Mountains of Veracruz, racialization operates to cast indigenous people as
lazy and violent, especially toward women. During my first visit to Zacatochin, I conducted an extended formal interview with Fermín Alonso,
the medical intern at the Mexican Institute of Social Security (IMSS)
clinic. As is the case in most rural areas in Mexico, the clinic is staffed
by a nurse and a single medical intern who is required to complete a one-
year internship as a graduation requirement for medical school. Over the
course of the interview, I increasingly felt that Fermín was suffering from
social isolation and was eager to speak to someone about his loneliness
and anxiety. He explained to me how frustrated and exhausted he felt.
He arrived at Zacatochin full of anticipation and an enthusiastic desire to
help and heal, but he opined that the "cultural problems and lack of education" have destroyed his hopeful outlook. According to Fermín, the medical knowledge he learned in medical school is worthless when confronting
the medical and social problems of rural, indigenous regions. Medical students are taught prevention, but the idea of prevention is useless in these
areas, given the dire living conditions and the blameworthy mentality toward health of the people.

His interactions with the local villagers are primarily motivated by the

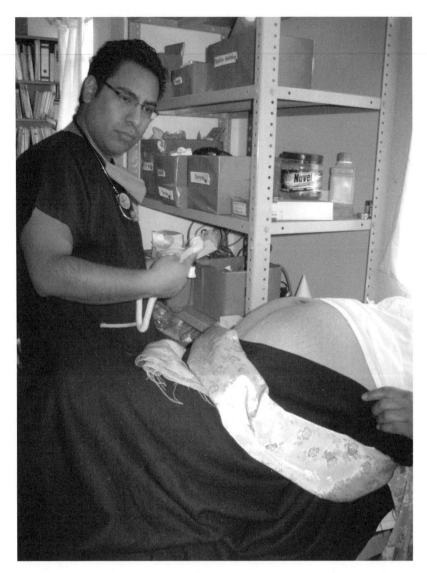

Figure 3.4. Fermin preparing to perform an ultrasound on an indigenous patient

fact that virtually all the villagers are IMSS Oportunidades recipients, and they are required to submit to certain medical screenings in order to receive their Oportunidades stipends. He said that the only reason villagers come to the clinic is because they are accustomed to state-run cash-transfer programs and expect to "receive, receive, receive," without any effort on their part. As a result of the conditionality of Oportunidades cash transfers, during medical exams, his patients act as if they are there "by force."

Fermín was struggling with the solitude of being a man from Mexico City and working in a rural clinic in an indigenous village. Nonetheless, his experience paled in comparison to the violent experiences of his female schoolmates. One of his classmates suggested to a female patient and her family that she go to the hospital immediately. She filled out the transfer papers, but the family decided not to take the woman to the hospital and returned home instead. The woman died in the night, and her family blamed the doctor for not insisting and accompanying the woman to the hospital. Soon after, the intern woke up during the night when she heard the woman's bereaved husband cutting through her window screen with a machete. She was able to call for help and the man was apprehended without having inflicted any physical harm on the intern.

Conflicts like these, along with stories of attempted rape, penetrated Fermín's perceptions of the indigenous community surrounding him. Although he decided to study medicine because he longed to help people in need, this commitment to altruism was overshadowed by depressing judgments about indigenous villagers shortly after beginning his yearlong internship. He told me, "Here there are no values." He felt deflated by the gender inequity, domestic violence, sexually transmitted disease, infidelity, and alcoholism among the villagers. He criticized Zacatochin villagers for not spending their Oportunidades money on adequate nutrition, but yet they all have cable television!

Toward the end of our interview, Fermín confessed a secret to me. Fermín wears a wedding ring and tells the villagers he is married when this is not the case. According to Fermín's sham, his wife lives in Mexico City, where he went to medical school, and where he spends his weekends. In reality, Fermín lies about being married as a strategy for preventing or at least diminishing accusations of sexual molestation from villagers. If the people in the village knew he is not married, he reasoned, they would say that he only wants to perform pelvic exams because he wants to touch the village women. Fermín's secret points to how men are also gendered subjects who face expectations shaping their habitus and restricting their relations with others.

I wanted to measure the desperate image Fermín painted against descriptions of social problems from people with a different set of engagements with the community. I asked Doña Eugenia for her opinion on the matter. Her primary concerns had to do with how women are treated and related effects on their physical and emotional health. She told me that her own marriage was arranged and though her husband has become a friend with whom she lives in harmony, there has never been a romantic connection between them. In general, the custom of arranged marriages has given way to more "modern" pairings in which couples pick each other. However, this does not mean that women's choices are not restrained in other ways—once married, a woman's decisions can be severely restrained by her husband's family. Doña Eugenia gave me an example of a woman "in the next village." (I wonder if the woman actually lived in the next village, or whether Doña Eugenia was attempting to anonymize one of her own fellow villagers.) She told me that after her husband died, her husband's family told her that if she ever remarried, they would take her children from her and prevent her from ever seeing her children again.

In another case, Doña Eugenia provided treatment to a woman who was badly bruised. When she insisted that the woman tell her the source of her bruising, the woman admitted that her husband had been beating her. Angered, she told her patient, "Tell him that if he wants to hit someone, he should come to my house and hit me!" When she encountered her patient's husband in the street, she told him, "I know what you've done, and if I ever find out about you hitting your wife again, prepare yourself, because I will report you to the authorities!" The man promised never to hit his wife again, and his wife continues to reassure Doña Eugenia that he has remained true to his word. Doña Eugenia is the descendant of a long line of *curanderas* and *parteras*, so she commands respect within the community, and she uses her authority to demand nonviolent treatment of the women in her village.

I also interviewed Padre Filadelfo Torres to assess his opinion of residents of Zacatochin and the surrounding communities. As the priest for twenty-eight chapels in the region, he has accumulated many experiences with the locals and is often the keeper of their secrets. He told me that when he arrived in the region, he was fearful because he had never interacted with indigenous people before. Over time, however, he discovered that the people in these communities compose a spectrum, and like anywhere else, there are people at either extreme. Before he arrived, he explained, "they described the place to me as being really ugly with respect to the people [who live here]. [The villagers] fight for their rights—for sure—especially when politicians deceive them to get their votes and when the time comes do not fulfill their promises. It is not violence for the sake of violence."

According to Padre Filadelfo, the previous priest was never able to gain

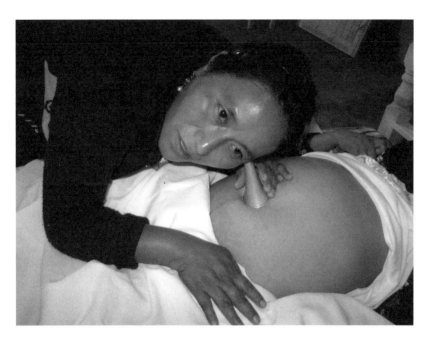

Figure 3.5. Doña Eugenia listening to fetal sounds

Figure 3.6. Doña Eugenia during a postnatal visit with a mother whose birth she attended

the communities' trust. That priest was a *güero* (fair-skinned) and had a French surname. When Padre Filadelfo arrived in the region, he made a concerted effort to treat the villagers as equals and to prove that he was different from his predecessor.

Padre Filadelfo has learned that, in general, the community members are primarily Nahuatl speakers and possess limited fluency in Spanish. They understand the meaning of the messages he delivers from the pulpit but are not familiar with all of the Spanish words. Padre Filadelfo is working on learning more Nahuatl so that he can better communicate with the community he serves. Instead of wishing that villagers become more like nonindigenous people living in cities, he hopes that they preserve their linguistic and cultural traditions, and considers it a "defect" when mothers don't dress their young daughters in traditional *bata*. Although some mothers appreciate the time they save when their young daughters dress themselves in pants instead of having to facilitate wrapping the *bata* and others consider pants to be a warmer option during the cold winter months, Padre Filadelfo frowns upon this potential loss of cultural heritage.

The padre explained to me that even though men often have to go to the cities to find employment, they tend to marry girls from their own villages, and this practice preserves the coherence of the community. That is, men perceive of city women less favorably than village women when it comes to finding a spouse. Once married, marriages tend to last a lifetime. Padre Filadelfo commented that marriage continues to be endogenous, but gendered relationships are evolving with time. Just in the time that he has been priest in the region, he has noticed a drop in alcoholism, and a related reduction in domestic violence. The padre counsels his young female parishioners to consider possibilities outside of motherhood and marriage; likewise, he urges fathers to send their daughters to school along with their sons. He told me with confidence that in the short time he has preached in this region, the interrelations between the villagers and within families have improved, and this is evidence of the positive effects of the church's teachings.

Although Padre Filadelfo described most of his communication with villagers as being effective, this had not always been the case. The first time he was invited to a baptism, he noticed that the head of the table was set with the most abundant food. Assuming that he was the guest of honor, he sat down at the head of the table, only to be informed that that spot was meant for the *padrinos* (godparents) of the baby, and he was asked to choose another seat. His assumption signals the patriarchal (and postcolonial) hierarchy of the Catholic Church with respect to its parishioners.

Figure 3.7. Doña Eugenia, godmother and guest of honor at a baptismal banquet

Although the perspectives of Fermín, Doña Eugenia, and Padre Filadelfo coincide in pointing to gender inequity and violence, they differ in
what is presumed to be the origins of social problems. For Fermín, the
problem is cultural. He locates the cause of social problems as emerging from the villagers themselves—since their indigenous culture is the
source of the social pathologies that plague the community, he is convinced that nothing can be done to improve the situation. As I listen to
his assertions, I wonder about his portrayal of culture-as-race and the degree to which culture "can be appreciated as 'data about individual racial
thoughts and fantasies' insofar as culture and race have begun to proceed
to the same effect" (Bridges 2011:136).

For Doña Eugenia, positive change is already underway. She considers
herself to be an agent of change and wields her authority to command nonviolent treatment of women among her fellow villagers. In her perspective, social problems are not rooted in indigenous culture—rather, they
are outdated remnants of the past and antithetical to a "modern" future.

Finally, for Padre Filadelfo, indigenous culture is something to be celebrated, and he considers it his job to learn Nahuatl to overcome the language barrier instead of his parishioners having an obligation to learn
Spanish. He also sees a positive change in the community, but the change

he identifies is a result of the church's teachings and not a "moderniza-tion" that originates from within the community. His assumption that he was the guest of honor at the baptism points to the potential difference between the role he feels he plays in the community and the role the vil-lagers feel he plays. At times, his perspective takes on a missionary flavor, and he positions himself as the person who "saves the Indians" by enlight-ening their lives with the teachings of Christ. Fermín and Padre Filadelfo have assigned differential values to Nahua culture, but both enact "ra-cial distancing" (Ikemoto 2009), even while attempting to serve the local community.

By juxtaposing locals' experience of rejection and dispossession result-ing from San Miguel's tourism economy with the struggles of medical pro-fessionals and clergy to gain entrance into "closed" indigenous commu-nities in the Nahua High Mountains of Veracruz, I again seek to balance politico-economic power structures with the agentive dynamism of indig-enous informants. The pluri-politics of inclusion/exclusion are dependent on spatial contexts—that is, definitions of race, gender, and identity shap-ing the encounters of difference are themselves nested in places. Although intersectional hierarchies provide the rubric that naturalizes the discor-dant experiences of individuals living in solitary contractuality and limit the realm of possibility; the underlying algorithm includes class, educa-tion, the color of one's passport (indeed, whether one possesses a passport at all), and cultural capital accrued from participation in transnational, consumption-oriented networks such as humanized birth.

Why, then, have I not just argued that what is truly at stake is habitus (Bourdieu 1984)? I insist that multiple, overlapping, structural inequali-ties are unfolding; thus, I offer intersectional racialization processes as a multivalent conceptual tool because I refuse to disregard the visually bla-tant discrepancy between servers and patrons in San Miguel, and between institutional representatives and Oportunidades recipients in the High Mountains of Veracruz. Race, gender, and class in Mexico are intimately imbricated, kaleidoscopic categories. Processes of intersectional racializa-tion collapse and incorporate a multitude of social factors, yet reducing these processes to a discussion of habitus would obscure apparent pheno-typic gaps readily observed throughout my ethnographic research.

CHAPTER 4

A Cartography of "Race" and Obstetric Violence

Nowhere is the dynamic of othering more salient than between health providers and the people they are meant to serve. While in San Miguel, I was invited to a directors' meeting at an NGO focused on community health. The directors considered "ignorance" and lack of responsibility to be primary obstacles to helping community members improve their health. Their list of examples included parents who don't teach their children to eat vegetables and themselves do not eat vegetables; individuals with poor health who do not seek treatment until it is too late; adolescents who forgo using contraceptives despite the availability of information about their use and effectivity; and mothers who stay home with their newborn during the first week after birth instead of having their neonates tested for hypothyroidism during the short period when long-term consequences can still be prevented. Whether healthy food is available to lower-class families, insufficient infrastructure in hospitals, accessibility of contraceptives given Mexico's Catholic underpinnings, and the benefits and limits of women's embodied knowledge were left out of the discussion. It is not only in boardrooms that "ignorance" is used as the explanatory variable for negative health outcomes—elsewhere in San Miguel, a woman shared a painful miscarriage experience with me, explaining that the nurse at the public hospital scolded her, saying, "You should have known that you were miscarrying. It is your fault that you didn't come sooner." The othering I observed during fieldwork often lapsed into blaming the victim.

In Veracruz, health professionals blamed vaginal infections on poor hygiene, whereas women insisted that "it is not the woman's fault." In essence, they criticized their patient population for being bad sanitary subjects (see Briggs and Mantini-Briggs 2003), placing themselves at risk, not

Figure 4.1. Meeting of Secretariat of Health officials about professional midwifery in public hospitals

understanding medical advice, and needing to be told things "real slow." Throughout my fieldwork, I noticed how physicians explained their diagnoses and treatment options in "colloquial" terms, which often meant giving incorrect information. In turn, this was interpreted by patients as lying and bred distrust and avoidance of hospitals altogether. Examples of this include telling indigenous people that an injection contains "vitamins" and that a baby must be born quickly or it will die.

In Guerrero, I sat in on a meeting between Secretariat of Health officials about incorporating professional midwives into public hospitals and rural clinics. At the conclusion of the meeting, one official summed up the Secretariat of Health's progress in the area of women's reproductive health by saying that people in villages are "too closed-minded," making it impossible for them to do their work. I visited a regional hospital in one of the impoverished, indigenous regions that these officials are responsible for overseeing and spoke to a physician about the difficulties he faces when treating patients. He said, simply, "Their problem is themselves. They are their problem." Again and again, health professionals told me how difficult it was to work with *indígenas* (indigenous people) because of their "distrusting" culture.

In San Luis Potosí I visited a rural hospital in a Huastec region. The professional midwife working there—herself a person of Huastec heritage and a speaker of the Téenek language—told me that a large number of adolescents are giving birth in that hospital. Some of the birthing mothers she attends, she asserted, do not even know what body part the baby is coming out of. "The people around here do not know much." I am interested in the way this professional midwife positioned herself vis-à-vis the community in which she works and in which she herself was raised. Having graduated from a professional midwifery school in another state, she no longer grouped herself with "the people around here." I suggest that the implicit contrast embedded in her word choice served to socially whiten her, thus distancing her from her indigenous roots, even as her "indigeneity" and linguistic ability (and, implicitly, her gender) serve as primary criteria for her placement in that hospital.

Elsewhere in San Luis Potosí, I asked two professional midwives what they hypothesized to be the cause behind a curious number of birth complications and congenital abnormalities in the region. They began listing their hypotheses: Women are not educated, have poor diets and don't drink enough water, don't take folic acid; they don't seek regular prenatal care, have poor hygiene leading to vaginal infections, and perform physical labor during pregnancy. Notably absent from this list of hypotheses are environmental toxins resulting from mining in the region. One professional midwife said, "The patients are uncultured. They don't come for medical examinations. Also, they lack education. A lot of women don't even know they are pregnant thirty-two weeks into their pregnancy." They went on to describe to me how a mother was nursing her newborn in the hospital when a nurse noticed that the baby was purple and not moving and took the baby from the mother. The medical team was able to resuscitate the baby, but if it had not been for the nurse's intervention, the baby would have died in the negligent mother's arms.

After they told me this story, I joined them in the Operating Room, where a woman was having the remnants of a miscarriage scraped from her uterus. Doors on both sides of the operating room were propped open, leaving the woman's naked genitals exposed to those passing by in the hospital corridor.

In Chiapas, I spoke to a health official about maternal deaths. He described recent cases, explaining that the first was a woman whose eclampsia was not identified opportunely because she didn't attend prenatal checkups. In a second case, he was not sure what the cause of the woman's death was, but he knew that the traditional midwife was to blame. In another case, he again was not sure as to the actual cause of death but knew

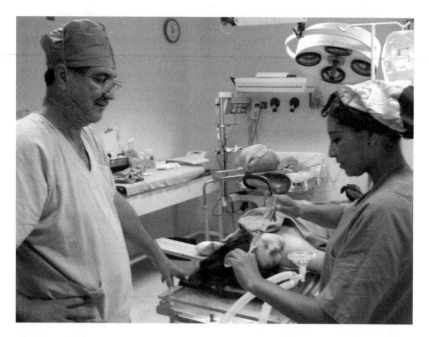

Figure 4.2. Anesthesiologist teaches professional midwife how to deliver medication through an IV drip

that it was an uneducated woman from a rural area. Lastly, I was told about a maternal death involving a traditional midwife who belonged to a civil association of traditional midwives and had been trained by a local NGO. The traditional midwife attempted to deliver a dystocic baby and broke the baby's neck. I met with many of the traditional midwives in the civil association. They resented being charged with causing maternal mortalities when no investigation is made into the individual cases.

I later spoke to a physician who sees a large number of indigenous female patients. He said, "They lack the economic support to come to the health center and buy medications, but the culture of the people living in the countryside does not allow us to go to them." He identified indigenous peoples' traditions and lack of education as the main reasons that patients and doctors are unable to understand one another. As our conversation broached the overlap between resource scarcity and indigeneity, the doctor reflected aloud on how he chooses whom to attend next from a crowded waiting room. Indigenous patients are less likely to have ready and reliable access to bathing water, and he is more likely to pick someone from the waiting room who has bathed on that day rather than three days ago; therefore, he tends to pick indigenous patients last, causing them to wait the longest.

In Michoacán, I interviewed a leader of an NGO that advocates for women's health, especially among Purépechan women. He spoke at length about inequality, and his words point to how easily indigeneity is collapsed with poverty: "If you ask 'Are the Purépecha discriminated against?' some people will say no. But . . . the majority of Purépecha would say they are routinely discriminated against and looked down upon, or refused service, or delayed service. It's common to have that kind of discrimination. Class is probably, I think, the major issue in Mexico. The disempowerment of poor people."

Although I am sensitive to the effects of colonial legacies unfolding in the present day, I resist carrying out a Fanonian or Hegelian analysis of mutual recognition (see Hegel 1977; Fanon 2008 [1952]; and Villet 2011)— not because I do not consider these analyses valuable, but because I recognize that many others have done illuminating work in this field, and I think it is more productive to use an intersectional approach to address the questions at hand instead of applying the concept of mutual recognition to a Latin American context. In this present analysis, I am positioning myself as a medical anthropologist, and more specifically, as an intersectional scholar of the anthropology of reproduction. Thus, I bring ethnographic tools and anthropological theory to bear on intersectional racialization processes in Mexico. What can stratified reproduction (Colen 1995) tell us about race?

Raza

My argument is not about deciding whether race is essentially biological or primarily a social construct—rather, I am concerned with how a history of colonialism in Mexico has resulted in the lingering concept of race, thus opening a space for intersectional racialization processes that lead to the consumption of "culture" and the production of differential (race-infused) identities.

My resistance to this binary construction of race harks back to Michael Montoya's work on diabetes, while adapting his perspective for the field of reproduction and building upon it to evaluate the agency of women in their negotiations of racialized citizenship. Montoya ethnographically examines the geneticists who socially produce US-Mexico border residents as biological Latino/as. At first glance it seems he is arguing against reductionism, determinism, and geneticization, but his work turns out to be even more subversive.

> I share with [Clarence] Gravlee the desire to push beyond discussions that reiterate that race is a social construct about which biology can tell us little. While true, this insight closes rather than opens the conceptual terrain about race and how it relates to biology. . . . I find it more productive, more faithful to my field encounters, to resist dualistic side-taking of biology versus society. (Montoya 2011:30)

Although I resist reducing race to a matter of biology, biological race is used to define the right and wrong types of reproduction, which in turn shapes policy and practice both nationally and transnationally (see Morgan and Roberts 2012). Whereas medical anthropologists have extensively studied these effects in the realms of international population policy and migration;[1] and have analyzed how nineteenth- and twentieth-century battles about slavery, miscegenation, immigration, population control, and eugenics resulted in the categorization of people into fit and unfit reproducers;[2] my work addresses Sarah Brubaker and Heather Dillaway's call to

> conduct comparative research on the subjective experiences of pregnant and birthing women at multiple social locations and multiple contexts, as well as the experience and perspectives of midwives and medical providers in order to provide a more critical and meaningful analysis of the complicated intersections of ideology, politics, practice and bodily experience. (Brubaker and Dillaway 2009)

My work holds the perspectives on race of several Latin Americanist anthropologists under one lens to then engage binational literature on citizenship and interculturality. In doing so, my work is informed by a binational discourse critiquing public-health systems in Latin America.[3]

I employ Elizabeth Roberts' notion of *raza* and provide ethnographic examples of how "reproductive governance" is applied to the supposedly hyperfertile indigenous women while whitening is sought through private medical care by educated, urban women. Roberts concentrates on the constitution of race, especially whiteness, through the "crucial economic and moral significance of care relations, in which life chances are forged" (Biehl and Eskerod 2007:110). Even though the collective goal of *blanqueamiento* is not often spoken about through the idiom of whitening, it is sought through practices of education, clothing, language, and occupation[4] and is reinscribed within private gynecological care. Roberts writes about how, in Ecuador, middle-class and increasing numbers of working-class women eagerly pay to be scarred (Roberts 2012b). Cesarean sections carried out in private clinics serve as a physical mark identifying women as superior to the indignities of devalued public medical services. By including medical care as another means to mark and transform race, Roberts is calling our attention to the malleability of material reality and thus provincializes North American tendencies to mark a divide between nature and culture, and assumptions about the universality and fixity of biological processes.

Whereas in North America race is understood as inherent to the person, despite scholars' emphasis on how race is constructed and performed (Hartigan 2010; Crenshaw et al. 1995), the materiality of *raza* in the Andes is malleable[5] and can be changed through changes in body and comportment. *Raza* is a "political economy of the body" (Lancaster 1992)—not an ahistorical, unchanging interiority. Roberts writes, "In Ecuador, medical care makes race" (Roberts 2012b:217). Furthermore, public-health services were developed to intervene in poor and indigenous populations, and especially hyperfertile indigenous women.[6] Thus, though *raza* is more pliant, plastic, and cultivatable in the Andes than in North America, it is still used to justify inequality.

With respect to the Mexican context, I do not deny associations between phenotype and how people are identified as racialized beings; however, as an intersectional scholar, I expressly resist the idea of race *as* phenotype. Instead, I signal how "social whitening" is partially achieved through the accumulation of cultural capital via commodified birthing practices. Similarly, de la Cadena explains how pervasive racism in Peru is erased, using a rhetoric of cultural difference: "These exculpations of racism are embedded in a definition of *race* rhetorically silenced by the historical subordination of phenotype to *culture* as a marker of difference. In other words, Peruvians think their discriminatory practices are not racist because they do not connote innate biological differences, but cultural ones" (de la Cadena 2000:2). For de la Cadena, cultures are vessels of immanent inequalities, leading to the mystification of racial discrimination and "racism without race." Culture is achievable, and categories such as Indians and mestizos emerge from interactions and not from evolution. One's phenotype can be subordinated to one's intelligence and morality if these have been corrected by "education." For example, Kim Clark focuses on how educating Indians produced them as national citizens: "By definition Indians were seen as ignorant, because it was assumed that Indians who were educated would automatically become mestizos" (Clark 1998:230). By the same token, a brown-skinned individual who is sufficiently educated can influence how he or she is perceived and, depending on the context, may be accepted as "socially white" (see Bashkow 2006).

Roberts argues that the saying "money whitens" is not about misrecognition, but about how accumulating money results in whiter relations of care, such as private medical care. Roberts is pointing to how women become whiter reproducers, not only through education and professional advancement, but through being cared for as whiter women. This care does not cease to be patriarchal, since women are cared for by surgeons who cut them tenderly, like a father toward a privileged daughter, instead of public medical patients. Roberts writes, "Raza entangles what in North America is understood as class relations. . . . However, disentangling class and raza would do damage to an ethnographic understanding of care relations in Ecuador. Identifying the kinds of food ingested or care received as social markers of class, misses the way that raza is produced within economic relations. Private gynecological care cultivates female whiteness, which is simultaneously a political, economic, and physiological state" (2012b:230). My intersectional reading and ethnographic experience in Mexico have shaped my argument that race is both produced by and shot through with class differences among gendered individuals.

Citizenship is fertile terrain for negotiation between indigenous women and the Mexican government.[7] These women are recruited into Oportunidades (a conditional cash-transfer program that shapes poor indigenous women into obedient mothers and "modern" citizens, see Smith-Oka 2013) and required to give birth in government hospitals. At times, my observations coincided with those of Smith-Oka—some indigenous women eagerly seek biomedical attention while giving birth—but I interviewed many others who resist mandates because of prior experiences of racial discrimination. In this book, I also address how citizenship fails to encompass the way privileged women are proactively constructing whiter subjectivities through natural birth in the private sector and participation in the humanized-birth transnational network.

These very different engagements with medical care undermine ubiquitous arguments for "interculturality" among Mexican medical anthropologists. Interculturality in Mexico aims to reduce the effects of xenophobia by incorporating indigenous cultural elements into government-provisioned services. My framing signals the inadequate attention of "interculturality" to gender, racial discrimination, and political economic factors.

Figure 4.3. Medical personnel teaching workshop in Zongólica, Veracruz

My perspective on intersectional racialization processes questions the rei-fication of cultures upon which "interculturality" is premised.

Deadly Consequences of Intersectional Racialization

When I attended a training workshop for traditional midwives given by the Mexican Institute of Social Security in Zongólica, Veracruz, I wit-nessed a striking moment when a single woman's body became a site of contestation about race, class, gender, and power. The room was divided into two glaringly distinct spaces—male doctors with white coats stood in front of the room, and traditionally dressed indigenous midwives sat in the audience. An elderly midwife, Paloma Domínguez, stood up in the very last row. Paloma told a story about how the neglect of medical doc-tors and staff led to the unnecessary death of an indigenous woman's baby. The pregnant woman had arrived at the hospital in active labor, and the nurses refused to attend to her. The desperate mother rushed to the restroom and gave birth to a stillborn child. The dead infant was born into the toilet. Having never been assigned a hospital bed, she left pools

Figure 4.4. Traditional midwives in attendance at the workshop

of blood on the hallway floor, and the nurse scolded her for making a mess and forced her to clean up the blood. Paloma ended the wrenching tale by yelling, "I, too, could put on a white coat!"

The hospital director asked Paloma the name of the community worker involved in the case. When she answered him with the female, indigenous community worker's name, he nodded, as if to say, "Ah, yes," and stated aloud that this community worker has been involved in several unfortunate cases. If the community worker had succeeded in getting the birthing mother to the hospital sooner, he suggested, the case would not have ended tragically. He promised Paloma that he would reprimand the community worker. Although this seemed to appease Paloma somewhat, I was less satisfied with this resolution. In a matter of seconds, the female, indigenous community worker became the scapegoat for a health system that is failing at multiple levels. The medical personnel at the hospital were, by sleight of hand, let off the hook. The hospital director quickly directed the workshop attendees away from this "disruptive" anecdote and toward other matters. However, the incident lingers in my mind. The woman's hemorrhage and the infant's life-that-never-was had been the site of contestation, but they were not the real objects of the debate.

This anecdote, combined with a description of "intercultural" health-care delivery in Capulalpam de Méndez and discussion of the politics of portraying indigenous identities, provides ample grounds for the analysis and critique of the assertion by Austreberta Nazar-Beutelspacher, Benito Izaba, and Emma Zapata Martelo (2007) that in Mexico, the approximation of institutional services to indigenous populations is an encounter between two cultures and is embedded in unequal relations with respect to the value of knowledge and distinct medical practices. My ethnographic observations suggest that indigenous and mestizo cultures unfold and evolve through engagement with one another, and are, thus, co-constituted. Indigenous informants contest and shape how their medical practices are valued, at times leveraging "indigenous" knowledge in entrepreneurial ways. At the same time, social collectivities are differentially nested in geographic places and even racially segregated in clinical spaces, signaling how the social construction of race undergirds structural inequalities and produces material disparities.

The Incoherency of Oportunidades

One particularly elucidative pathway for understanding the relationship between the Mexican government and indigenous groups is through detailed examination of Oportunidades conditional cash transfers. After initiating her public dispute with the hospital director in Zongólica, Paloma backed down and did not argue her point further. Throughout my research, I observed many midwives' disparate behavior in public and private realms. Traditional midwives and indigenous Oportunidades recipients performed obedience in workshop settings while enacting resistance to government mandates in their daily lives. Program successes "front stage" (such as widespread attendance at Oportunidades-mandated workshops) did not easily translate into changes in social behavior "back stage." Maxine Molyneux goes so far as to argue that Oportunidades puts mothers at the service of the "new poverty agenda" and inadvertently exacerbates gender inequality when it holds mothers accountable for their children's well-being, excuses fathers of responsibility toward their offspring, and provokes marital discord (and potentially, domestic violence) by putting cash stipends in the hands of women amid widespread unemployment of male "providers" (see Molyneux 2006).

The conditionality of cash transfers evidences differential valorization of knowledge and medical practices while also serving to extract obedience from Mexico's racialized "Others." According to Rodrigo Vázquez, a physician turned Mayan-rights advocate and board member of an indigenous association in Chiapas, training workshops offered by the state are meant to reinforce inequality in existing power structures. Although the Oportunidades program has been lauded within the public-health realm,[8] from Rodrigo's perspective, "Oportunidades is really [an example of] the dominant society practicing coercion over indigenous people." As an outspoken critic of biopiracy and a proponent of indigenous knowledge, he argues that although traditional midwives' resistance to biomedical methods is deemed "backwardness" by medical professionals, traditional midwives are not interested in learning new techniques because they are confident about the effectiveness of the techniques they have been using for generations. He explained that though traditional midwives may attend training programs in order to continue receiving cash transfers and other government-provisioned services, they often do so with no intention of changing the methods they employ in their everyday practice of midwifery.

Rodrigo's assertions are supported by traditional midwives like Yanira, who, during an in-depth interview, explained that women's participation in cash-transfer programs has resulted in changes to what she reveals about her practice to authorities, but it has not altered the substance of her midwifery. That is, women who receive support from Oportunidades tell her, "Don't give me a birth certificate. I am going to say that [I couldn't make it to the hospital in time] and gave birth alone at home. I am going to say that I was not attended by a midwife."

However, my ethnographic research did not point to wholesale resistance. Indigenous informants often complied with Oportunidades mandates in ways that suggested engagement at the level of form instead of substance, but I also observed how Oportunidades mandates structure the rhythm of indigenous women's daily lives. At the same time, I observed that when government health professionals detect what they perceive to be shrewd disobedience on the part of indigenous mothers (sometimes in the form of medical pluralism), they are more eager to carry out medicalized procedures. At times, I observed physicians disregarding medical guidelines and manipulating indigenous mothers with false information (i.e., telling a pregnant indigenous woman that her baby is at risk and needs to be delivered by cesarean immediately when, in actuality, the physician is trying to prevent the woman from returning to her village and receiving midwifery care). This is but one additional example of how the incoherency of Oportunidades contributes to obstetric violence and violence against women more broadly.

During my first trip to Zacatochin, I joined Francisca Serrano as she completed the requirements for her two-week "field practice"—part of her ongoing CASA training at the time. Among the requirements was to deliver a workshop to the villagers, educate them about reproductive health, and document the number of attendees as a measure of her "impact." Francisca went to the municipal offices to sign up to have her workshop announced throughout the village. Since there are no telecommunicative services in the village (no telephone, Internet, etc.), announcements are made via an old Volkswagen Beetle that drives slowly along the winding mountainous pathway, blasting information through a megaphone attached to the roof.

The next day, Francisca and I went to the gathering place where communitywide workshops are held—cement basketball courts covered by corrugated metal, built with government funds to foster "community development." We waited, and no one arrived. Francisca decided to wait half an hour past the announced start time, and two women arrived. Disappointed in the meager turn out, Francisca half-heartedly delivered the workshop materials she had prepared, and then we walked back to our host's home.

That night, Francisca reflected on the disinterest in her workshop, and she decided that if villagers were uninterested in learning information that was to their benefit, they would have to be coerced. Furthermore, she refused to return from her "field practice" to report that the impact of her workshop had been the delivery of educational materials to two people. The next day, while I was at the village clinic interviewing Fermín, Francisca returned to the municipal offices to announce another workshop. This time, she identified herself as someone who was coming to the village on behalf of the state-level Secretariat of Health and that her workshop was mandated by Oportunidades. The next day, we returned to the basketball courts and prepared for the workshop. This time, over 130 members of the community, mostly women, attended. At the outset of the workshop, Francisca announced that at the end of the workshop she was going to take roll by asking to see each participants' voting registration card and cataloging each person's name. This list, according to what she told participants, was going to be reviewed by the authorities at Oportunidades to determine compliance. In this way, Francisca insured that her audience remain captive until the end of her workshop.

As a professional midwifery student, Francisca was trained in medical terminology, and the intention of this "community engagement" experience was to allow her to develop the skills necessary to practice intercul-

Figure 4.5. Workshop on sexual and reproductive health, "required" by Oportunidades

tural midwifery in rural settings. Francisca's presentation of reproductive health was littered with biomedical terms that were incomprehensible to workshop attendees, and she failed to explain underlying physiological properties. The workshop "participants" stared blankly at her during most of the workshop. At the conclusion of the workshop, attendees lined up as Francisca took their identification cards one by one to write down their names.

This anecdote clearly highlights Francisca's abuse of power, evidencing how women with relatively greater privilege can also act as agents of structural inequality against other women. Moreover, it points to how conditional cash-transfer programs like Oportunidades extract obedience from women recipients on the basis of their poverty and dependency on government-provisioned stipends. When the workshop was not a requirement for continued receipt of Oportunidades stipends, community members were almost universally disinterested. Subsequently, threatening their Oportunidades stipends elicited compliance from village members. During private conversations, informants have expressed their annoyance at having their daily routines disrupted and dictated by Oportunidades mandates. One mother reported feeling like "a ball, bouncing from one place to another." Instead of validating the intended positive effects of obligatory social services, the Oportunidades recipients I interviewed pointed to their frustration with the conditionality of the cash transfers and with forced compliance. Programs like Oportunidades are shaped by notions of "interculturality" that are valuable in theory but contradictory in practice.

Interculturality

In Mexico, "interculturality" had emerged as a buzzword in government offices, academic circles, and a few hybrid clinics to describe respect for cultural differences through the merging of traditional indigenous medicine and biomedical methods. "Interculturality" is explicitly mentioned as a priority in the second article of the Mexican constitution. The article states, "The nation has a pluricultural composition originally sustained by indigenous peoples who are the descendants of those who inhabited the present-day territory of our country at the initiation of colonization and who preserve their own social, economic, cultural, and political institutions. . . . Awareness of their indigenous identity should be a fundamental criterion for determining who undertakes the ruling over indigenous peoples" (my translation). The article goes on to state that in an effort to ameliorate the *rezagos* (backwardness) in indigenous communities, authorities are obligated to ensure effective access to health services that make the most of traditional medicine, as well as support the nutrition of *indígenas* through food programs, especially for the child population (Article 2, Section B III). Furthermore, authorities are obligated to foster the incorporation of indigenous women into development through support for productive projects, the protection of women's health, and granting incentives to boost women's education and participation in decision-making related to community life (Article 2, Section B V).

Notions of "interculturality" are ubiquitous in Mexico and are thus woven into development programs such as Oportunidades even when not explicitly stated. The Mexican government engages with its indigenous population through the (supposedly) benevolent and equitable framework of "interculturality." However, I examine the textual politics of "interculturality" to uncover how this concept has been authored from positions of power as an approach to communities that are presumed inferior (see Haraway 1991). The use of the word *rezago* in the Mexican constitution while describing various "intercultural" strategies points to the contradictory way *interculturalidad* in Mexico purports to equitably grant citizenship-based rights to indigenous community members while simultaneously casting indigenous people as "backward."

To try to understand the concept of "interculturality" better, I shared my observations and compared experiences with Jaime Breilh, director of Health Sciences at Universidad Andina Simón Bolívar, in Quito. He explained to me that in Ecuador, interculturality emerged as an indigenous movement, originating from the indigenous people. It has transformed not only into a political juncture, but an intellectual one as well. The people of Ecuador began applying their critical perspective to a colonial past, and the result was an epistemological and philosophical proposal for the future. In contrast, in Mexico "interculturality" did not originate from indigenous people; rather, it emerged as a theoretical debate in academia and a bureaucratic strategy in public-health policy and development.

My ethnographic fieldwork suggests that "interculturality" is a powerful force for producing racialized subjects, arranging them hierarchically, and extending the material effects of those hierarchies. I am arguing against a naïve reading of interculturality—a liberal formulation that creates a utopian vision of a world of harmonic difference that exists apart from power. That is, traditional medicine and biomedicine do not come together on a level playing field, penetrating each other equally and evenly. The expert knowledge and abilities of physicians and traditional medicine doctors are not equally valued, they are not equally remunerated, and they are not equally supported by healthy policy and infrastructure. Often, when "interculturality" is celebrated, persistent inequalities are ignored. I am wary of how unequal power dynamics, disparate perceptions of value, and ongoing racial discrimination can potentially be masked by emphasis on "interculturality," whether it be at the level of academic debate or public-health policy.

When performing fieldwork, I spoke to a variety of people in order to think through how "interculturality" is put into practice. A physician turned NGO leader and traditional medicine advocate spoke to me about different "intercultural" clinics around the country where traditional medicine is "butchered," and decontextualized and deauthenticated techniques are applied in isolated and incoherent ways. For example, in La Riviera Maya, one hospital installed hammocks in the waiting area as a "intercultural" strategy, while nothing was done to make the actual delivery of health care and therapeutics more culturally appropriate.

Meanwhile, efforts to develop more substantive forms of interculturality encounter obstacles when seeking funding. These obstacles stem from the fact that despite the rhetoric of "interculturality" within policy, the legitimacy of counterhegemonic models is severely questioned. One midwife, an adjunct professor at the Intercultural University of Quintana Roo, told me "intercultural models are not respected at all." The university at which she works is part of an emerging university system that attempts to incorporate indigenous knowledge into university-level education and requires students to study the Mayan language and learn about traditional medicine alongside biomedical methods. Nonetheless, the intercultural university model struggles to be acknowledged and valued within Mexican academia.

The realm of "interculturality" has become increasingly heated over the course of my research. At the time of this writing, not only are intercultural universities facing the challenges of limited funding, the Intercultural University of Chiapas (UNICH) is under attack by a local indigenous organization. In 2017, the Organization of Indigenous Doctors of the state of Chiapas (OMIECH) circulated a letter via e-mail listservs addressed to the researchers and instructors at UNICH, academics at public and private institutions, the members of the State Commission for Higher Education Planning (COEPES), the media, and the general public. In the letter, the midwives, indigenous doctors, and health promotors of OMIECH identify themselves as defenders of traditional indigenous medicine in the state of Chiapas. As such, they denounce the premeditated "ethnocide of indigenous midwifery" being promoted in UNICH and the Comitán Center for Health Research (CISC) through their Obstetrics and Midwifery undergraduate program. OMIECH further implicates COEPES in the ethnocide, citing its role in approving the undergraduate program at UNICH.

The Obstetrics and Midwifery undergraduate program identifies its objective as "reducing the maternal mortality rate through the professionalization of midwifery." To accomplish its stated goal, the program aims to enroll young indigenous women—with a preference for daughters of indigenous midwives, and especially those who have received their calling to midwifery through a dream-vision. The members of OMIECH argue that UNICH and CISC have overlooked how their educational model favors biomedical ideology and "scientific bases," thus displacing theoretical and practical elements of traditional midwifery. This ideological gap has led to conflict between traditional midwives and the graduates of the UNICH program, as evidenced by significant disagreements between these two groups in the municipality of Chenalhó.

The members of OMIECH subsequently critique how maternal mortality "metrics" have been recruited and unleashed to further reinforce the hegemony of biomedical ideology and the undoing of traditional midwifery (see Adams 2016). They further point to how both the state and federal health sectors lack the financial and structural resources to employ UNICH graduates, thus contributing to the privatization of midwifery, to the detriment of core values.

Obstetric Violence

During a visit to San Luis Potosí, I stayed for a few days with Daniela Blanco, a nurse and public-health officer whose life work has focused on maternal mortality. She facilitated my participant observation in a large public hospital where professional midwifery is beginning to be incorporated. After hours interviewing expectant mothers in the labor and delivery area, I was invited into the delivery room to participate in a birth. When I arrived, the woman had been in the delivery room for four minutes and the baby was crowning. The young male intern attending the birth was visibly impatient, and a minute later he performed an episiotomy, slicing through the woman's perineum with a scalpel. During the woman's next contraction the woman pushed, but the baby did not emerge. As the contraction subsided, the intern ordered the mother to continue pushing, but a nurse interjected that since the contraction had passed, it would be better for the mother to take advantage of those few brief moments to rest until the next contraction. When the obstetric team had been in the delivery room for seven minutes with the birthing mother, the intern hastily performed another episiotomy, this time slicing the woman's vaginal opening down to her anus. He was not satisfied with the lack of apparent progress and considered using forceps to clamp the baby's head and yank it from the mother's womb.

At this point, the attending physician popped his head into the delivery room and asked the intern to report the woman's progress. The intern suggested using forceps to deliver the baby. The physician asked how long the woman had been in active delivery, and the intern responded "eight minutes." The physician instructed the intern to wait a while longer before using forceps, since in his view, all the woman needed was a little time.

The attending physician then entered the delivery room and instructed the two nurses to each grab one of the woman's legs and to push them back toward her body. Having audited many professional midwifery courses, I knew that this would shift the woman's pelvis, thus widening her vaginal canal, potentially allowing the baby to be delivered with no further intervention during the woman's next contraction. However, I could not anticipate what happened next. The doctor told the woman, "I am going to help the baby be born." Then, he began performing the Kristeller maneuver by jamming his fists into the woman's uterus, using all his body weight to push down sharply and repetitively. The mother began screaming, "I can't!" Reacting to the pain, she grabbed onto my hand and began squeezing hard. The Kristeller maneuver is an "extinct" practice in the developed world because it is widely recognized to carry the risk of uterine rupture. Even in Mexico, it is considered an option of last resort.

I asked the physician why we could not turn the woman over and allow her to give birth on all fours, thus widening her vaginal canal an additional two centimeters. He looked at me as if such an inane comment did not even warrant a response, but then he retorted, "Do you think with this [delivery] table she could turn over?" The woman was lying on a metal table with stirrups for giving birth in lithotomy position. I responded, "No, but if it were not for the table, she could turn over and the baby could emerge more easily." After the baby was born, I congratulated the woman. No one else spoke to the mother, and the baby was whisked off for health assessments.

This experience, among many others, is evidence to me of systematization of obstetric violence in Mexico. Although physicians are also aware of systemic violence in public-health care, some have shared their feelings of helplessness to change it. I interviewed one humanized-birth obstetrician, Maricelda Sanz, about her internship experience in a Mexican Institute of Social Security hospital. At the time, her attending physician told her to insert intrauterine devices during pelvic exams with or without the consent of indigenous patients. On one occasion, she reported to him that she had requested an indigenous woman's consent and was refused. The physician ordered Maricelda, "Go get the patient and put it inside her!" Maricelda had to come up with a false reason to perform a pelvic exam and illicitly placed an intrauterine device without the patient's knowledge. She ended her recounting by exclaiming, "That's violence!"

I was left reflecting on the potentially double meaning of her assertion—forced contraception is undoubtedly an act of violence against indigenous women, but what about the trauma and years of lingering culpability Maricelda has experienced? At the same time, Maricelda's life does not unfold at the intersection of racial discrimination and gender discrimination—though she suffers from the emotional sequelae of her traumatic experience, as a fair-skinned woman, she would not be the victim of forced sterilization.

The incident Maricelda described is not unique to obstetric internships.

Figure 4.6. The area in her home that Pamela uses to attend births

Camelia Castro, the daughter of a traditional midwife and a CASA graduate, shared guilty feelings at having to practice episiotomies on women as part of her professional midwifery internship in a government hospital. As a child, Camelia first learned midwifery by watching her mother attend countless episiotomy-free births and lending a helping hand when necessary. From this experience, Camelia knew that episiotomies are, at best, unnecessary procedures, and at worse, mutilations of normal female anatomy. When Camelia confessed to her mother that she was practicing episiotomies as part of her training, her mother began acting "strangely" toward her. Later that day, I traveled to Camelia's natal village to spend some time with her mother, Pamela Ramos, in her home. At the height of her practice as a traditional midwife, Pamela attended twenty to thirty women a month. These days, Pamela is one of two midwives who have not ceased attending births—the rest have stopped practicing in reaction to the threat of criminal charges being initiated, were an infant death to occur on their watch. Pamela takes her chances and continues to attend pregnant women who refuse to deliver at the regional hospital where personnel routinely perform episiotomies.

Maricelda and Camelia's guilt-ridden internship experiences demonstrate that as violence is unleashed on indigenous women's bodies, it also weighs on health-care providers who feel helplessly drawn into its systemic nature. Their complicity in physically violating racialized women points to the powerful reach of racism and discrimination, as well as different women's positionality with respect to systemic, intersectional forms of oppression. Maricelda now considers defending women's rights a part of her job as a private practitioner. Unfortunately, I suggest that her educated, affluent patients are not the individuals who most need their rights defended. Maricelda's positionality as a private practitioner who "empowers" women who are already relatively empowered by their socioeconomic and racial privilege highlights how intersectional racialization processes are (re)produced.

What is the utility of the citizenship concept for capturing the disparate experiences of, on the one hand, racialized "Others" for whom Mexican citizenship fails to insure even the most basic medical interventions, and, on the other hand, global bioconsumers engaged in medical migrations for (ethno)medical tourism? How might we explore (im)mobility by simultaneously casting our critical gaze toward both ends of the socioeconomic spectrum?

CHAPTER 5

(Ethno)Medical (Im)Mobilities

Medical migration has emerged as a vibrant topic of ethnographic inquiry within medical anthropology. Many of these studies analyze how medical therapies are reshaped and modified when both the therapies and health-care seekers travel across geographic and political-economic terrains (see Roberts and Scheper-Hughes 2011). In response, I query not only the effects of migration on medical therapies, but how geographical and political-economic terrains are themselves reshaped and modified in the process. My investigation of Mexican midwifery analyzes how traditional Mexican midwifery is transformed into a series of commodified practices that are then marketed in other countries, and how humanized-birth techniques originating in the Global North are combined with "traditional" methods through a New Age logic that confounds Euro-American notions of chronology and progress. That is to say, the humanized-birth movement in Mexico provides a salient example of how transnational mobilities foster emergent traditionalities, thereby disrupting reified ontologies of time and reconfiguring how "modernity" is defined and desired.

Although others have pointed to the tension and multiple imbrications between "the global" and "the local," my observations of Mexican midwifery's movement across geographic space, border crossing, and deployment led me to contemplate how "the local" (in the form of traditional Mexican midwifery) is usurped by transnational individuals and marketed across the globe for economic profit. My ethnographic observations evidence how "medical migrations are increasingly part of the very fabric of the transnational world order" (see Thompson 2011:205). I heed Laura Nader's 1972 call to "study up" socioeconomic grades and combine this strategy for understanding the reproduction of inequality within society with Rayna Rapp's (2000) multi-sited method for following the object of human reproduction as it is embedded within different social contexts. I thus critically analyze the interaction between spheres of affluence and racialized Others. This method led me to ask: How does ethnomedical culture travel and who is able to perform a simulacrum of traditional culture as culture-in-motion? Conversely, what are the mechanisms that confine others to practice ethnomedicine as culture-in-place?

Medical Migrations: From San Francisco to San Luis Potosí

In November 2012, while attending the American Anthropological Association (AAA) Annual Meeting at the Union Square Hilton in San Francisco, I unexpectedly received an invitation from Martha Lipton, "water birth educator, gentle-birth guardian, and celebrity" within humanized-birth circles, to visit her workshop at the Kabuki Hotel in Japantown as part of the Association for Prenatal and Perinatal Psychology and Health (APPPAH) Conference. Over the past five months, Martha and I had exchanged several messages and discovered we had traveled to all the same places across Mexico and, on several occasions, had missed each other by a matter of days. Finally, our presence coincided in San Francisco! Not letting this opportunity pass, I briskly footed to the APPPAH Conference. At the hotel, I wandered past various vendors' tables, replete with educational books and videos, and birth-related artisan jewelry, bookmarks, postcards, et cetera, and located the workshop hall.

Moments later, Martha Lipton, earrings dangling and flowered shawl streaming, burst in with a bevy of followers. Among them was David Chamberlain, renowned author of *The Mind of Your Newborn Baby*—which has sold worldwide and is available in thirteen languages. Martha immediately began her talk, "Birth and Bonding: How First Hour Programming Will Shape Your Baby's Life." Her presentation was peppered with personal anecdotes, including a few specific experiences in Mexico.

Drawing from her recent travels, Martha described a workshop in Monterrey, Nuevo León, where she probed eager parents in her audience, "If I could guarantee a self-regulating, talented, intelligent, precocious child, . . . I'm currently accepting clients." Judging from their reactions, Martha said, "These parents would pay any price." She explained to the parents they were too late, as some of this programming already happened at birth. She also spoke of a married couple, both obstetricians, who were attending gentle birth in Puerto Vallarta. "What a wonderful place for a destination birth!" she exclaimed. "You could give birth and swim with the dolphins, all on the same trip!"

Martha then described ways she uses her "celebrity status" to leverage power when instructing directors of private hospitals in Mexico on how to properly attend births and preserve the connection between mother and newborn. She recounted her recent experience at a hospital she inaugurated as a water-birth center. When she saw newborns isolated in a nursery, separated from their mothers, thus losing valuable opportunities for first-hour "programming," she authoritatively demanded of the director, "You must stop this immediately! You must take these babies to their mothers right now! I'll wait right here!"

When her three-hour lecture concluded, Martha and I retreated to a quiet hallway where she granted me a two-hour interview, describing in rich detail how she became a humanized-birth advocate. Her journey began with a search in France for Fréderic Leboyer and Michel Odent. After a successful water birth sans physician in her own home in the United States, Martha's prenatal care OB/GYN called Child Protective Services, denouncing what he considered to be child endangerment. According to Martha, when police arrived at her four-bedroom home with two Mercedes Benzes out front, it was obvious to them this was not the typical home where abuse happens—as she put it, "the total opposite of what you look for when you're looking for abuse." Next, Martha apprenticed with spiritual midwives and certified nurse midwives from around the globe. People began arriving from England, France, Sweden, and Norway to give birth in the Jacuzzi installed in her living room.

After a trip to Russia, where the Russian Orthodox patriarch anointed her, Martha had a dream while dozing in the park with her baby. "In that dream state I folded time and I saw the future." She envisioned a vibrational birth: A woman walks into a pyramid and descends into a pool of water, where she "let the baby out." Then, the woman "picks up the baby into the 'habitat'" (skin to skin), walks out of the pool, and is cloaked by singing observers. When Martha awoke, she thought, "I have to start a nonprofit organization and spread the word about water birth." She hired an attorney, wrote the bylaws, and paid the fees, putting at least $2 million of her own money into the project—which was fine, she explained, because she was married to a millionaire when the nonprofit was created. "From that day until this one, I haven't stopped." She has since spread the word in forty-nine countries, spoken with health ministers and presidents (for example, of Russia and Costa Rica), and developed projects in Germany, Denmark, and Norway.

Martha suggested I meet with Larissa Rubio and Jose Felix Ibáñez, founders of the Mexican water-birth organization Tranquilo, and entrepreneurs of Port-a-Pool. After returning to Mexico, I traveled to San Luis

Potosí to interview them at their home. Arriving early with no one home, I waited, admiring the ornately carved sun on their heavy wood door. Minutes later, Larissa returned in a minivan with their five-year-old daughter from Montessori school. Their little girl popped out of the van, a picture of perfection—red ribbons in her hair and wearing pretty white shoes with beading. Then I met Jose Felix—together, he and Larissa made a handsome, fair-skinned couple that could pass for Anglo.

The grandeur of their enormous home was impressive—wood and tile floors, marble countertops, luscious couches, and fine furniture oozed luxury. The family ate only organic, vegetarian food, and offered me chocolate-covered amaranth, nuts, and fresh fruit. Their dining-room table held a wooden box with an assortment of teas and a silver hot-water thermos. A Michael Kors shopping bag was perched on a couch armrest in their living room. There were children's toys scattered around the house and a jungle gym in the backyard; yet their baby was more interested in playing with Jose Felix's iPhone, promptly dropping it on the floor. Jose Felix did not flinch.

When Larissa and Jose Felix met in New York City, he was working at a stock brokerage firm and she was studying international relations at Barclay College. Both come from entrepreneurial families—her family owns numerous beachfront hotels, his owns funeral homes and crematoriums. They recounted how they were drawn to humanized birth five years ago while attending a conference in Monterrey, Nuevo León. Barbara Harper, Michel Odent, and David Chamberlain were in attendance— "the humanized-birth leaders of the world." So far, Larissa and Jose Felix have coached thirty couples in the city of San Luis Potosí over the past two years. They teach relaxation and self-hypnosis strategies, and help women trust their bodies and stop fearing labor pains. Their Port-a-Pool business required a significant initial investment, and it does not generate enough revenue to support their lifestyle. For them, it represents a hobby that, in Larissa's words, "inspires me, and I have come to see it as a social responsibility. I not only feel that I *have* to and *want* to do it, but I *like* doing it" (my translation). Jose Felix enthuses that water-birth education fascinates him, and he hopes to grasp important opportunities to present their courses to large companies and influential people.

Couples taking their course began arriving. They are all educated, English-reading, and working professionals in the fields of real estate, mortgage assessment, law, graphic design, and human resources. When I asked what drew them to water birth, the human resource manager joked that his conjugal family's religion is water birth and Montessori school;

for those who wish to marry into this family, it does not matter what else they believe, as long as their children are born by water birth and attend Montessori school. Larissa began her workshop by describing character- istics of "tranquil birth": no unnecessary interventions or manipulations, privacy, silence, accompaniment, freedom of movement, and freedom to eat and drink during the birthing process.

Meeting the couples was instructive, and following up on the history of Larissa and Jose Felix's three home births was also elucidating. Their births were attended by Dr. Maricelda Hernández Tellez, an obstetrician who "converted" to gentle birthing after witnessing Larissa give birth with zero intervention and now attends water births at Hospital Lomas, a pri- vate hospital nearby. (Throughout the course of my fieldwork, the analogy of religious conversion reoccurred in interviews with informants.) Hop- ing to tour the facilities, I walked to Hospital Lomas and explained my re- search to the head nurse. She told me all the birthing suites were occupied and could not be viewed but ceded to a general tour. I was quickly flanked by two nurses assigned to guide me. I perceived from the doctor's tone of voice and gestures that she was signaling to them to guard me and ensure I did not pry.

As luck would have it, both nurses enjoyed boasting about their top- notch facilities. "This hospital is 100 percent private, so it's targeting a cer- tain clientele, which is the upper-middle and upper class. It is a very exclu- sive hospital." As we toured the labor and delivery area, I complimented them on their hospital's amenities, which, truth be told, were quite im- pressive. This fueled them to show me the birthing suites: a regular suite, a junior suite, and a master suite—complete with flat-screen TVs, sofa beds, closets, full bathrooms, living rooms, second bedrooms, large balco- nies, refrigerators, and minibars. Bottled water was placed in pyramid for- mation on dressers, Kleenex was fashioned into shapes of fans, and ends of toilet paper rolls were folded in triangles.

During my next visit to San Luis Potosí a year later, I was finally able to interview Dr. Maricelda. Her office building appeared to be a private prac- tice where a group of physicians work. Seeing only Dr. Maricelda's name in enormous metallic letters across a marble wall in the reception area, I realized the entire space—which includes a multimedia room, a multi- purpose classroom, a playroom and jungle gym for patients' children, an exam room, and several offices—was solely hers. Dr. Maricelda's recep- tionist led me to her "main" office.

In describing her patients, Dr. Maricelda explained that since hers is a private practice, her patients are middle class and above. Their average ed-

Figure 5.1. Dr. Maricelda with photos of the children whose births she has attended

ucational level is university. Generally, the women are in their late twenties or older, communicate via e-mail (a distinguishing factor in Mexico), and are first-time mothers. She tends to deliver children for couples in stable marriages, and rarely does she see single mothers.

My interview with Dr. Maricelda spurred me to seek out other humanized-birth obstetricians and inquire about their clientele. In Guadalajara, I entertained myself while waiting for an audience with a renowned humanized-birth obstetrician by counting the number of iPhones being used by patrons in the reception area: five. As I waited a little longer, I could hear different couples speaking English and French, as one of each pair was a foreigner. When I asked the obstetrician about the sociodemographics of his clientele, he explained that though his clients all have a high "cultural level," he does not consider many of them to be wealthy. Bolstering Currid-Halkett's theory that the aspirational class derives cultural capital through education, he explained that his patients have at least a bachelor's degree, with some speaking five languages, some with multiple postgraduate degrees. (Even a bachelor's degree is a distinguishing factor when compared to the general population in Mexico.) He emphasized, "My patients are more cultured than rich." In line with Brooks' 2000 argument about how those in the new upper class aspire to transcendence and nonmaterialism, the obstetrician openly criticized those who seek medicalized care: "All of those who go to really expensive places [to give birth], it is because they have a lot of money to pay, but not enough brains to ask questions."

In Mexico City, I asked another humanized-birth obstetrician to describe his clientele, and he responded that they are middle-upper and upper class. About 50 percent pay a portion of the cost of birth with health insurance, with the other 50 percent paying the entire cost out of pocket. Nearly all his patients have studied at the university level, and many have earned postgraduate degrees. Most of his clients are bilingual and articulately express as a unified couple exactly what they are seeking from his humanized-birth practice. Like his clientele, he himself is a transnational, holding dual US-Mexican citizenship, and is married to a Spanish woman who earned a master's degree at Duke University before working for the World Wide Fund in Washington, DC. His daughter was born in water.

I interviewed several humanized-birth obstetricians whose lives also included transnational experiences, including a tall, blue-eyed obstetrician-entrepreneur who studied English at the University of California–Berkeley, medicine at the University of California–Irvine, and genetics in Switzerland before opening a private hospital for patients seeking "natural" medical alternatives. My interactions with humanized-birth obstetricians, Martha Lipton, Larissa, and Jose Felix highlight how their social class and economic capital have allowed them to open nonprofit organizations and for-profit businesses through which they meet their "social responsibility" to promote humanized birth. I do not deny the authenticity of these individuals' desire to improve the way children are born and the noble intentions behind their work, but I do recognize that a definitive tendency toward "aspirational-oriented" consumption—the idea that parent-clients would pay any price for a certain type of child; that couples might plan a "destination birth"; the fact that hospital suites where humanized births take place resemble those of a five-star hotel; and all the merchandise related to humanized birth—acts as a filter, in addition to a couple's level of education and exposure to birth in other countries, resulting in some couples with a certain profile becoming members in the transnational movement for humanized birth while others are excluded.

Eventually, I ended up across the desk from Dr. Horacio García, a National Autonomous University of Mexico (UNAM)–trained OB/GYN and perinatal expert whose private medical practice near Estadio Azteca in-

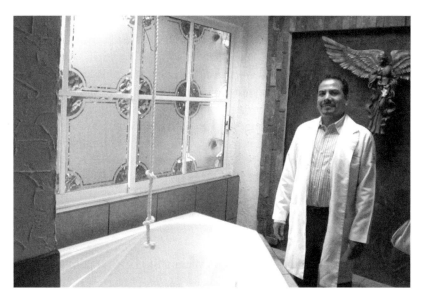

Figure 5.2. Dr. García's garden-view birthing suite with Jacuzzi, skylight, and fountain

cludes a birthing suite with a queen-sized bed, bathroom, Jacuzzi, skylight, and fountain with the statue of an angel. I was struck by how reasonable his prices were when compared to everyone else I had interviewed (8,000 pesos [about US$640] for a water birth, including postnatal care). The services he offers at his private practice are still inaccessible to lower-class Mexicans (across Mexico, minimum wage ranges from 61.38 to 64.76 pesos daily; thus, his water birth package costs the equivalent of about six-months salary at minimum wage) but is approximately a quarter as expensive as Paula's midwifery services. Dr. García spoke to me about his desire to "give back"—as someone who received a stellar public education, he now teaches UNAM medical students for virtually no pay. His comments led to a sense of solidarity during the interview since at the time, I was also teaching UNAM medical students—an invaluable and rewarding experience with little economic benefit.

When I asked him to describe the women he attends, he looked into my eyes and said, "women like you." He went on to say that his patients are women who hold advanced degrees in the humanities and sciences (as opposed to technical fields), are foreign or transnational, bilingual or multilingual, and who place more emphasis on values than aesthetics. A year later, when I had a gynecological emergency, I thought back to all the obstetricians I had interviewed over the course of my ethnographic research and the one who sprang into my mind was Dr. García. What this says about my own subjectivity is for the reader to decide. At the very least it signals that as much as I am committed to uncovering social mechanisms that marginalize and disenfranchise, when it comes to my own health emergencies, I revert to my own transnational identity, education, and privilege. Thus, although hyper-self-reflexivity mandates that the ethnographer attempt to "shed privilege" while adopting the lifestyle of informants, it is impossible to entirely transform the embodiment of difference into sameness. Throughout the course of my fieldwork and during the process of writing, I was careful to recognize, confront, and explore the implications of my "complicity" (see Kapoor 2004).

Bioconsumption and the Limits of Citizenship

Martha Lipton is the quintessential medical traveler: her combined geographic and social mobility buttress her authority as a leader in the transnational humanized-birth movement. CASA has emerged as a special site in the transnational network for humanized birth—it has earned a great deal of recognition and attracts volunteers and visitors from around the world. Some of CASA's credibility rests on the fact that it has been certified by Martha Lipton as a water-birth center—her name appears on a plaque prominently displayed in CASA's main hallway. Thus, CASA deploys the social capital of its association with someone whose privilege has allowed her to become a humanized-birth "celebrity" and a representative of expert knowledge from the Global North.

Martha's influence in the humanized-birth movement unfolds across the Mexican landscape. Through followers like Larissa and Jose Felix, her teachings are spread among affluent, professional couples that, through reading English- and French-language texts about birth practices originating in the United States and Europe, seek inclusion in a transnational community of bioconsumption. Not only couples, but humanized obstetricians and birth attendants, position themselves as transnational subjects. Couples and birth attendants encounter each other as resources for enhanced mobility within a social network that emerges outside of the realm of national citizenship. The privatized lives of participants in the humanized-birth movement decenter citizenship as the primary mechanism for obtaining health-care services. Instead, their bioconsumption of specific bodily practices associates them with consumers who are giving birth elsewhere.

Throughout my research, I was struck by socioeconomic and georacial patterns distinguishing participants in the humanized-birth movement from those the movement references but does not include. I offer the concept of (im)mobility as a tool for thinking about how some people are able to position themselves as consumers within transnational networks, while others continue to make their lives out within the citizenship modality. Considering the intersections between (im)mobility and neoliberal consumption helps test the limits of citizenship, thus highlighting when it is an appropriate analytic, and when it is inadequate for describing people's behaviors and motivations.

The concept of biological citizen is premised on the responsibility of the nation-state to care for its citizens, and the conviction that basic health care is a citizenship-based right (see Petryna 2002). I am specifically pushing against biological citizenship by observing how health (in this case, ethnomedicine) is deployed as a commodity instead of an entitlement. My focus on (ethno)medical migrations brings into view a transnational political order in which biological and medical practices produce both mobile transnationals and comparatively immobile counterparts who are socially situated in ways that encourage them to seek government-provisioned services through citizenship.

This book explores processes of inclusion/exclusion and patterns of bioconsumption. Thus, it critiques tendencies to apply the concept of citizenship too broadly. My perspective is very similar to Scheper-Hughes' 2000 framing of "super-citizens" and "sub-citizens," but I signal subtle but important differences. Scheper-Hughes' terminology suggests a hierarchical scaling of citizens in which some individuals have access to more citizenship rights than others. I problematize contemporary anthropological notions of citizenship by describing individuals whose lives unfold at the edges of citizenship—marginalized individuals for whom citizenship is always just out of reach and transnational elites whose privatized lives render public services undesirable. This ethnography signals how belonging may partially occur beyond the scope of coinstantiation between territory and polity. The ways in which many of my informants sought inclusion in transnational communities of consumption led me to ask: What are the productive ferments caused by friction between citizenship and bioconsumption (see Tsing 2005)? The two elements truly at stake for the bioconsumers I observed are presentations of self (see Goffman 1959) and the accrual of cultural capital, not government-provisioned services.

I am not discarding the concept of citizenship—"papers" are immensely important for millions, especially in an age of intense criminalization of undocumented migrants. In the case of traditional midwives, being "undocumented," or "without papers" is an interesting metaphor to consider, given that they are denied entrance into the guild created by the Mexican Midwifery Association for professional midwives. At the same time, building on Aihwa Ong's 1999 argument, the cultural logics of transnationality make citizenship "flexible" for some more than others. Thus, I examine the contours of biological citizenship and explore the circumstances under which it is overtaken by bioconsumption as the primary strategy for acquiring health-care services and accruing cultural capital. This framing signals how the very presupposition of equality embedded within citizenship as a concept must be reexamined in our neoliberal age. Essentially, this perspective draws attention to the multiplicity of citizenship as it unfolds in the present day.

The ways in which global elites seek and promote privatized humanized birth while the births of indigenous women (whom the movement references) are subject to the mandates of conditional cash-transfer programs serve as fleshy ethnographic evidence of Rose and Novas' (2008 [2005]) reinterpretation of biological citizenship. They emphasize the transnational nature of emerging citizenship projects and the partial delinking of citizenship and nation. I find their proposal provocative, but I am committed to matching the transnational content of my ethnography with transnational content in my theory. Thus, I bring Latin American (and especially Mexican) scholarship to bear on the concept of biological citizenship, thereby drawing attention to the roles consumerism, socioeconomic class, and representations originating in the Global North play in the construction of global, biological, consumption-oriented communities.

Néstor García Canclini (an Argentina-born anthropologist at the Universidad Autónoma Metropolitana in Mexico City and director of its program of studies in urban culture) argues that citizenship used to signify equality of abstract rights and collective participation in public democratic spaces, but nowadays questions of belonging, information, and representation are answered in the realm of private consumption and mass media—effectively rendering citizens of the eighteenth century into consumers of the twentieth (or twenty-first) century (see García Canclini 2001). Signaling the decline of nations as a meaningful unit of social analysis, García Canclini notes how people's sense of belonging and identity is increasingly defined by participation in transnational or de-territorialized communities of consumption. Identity is now configured by consumption—how much one possesses and is capable of appropriating. Thus, García Canclini argues that the neoliberal conception of globalization reserves the right of being a citizen for elites.

I consider neoliberalism to be a mode of global governance that has led to consumption as a primary way the "haves" construct identities, leading to a regime of inclusion-exclusion that, in the case of Mexican midwifery, feeds off the "have-nots" in a symbolically cannibalistic or vampiric way and (re)produces uncritical notions of "indigeneity," thus reinscribing inequality and disparity. Merging "biological citizenship" and "consumer citizenship" (thus combining US and Mexican perspectives on how citizenship operates in our contemporary era) is a useful analytical maneuver for understanding how bioconsumers seek therapies and make claims to health resources in numerous contexts. However, this framing is insufficient for assessing the mobilities and immobilities that emerged among informants during my ethnographic research. My twofold method of simultaneously conducting ethnographic research at both ends of the socioeconomic spectrum serves as a lens for examining how (im)mobilities are not just geographic, but also reference *upward* mobilities. I am signaling the operative relationship between social geographies and citizenship projects. The parenthetical composition of (im)mobility is a permanent signpost for the complexity of mobilities afforded by immobility, and vice versa. Beyond that, it signals that agency and power are not entirely about who moves and who does not (see Deomampo 2013).

Mobile Humanized-Birth Practitioners and Participants, Immobile Mexican Midwives and Families

After a few phone and e-mail conversations with Sagrario Villareal to arrange institutional access for research performed at the Center for the Adolescents of San Miguel de Allende, I traveled to San Miguel de Allende for the first time in December 2010. Sagrario later told me that as general director of CASA, she received an endless stream of solicitations from *gringa* researchers and volunteers wanting to involve themselves in CASA's work. Her answer is always the same—a cordial but uninvested "yes." She has found that though many foreigners express their desire to collaborate, their help is often ineffectual or fleeting and may at times even be detrimental. As an assistant professor who is focused on developing the global-health curriculum at my institution, I have engaged in ongoing debates addressing the challenge of designing and implementing service learning projects that are culturally appropriate, meaningful, and sustainable. All too often, global-health projects are ineffectual and can even produce harmful unintended effects.

Sagrario had been on the receiving end of short-lived volunteerism. Unbeknownst to me, I surpassed her expectations when I followed through with my offer to spend four months over the summer of 2011 volunteering at CASA, faithfully arriving every day to perform video editing and translation as well as liaising with the country's sales manager for Laerdal International, thereby obtaining experiential learning materials for the midwifery students. In exchange, Sagrario allowed me to audit CASA's professional midwifery classes, sit in on administrative meetings, and interview all the students. By the end of summer, I had performed at least one in-depth interview with nearly every student. Shortly before I returned to Berkeley to begin the academic year, Sagrario granted me an in-depth interview (the first of many, deeply personal conversations we shared over the next several years) and told me how pleasantly surprised she was to see my sustained commitment to volunteering and carrying out research at CASA. She has had experience with many eager foreigners over the years, but these experiences had not resulted in mutual collaboration and ongoing partnership. Sagrario emerged as a key informant throughout my fieldwork; thus, my commitment to volunteering reflects both the importance my involvement at CASA played in accessing the transnational humanized-birth network, and the deep friendship that we developed.

Her experience with other volunteers has not been as positive: she shared how resentful she felt when American student volunteers came to CASA, believing that they could touch and manipulate Mexican women's bodies, knowing very well that they were not trained to do so and would not be permitted to perform these procedures in their home country. However, her fraught relationship with foreigners does not stop with entitled volunteers but extends to donors as well. Sagrario expressed her frustration and exhaustion—she is tired of perpetually conforming to the desires of Americans and pleasing Americans at fund-raising events. Why don't Americans living in Mexico try to adapt to Mexican standards of living?

This tension also unfolds in her daily life, outside the confines of her work post. She talked to me about the injustices she has personally suffered as a Mexican woman living in San Miguel. She explained that if she hails a taxi on any street in San Miguel and a white person is also hailing a taxi half a block ahead, the taxi will bypass her and pick up the white client. In that moment, Sagrario's social and symbolic capital as general director of a renowned NGO disappears as the taxi driver makes a racialized judgment based on a centuries-long history of imperialism leading to present-day socioeconomic differences between Mexico and the United States. This same phenomenon was readily admitted to me by a taxi driver—he will often pass up Mexican passengers to pick up "gringo" passengers instead. Although he admitted aloud to me that he engages in "reverse-discrimination" (his term), for him the determining factor is which passenger is more likely to pay a larger fare.

Subsequently, Sagrario resigned from her position at CASA and accepted a contract as an adviser at the Center for Gender Equity and Reproductive Health in Mexico City. Soon after she left CASA, the clinical and academic directorships were filled by American women. She scoffed, saying that when she was general director, she was careful not to hire foreigners for key administrative posts as, in her opinion, such an organization should be run by Mexican women for Mexican women. This theme of bowing down to foreigners has followed her to her new job. Recently some "gringo people" came to visit her center. She prepared a presentation for their visit but had no luck explaining any of the current programs to them since they didn't speak any Spanish whatsoever. They wanted to see statistics on reproductive health in the state of Puebla, so Sagrario assumes they are considering investing development funds in Puebla. In spite of the language barrier, Sagrario perceived that their intention was to show Mexicans "the right way" of doing things—she was very critical of their stance, stating that America's lacking health system produces poorer health outcomes when compared to its neighboring country, Canada.

While Sagrario was working in Mexico City, she returned to San Miguel often to visit her teenage and adult children. Whenever she returned to town, she invited me to her home. On one such visit, she expressed her frustration at being a "second-class citizen" in midwifery circles when compared to foreign midwives who are not licensed to practice midwifery in Mexico. Several times she asked me the same rhetorical question: "Why, why, *why* do foreign midwives come to Mexico to practice midwifery? She commented extensively on the privilege these midwives enjoy, which she argued is based entirely on their cultural capital and not actual training or skill.

Sagrario offered the following anecdote to illustrate her point: Recently, she attended a birth with two midwives from Europe. Although the first-time mother had been in labor for quite some time, the European midwives did not want to check her dilation. Finally, at Sagrario's urging, they discovered that the mother was fully dilated but that the baby was not emerging due to a nuchal cord (a tangle in the umbilical cord). Sagrario suggested that they administer low-dose oxytocin, but the European midwives resisted for the next several hours. The birth had to be transferred to the hospital. Upon arrival, Sagrario asked the physician if she could administer low-dose oxytocin at four drops per minute and the doctor agreed.

Even though Sagrario considers that many foreign midwives are not as well trained as she is, she observes their elevated status in Mexican midwifery circles. For example, foreign midwives offer courses and workshops at high rates—hundreds of pesos if the course or workshop lasts several hours, and thousands of pesos if it lasts a few days. Sagrario asserted that a Mexican midwife would never be able to charge as much—if she did, no one would come.

Furthermore, Sagrario had recently attended one of the first Mexican Midwifery Association organizational meetings, discovering that despite the association's name, the group is composed almost entirely of foreign midwives, and that the majority of the women on the directive panel are from the United States and Europe. Even more offensive from Sagrario's perspective was that one of the association's leaders (a midwife from Spain) began her midwifery training under Sagrario's tutelage. Nonetheless, within the organizational structure of the association, it is as if this unlicensed Spaniard is more knowledgeable about midwifery than Sagrario— a possibility Sagrario deemed ludicrous. At the meeting, she confronted the issue, asking why she had not been invited to participate on the directive panel. Her question went unanswered, and for the following five or so years, she was not offered a place on the directive panel. (She eventually took an interim position amid accusations of embezzlement launched at her apprentice—who was president of the association at that time.)

Sagrario hypothesized that the Mexican midwives in the organization idolize their foreign counterparts, believing that they are more knowledgeable and better trained, just because of their US and European origins. In her opinion, what was happening within the Mexican Midwifery Association was an example of *neocolonialismo* ("neocolonialism," her term) occurring in the name of humanized birth and professional midwifery. Indignant, Sagrario told me that she was intent on fighting against this ongoing phenomenon of doors opening for foreign women living in Mexico and slamming shut in the faces of Mexican women. I asked her if I was included among the foreign women she was maligning, and she told me that I am an exception—an *"amiga"*—someone who is an ally and a supporter but who does not attempt to usurp positions of power based on "expert knowledge."

Traditional Midwifery Reimagined for Popular Tourism

My thoughts continued to circle around how certain women are able to construct lucrative, transnational identities as professional midwives within humanized-birth networks, while others are not able to do so. I realized that the middle- and upper-class lifestyles of transnational midwives had not only attracted the attention of Mexican counterparts such as Sagrario but also resulted in these privileged midwives being the targets of blackmail and kidnapping threats.

One well-known professional midwife, Adeli Hirsch, fled to Brazil from Veracruz after her children's private school became a target for kidnappings. Three years before, I too had been the target of kidnapping threats. I had failed to anticipate the sentiments my privilege provoked among the rural farmers whom I was attempting to study. After being targeted, I reflected on steps to prevent this same problem from recurring, and I conscientiously adapted myself to the socioeconomic level of my informants. This meant changing my habitus, the clothing I wore, and the very food I ate. When I heard about Adeli suddenly uprooting her family and relocating to Brazil, I wondered what factors contributed to her being identified as a target. Many of the individuals I interviewed mentioned Adeli—she has discursively emerged as an important figure in the Mexican humanized-birth movement, even in her physical absence.

I decided to seek her out in Florianópolis, the capital city of Santa Catarina, Brazil, known for its high quality of life, unparalleled Human Development Index score among Brazilian capitals, and its nightlife, tourism, and dynamism. Florianópolis is a second-home destination for many Argentines, North Americans, Europeans, and people from São Paulo. As a result, it is perhaps the "whitest" city in Brazil. After spending a week with Adeli in her home and around Florianópolis as a participant in a workshop she held titled "Traditional Mexican Midwifery," I had a better understanding of the decision-making process that led her to move to Brazil and forge a new life with the three children she has with her ex-husband, a Japanese artist.

Adeli is of mixed Jewish and Mexican heritage and was reared in the United States and Mexico. Her parents are writers and intellectuals. She has tight brown curls, piercing blue eyes, and the warmest of smiles. She exudes positive energy with her every word and gesture—the way she carries herself signals her training in dance at the University of California–Santa Cruz and in the Congo. Like other successful professional midwives in Mexico, she studied midwifery in Texas. I was excited to meet her, but as the workshop unfolded, I was equally intrigued by the other participants in the workshop, most of whom had specifically traveled to Brazil from other Latin American countries to learn from Adeli. I was surprised at how fair the group was—I was among the darker women in the room, and although we were in Brazil, there were very few women of African

Figure 5.3. Participants at the workshop on "Traditional Mexican Midwifery." I am second from the right.

descent. As we went around the room introducing ourselves on the first morning of the workshop, Adeli commented to the group that I was the only Mexican in this workshop. I quickly explained to the group that as a person of mixed ethnic heritage reared in the United States, I am not an appropriate representative of Mexico.

For most of the week, the group sat in a circle on the beach or in boats, listening to Adeli's anecdotes of births she attended and her personal reproductive experiences. Adeli is a remarkable storyteller—her anecdotes highlight the spiritual and emotional elements of birthing and are infused with symbolism and imagery. However, as the workshop transpired, I realized that very little of what was being taught is traditional Mexican midwifery. That is to say, the techniques that Adeli discussed represent her own style of midwifery, and most are not the traditional techniques of indigenous midwives in Mexico. For example, her workshop included New Age explanations of homeopathy and how to make tinctures from placentas and create placenta art.

Throughout the week, I increasingly wondered if what I was observing can be more aptly described as traditional midwifery popular tourism: middle- and upper-class women from across Latin America who are not midwives but are interested enough in New Age notions of traditional midwifery, indigeneity, and going back to nature to travel internationally and spend a week on Brazilian beaches with someone who offers herself as a representative of traditional midwifery knowledge. The fact that professional midwives go unquestioned when they stake claims to traditional knowledge, while traditional midwives are excluded from a national guild for professional midwives unless they undergo a formal course of study, speaks to the unequal power relations operating within Mexican midwifery.

Figure 5.4.
Participants on a boat headed for a beach restaurant where the workshop was held that day

Figure 5.5.
Using *rebozos* to manipulate the shape of the birth canal by applying pressure to the pelvis

Figure 5.6.
Participants watching, filming, and photographing Adeli prepare herbal cosmetic balms

My curiosity about whether the workshop was really an example of traditional midwifery popular tourism became more persistent after we went as a group to a spa and participated in a nighttime *temascal* ritual. Compared to the *temascals* prepared by indigenous people in Mexico for healing purposes, this *temascal* was decidedly mild. The temperature was not as extreme as the traditional version, the door was opened quite often to let participants cool off and breathe fresh air, and no flogging with fragrant herbs was involved. While I sat in the *temascal* dressed in a bathing suit, some of the women around me began stripping off their clothing. Ana Rojas, a young woman with dyed flaming red hair and a deep voice, laid her naked body across my lap and began touching herself, occasionally touching my arm and side. I was not certain what to do, but I felt uncomfortable being fondled, so after a few minutes I repositioned myself, lying down on the floor in a corner. Moments later I heard her moans in the pitch black as she reached orgasm.

I disappeared for a while in the darkness, listening to the sounds the others were making and remaining inaudible to them until Adeli called out my name and asked, "Will you sing 'Amazing Grace'?" I did, lying down, my lungs filling with hot rosemary-infused air, and my voice was stronger and throatier than ever, filling the small space with a palpable vibration. In this moment, my years of singing in church as a child lent a sense of closure to what, I would soon discover, represented an emotional journey for the other women. After the ritual was over, the women emerged, hugging and kissing each other, and crying. By the end of the night I was covered with the sweat and tears of two dozen women. I felt awkward with each embrace—the feeling of other women's naked breasts pressing against my body was strange and unnerving to me. The next day, as we sat on the beach and shared our experiences, most of the women recounted how being in the *temascal* had forced them to deal with old emotional traumas, and by the end of the ritual, many had let go of the fear and pain that they had been harboring.

What was striking to me about this experience was how the *temascal* ritual had been extracted from its original geographic and sociocultural contexts; usurped, transported, and manipulated for profit within Florianópolis' tourism industry; and infused with New Age meanings, which led to experiences of sexual liberation, emotional cleansing, and psychological healing among the participants in a way that is wholly distinct from the way my indigenous informants experience the *temascal*. Furthermore, my own interpellation to perform "Amazing Grace" made me wonder about the intermingling of traditional and indigenous practices with Anglo-

Christian elements. How does the New Age notion of healing allow for the mixing of concrete practices originating from disparate contexts and rooted in divergent ideologies? What are the unintended consequences of this ostensibly clean extraction of healing practices from the social milieu for which they were created?

After returning to Mexico, I looked over my financial account of the trip to think ethnographically about what the sum of money I had spent represented for the majority of Latin American women. In addition to the cost of international air travel and hotel accommodations, the base price for the workshop was US$795. The participants also had to pay for passage on two boats, a fee for the *temascal,* and food. Also, during the course, participants eagerly purchased birth-related jewelry, birth manuals, music, and *rebozos* from Veracruz (the iconic shawl worn by "indigenous Mexican midwives" and a "tool of their trade").

Rebozos are used by indigenous women in Mexico for many different activities—to carry children, to transport firewood, as protection from the beating sun, to provide warmth during cool evenings—the *rebozo* is like a backpack, handbag, coat, and umbrella all in one. Humanized-birth proponents told me about a "traditional" technique that involves wrapping a pregnant woman in a *rebozo* and forcefully jerking the material in order to jolt a misplaced fetus back into proper position (this technique is called *la manteada*), but during fieldwork I observed that traditional midwives are more inclined to use controlled hand movements to manipulate the fetus' position (a type of massage called *sobada*). Once I discovered that *la manteada* was not the most prevalent technique I observed among traditional midwives, I became curious about the *rebozo*'s "cult status" among humanized-birth practitioners. Upon typing *"rebozo parto"* in an Internet search (*parto* is the Spanish word for "birth"), Adeli's name appeared several times on the first page, along with that of a doula from Mexico City who trains doulas internationally (in the United States, Canada, Argentina, Chile, Uruguay, Puerto Rico, England, and Belfast, Ireland) and a Chilean midwife who was a fellow participant in Adeli's workshop.

After the workshop had ended and the other participants dispersed, I spent an extra day on the beach with Adeli and her boyfriend. I enjoyed getting to know them both outside of the workshop setting. Adeli shared with me her deeply held desire to improve women's birthing experiences, and I observed during my weeklong stay how she combines this passion with entrepreneurial spirit. Through the workshops she offers and ongoing speaking engagements, Adeli is able to provide her children with a comfortable upbringing and enjoy an affluent Florianópolis lifestyle.

However, as we spoke, her hesitance about how Mexican ethnomedicine is enacted in Florianópolis, as well as her thoughts on participants' reactions, arose. She identified the differences between a traditional *temascal* in Mexico and the less therapeutic, more touristic version we experienced during the workshop. For participants to truly experience a level of meditative consciousness resulting in healing from psychoemotional traumas, the *temascal* has to be very hot, pushing participants toward their physical limits. Nonetheless, participants expressed deep transformative experiences during the workshop *temascal*. Adeli wondered aloud if this had more to do with the social dynamic of the group than body-mind-spirit effects of the *temascal*.

Almost exactly two years after my first in-depth interview with Sagrario in 2011, I joined her on a supervisory trip of CASA graduates working in public clinics in the state of Guerrero. The CASA model envisions training indigenous women from rural communities in professional midwifery so that they may return to their places of origin, practice professional midwifery among a "vulnerable" and "at risk" population, and thus reduce maternal mortality, but I have observed that this is rarely the case.

The gap between what CASA aims to do (train indigenous women to reduce maternal mortality among indigenous women) and what actually manifests led to the inception of a pilot program in Guerrero, for which Sagrario was partly in charge, as a CASA graduate, an adviser at the Center for Gender Equity and Reproductive Health, and an expert on midwifery at the federal level. The program was developed to curb the trend of CASA graduates either abandoning the practice of midwifery after graduation, or solely attending births of nonindigenous women in the private sector.

CASA graduates who do actively practice midwifery have generally avoided working in rural regions for lifestyle reasons—after four years of intense study and clinical training, they generally settle in urban regions, where they receive higher remuneration for their services and their children can get a better education. In addition, the distance from urban conveniences (hot water, cell-phone signal, Internet, food other than beans and tortillas, etc.); the feeling of isolation produced by separation from friends and family; and the slow wearing down of the soul from routinely witnessing deep social pathologies such as widespread alcoholism and normalized domestic violence, are reasons that CASA graduates identify as deterrents, especially since they studied professional midwifery in hopes of "a better life" after graduation.

Through the public employment of CASA graduates at rural clinics in indigenous regions across the state of Guerrero, the Mexican government aimed to outweigh the detractions of rural living with economic balances (i.e., a salary of 12,000 pesos per month [about US$960], to be raised to 14,000 pesos [about US$1,120] in the second year of the program). Although the salary the Secretariat of Health has offered pales in comparison to the sums foreign and transnational midwives like Paula Marin of Mexico City and Montserrat Venegas, a former apprentice to Sagrario who now lives and works in Chiapas, earn per birth, it rivals the salary of other publicly employed medical personnel and is more than many Mexican midwives, professional or traditional, expect to earn.

María del Carmen and Ignacio

Sagrario and I spent two weeks together traveling across Guerrero, visiting and assessing CASA graduates as they provided prenatal care to indigenous women from their rural posts. On one sunny afternoon, we were lurching up a winding mountain road with our driver, a Secretariat of Health worker for the state of Guerrero. Sagrario and I crammed into the passenger seat of the truck, since neither of us wanted to get motion sickness while sitting in the truck bed. My eyes were glued to the pavement, which snaked back and forth along the mountainside. Suddenly, Sagrario saw something off to the side of the road, and our driver screeched to a stop. Emerging from the truck, we saw a short-statured, indigenous man—bewilderment and desperation in his eyes—holding the limp body of his unconscious wife. Sagrario ordered the driver to help her load the woman into the back of the truck, and she quickly grabbed a bag of IV saline solution from her purse. With the calmness and efficiency of someone with extensive clinical experience, Sagrario inserted the IV needle into the woman's arm as our driver jolted down the mountainside. (I later asked her why she carries IV saline solution in her purse, and she told me that she is always prepared for the possibility of someday intervening in a life-threatening situation.)

When Sagrario arrived with the patient, María del Carmen Campos, and her husband, Ignacio Prieto, at the closest semi-urban clinic in San Luis Acatlán, she was informed that though the clinic has an operating room, it does not have a surgical team to perform the procedure María del Carmen needed to stop her potentially fatal hemorrhage. During the ride to San Luis Acatlán, Sagrario had diagnosed the cause of María del Carmen's hemorrhage as miscarriage of an unknown pregnancy. Unable to access the necessary treatment in San Luis Acatlán, Sagrario decided to take María del Carmen and Ignacio to the closest urban hospital in Ometepec. Three hours after seeing the couple on the side of the road, Sagrario finally left them with hospital personnel, who were already initiating surgical management of María del Carmen's acute uterine bleeding. During the long car ride to Ometepec, Sagrario asked María del Carmen if she wanted to have any more children. María del Carmen answered no, and Sagrario sought her consent for tubal ligation, explaining that this would prevent any similar complication from happening in the future. María del Carmen consented, and Sagrario passed this information along to hospital staff, asking that they perform the ligation in addition to the surgical management of María del Carmen's hemorrhage.

Sagrario and I then took Ignacio to the Health Jurisdiction Offices in Ometepec to meet with the head administrator and discuss the case with him. I watched the encounter with the administrator unfold, as Sagrario insisted that the administrator personally look after María del Carmen's case, and as Ignacio slouched and stared sheepishly at the floor. Instead of locating the origin of the problem in María del Carmen's biology or in inadequate health resources and infrastructure in rural indigenous regions, the administrator complained about how difficult it is to provide health care to *"gente indígena por su cultura"* (indigenous people because of their culture). The administrator made harsh and discriminatory comments as if Ignacio was not present in the room—as if Ignacio did not even exist. Ignacio's facial expression never changed; he continued to stare at the floor until Sagrario and I signaled to him that it was time to leave.

The next day, we returned to check on María del Carmen, who was already being prepared for discharge. She had not received a tubal ligation. One staff member said that the operating room was not suitable for such a surgery due to a recent earthquake (the earthquake occurred two and a half months before), while another staff member indicated that the problem was actually blood. If they performed the tubal ligation, María del Carmen would have to be administered at least one pack of blood, but the blood bank's policy is to refuse blood to any patient whose family cannot replace the same amount of blood on the patient's behalf. Since Ignacio was assumed to be anemic like the majority of indigenous people in the region, he was not a candidate for blood donation, thus precluding María del Carmen from receiving blood or a tubal ligation.

Sagrario's blood began to boil. She was visibly angered by this news, and she stormed down the hospital corridors until she found the chief of staff and demanded that María del Carmen be given a tubal ligation im-

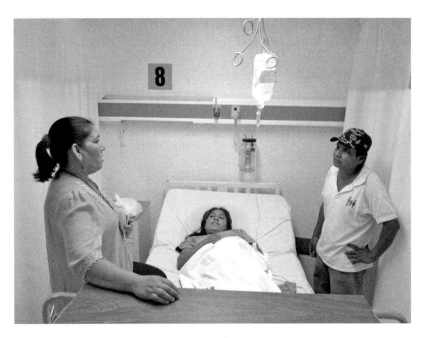

Figure 5.7. From left to right: Sagrario, María del Carmen, and Ignacio

mediately. She insisted, telling him that he knew perfectly well that if they missed the opportunity to ligate, the patient would not return and would likely have more children, in addition to potentially suffering another hemorrhage in the future. The chief acquiesced, and we left the hospital . . . for that day.

The next day, we drove to a small village tucked deeply into the Guerrero countryside. To get there, we had to ford four streams and small rivers, holding our breath while hoping that the water would not rush into the cabin of the truck or damage the truck's engine. Then came the biggest challenge: driving along a faint mountainside path that withered away until we found ourselves on a narrow ledge. The truck crept forward, cautiously, slowly . . . and then it happened. One of the wheels had slipped over the cliff edge, and for a second we were suspended, teetering in the air, throwing our weight toward the side of the mountain. The driver put his foot on the gas and the wheels spun until the truck climbed back to safety.

When we finally arrived at the tiny hidden village, we were famished. Perhaps our brush with death had unconsciously motivated us to fill our stomachs with whatever sustenance we could find. Arriving at a villager's house, we were welcomed into her kitchen (the area in her cabin around the fire she uses to cook) and promptly served *chipilis* (a weed that grows abundantly in the area, and a source of free food) in clear broth (I suspect that the broth was made from water and salt instead of meat or bones). Unboiled water is undrinkable in the area, so we all accepted Coca-Cola.

After satisfying our bellies, we paid the woman for the food and began a long trudge up the hill to visit a first-time pregnant woman. When we arrived at an adobe house at the top of the hill, we asked for Verónica Monteros, but Verónica's father-in-law emerged. He asked us to explain our business with Verónica, and when Sagrario explained that she wanted to perform a follow-up prenatal exam since Verónica had been totally absent from the San Luis Acatlán clinic, the father-in-law cocked his head to the side, considering Sagrario's proposition, before heading over to a cell phone sitting in a cut-off plastic water bottle, taped to the top of a wooden post. He dialed his son's cell-phone number and his son answered from the taxi he drives in Mexico City. They spoke in Mixtec, conferring about what to do. A couple of minutes later, the husband in Mexico City asked to speak to Verónica, to inform her that she should submit to the prenatal exam. Verónica came to the post, heard her husband's instructions, and hung up the phone.

Verónica led us to a woven-straw bed, similar in construction to a trampoline, in the patio of the family's adobe home. Sagrario performed the

Figure 5.8. Verónica's father-in-law talking to his son through the cell phone on the end of the wooden post

Figure 5.9. Verónica receives a prenatal exam from Sagrario and another professional midwife

prenatal exam and determined that everything was fine. She inquired why Verónica was no longer seeking prenatal care at the clinic in San Luis Acatlán. Verónica explained that on her last visit, she was told the baby was undergoing "fetal distress," displayed cardiac rhythm abnormalities, and had a nuchal chord. Verónica demonstrated a steely, unshakable confidence in her capacities to sense the well-being of her fetus and give birth to a healthy child (in contrast to Davis-Floyd's 2004 [1992] assessment of the American paradigm that mires women in fear). Relying solely on mother's intuition, she determined that her baby was perfectly fine and that the medical personnel were manipulating her in order to lure her onto the operating table. We asked her what she planned to do: how would she, a nineteen-year-old first-time mother, give birth in a small village with no midwife? Her answer was simple and matter-of-fact: "By myself."

After similar visits in other villages, we returned to the place where we found María del Carmen and Ignacio on the side of the road. From there, we beat our way through thick brush and foliage until we found a small one-room cabin tucked among the trees. María del Carmen's sister-in-law, Valeria Prieto, was in tears as she translated the story of the couple's jour-

Figure 5.10. Searching for María del Carmen and Ignacio's cabin in the woods

ney home from the hospital, late at night, with no money, no medicines, and no place to stay. To get home, the couple had to *engañar* (deceive) the taxi driver, only admitting they had no money to pay him once he had driven them home. It was the only way. Ignacio's mother also cried, saying that it felt so good to be treated well by *gente* and that she was touched that "*doctoras*" would come all the way to their home to offer help. *Gente* can literally be translated to mean "people." However, this term is often used to contrast "decent folk" from "the dregs of society" and use of that word evidences her presupposition that Sagrario and I are somehow superior people to Ignacio and the rest of his family.

After hearing about María del Carmen and Ignacio's tribulations during their return home, Sagrario was again on the rampage. We drove three hours to Ometepec, Sagrario fuming every kilometer of the way and planning a tongue-lashing for the Health Jurisdiction administrator. Our driver, anxious about what was in store, said, "I will take you wherever you want to go, but do not make me face those monsters." He explained that the administrator is a close friend of the governor, has support of the union, and his sister is the municipal president. As someone within the circle of power, he is accustomed to abusing the local population. Once we arrived, Sagrario reminded the administrator that he had personally

Figure 5.11. Ignacio helps María del Carmen sit up in the bedroom portion of the cabin

Figure 5.12. The inside of María del Carmen and Ignacio's cabin; their children and family members

assured her that he would provide María del Carmen and Ignacio with transportation home. She told him that he broke his promise and is not trustworthy, and then she threatened, "I am not leaving here without a solution." After some squirming on his part during Sagrario's tirade, the administrator was left speechless. He pulled out two 500-peso notes (approximately US$80) from his billfold and handed them to Sagrario as reimbursement for María del Carmen and Ignacio's travel expenses and had a nurse bring the postoperative analgesics and antibiotics María del Carmen required from the health center. Then he sent us to a restaurant in the town center, telling us to eat to our heart's content, "The bill is on me."

The Limits of Citizenship

While marginalized individuals like María del Carmen and Ignacio seek minimal government-provisioned medical services and are deeply moved by rare experiences of kind treatment by *gente*, their affluent counterparts are oblivious to the trials of state-issued health care. Due to their limited economic resources and ongoing racial discrimination, María del Carmen and Ignacio can only hope that their dire health needs will be met through the trope of citizenship. Since they are not positioned to leverage scientific knowledge and the performative medicalization of their suffering bodies as Petryna (2002) describes, biological citizenship is always just out of reach. For mothers like Verónica, being denied agency within government-hospital settings fosters agentive disinterest in pursuing ever-aloof biological citizenship and willful determination to go it alone. In contrast, Larissa and Jose Felix's privatized lifestyles unfold entirely outside of the realm of citizenship. For them, citizenship is neither unattainable nor aloof—it is simply not the mechanism through which they acquire services. Instead, their identities are linked to a transnational meritocracy around parenting and birthing that allows cultural capital to stealthily stand in for economic capital.

The experiences of Adeli, Sagrario, María del Carmen, Ignacio, and Verónica demonstrate the relative physical and social mobilities of a humanized-birth practitioner, a Mexican midwife, and impoverished indigenous patients and their families. The landscape I am describing is fraught with conflicting interests, and as mobilities collide into immobilities, social tensions surge. Each example offered here highlights a different aspect of this complexity. I dispute Appadurai's 1996 notion of "flow" and instead build upon Ong's 1999 portrayal of how power works in globalized contexts. I do this because my work not only describes (ethno)medically mobile travelers, on the one hand, and socially situated individuals, on the other, but rather, it highlights the tensions that emerge from physical propinquity and divergent access to transnational consumption and national citizenship.

I highlight moments that add complexity to the concept of medical migration in order to describe how people from disparate socioeconomic and georacial spectrums experience (im)mobility. For example, Sagrario comes in contact with foreigners whom she perceives as more privileged but less skillful than she is. Their mobility and her relative immobility, along with associated cultural and economic capital inequality, caused her to express frustration and resentment. Adeli, however, is an example of someone who has leveraged a transnational identity to accumulate both cultural and economic capital—she is a US-trained Jewish Mexican American whose livelihood depends on successfully portraying herself as a "traditional Mexican midwife." Adeli's experiences show that both physical and social mobility are premised on one's ability to position oneself in a transnational community of consumption vis-à-vis traditional and professional categories. Her "border crossing" was met with resistance in her community, leading her to flee to Brazil. The contrasting ethnographic examples of Sagrario's exclusion from the Mexican Midwifery Association advisory panel and threats to the safety of Adeli's children demonstrate that although some informants enjoy heightened mobility and others are constrained by immobility, the social categories that separate the two groups can sometimes be equally binding in emotionally challenging ways (see Deomampo 2013).

In Mexico, neoliberal economic restructuring has led to the dismantling and defunding of social safety nets. Cash-transfer programs such as Oportunidades situate poor indigenous women at the crossroads of multiple forms of oppression and require them to alternate between performances of need and performances of capacity (see Gálvez 2011 and Smith-Oka 2013). Others have suggested that the Mexican government holds its citizens responsible for self-care, and that Mexican citizens, distrusting of the government's provisioning of the necessities of life, have developed a sense of self-reliance (see Maldonado 2010 and Gutmann 2002); however, my ethnographic observations collectively suggest that neoliberal governance is not only premised on self-care but is redefining the limits of citizenship.

Although this former perspective links neoliberal models of self-reliance to Foucault's "technologies of self" (Foucault 1988) and Ong's dual technologies for the formation of neoliberal subject ("technologies of subjectivity" and "technologies of subjection" [Ong 2006:6]), the case of humanized birth in Mexico casts a light on the limits of governmentality. My observations from the field do not support the argument that self-government and internalized discipline reinforce power structures and further regulate populations. I aim to build upon recent scholarship pointing to how neoliberalism is resulting in the simultaneous expansion and delimitation of citizenship by exploring other forms of subject-making. My ethnography takes place at the edges of citizenship. I emphasize moments in which national citizenship is either not attainable or simply not the object of desire. Thus, I agree with scholars who critique the exceedingly narrow and racialized sphere of citizenship, but I depart from these critiques by asking what is unfolding beyond.

My rethinking of citizenship resists uncritical assumptions about how health as a human right unfolds in our neoliberal age. Countries like Mexico and Brazil are investing in nascent universal health systems, and yet medical migrations point to the transnational nature of health care in the contemporary world and the delinking of nation and health provision. Recognizing the disjuncture between national health systems and legal citizens—that is, attending to how some individuals seek "citizenship" that is always just out of reach while others secure inclusion in transnational health-related communities through consumption—throws into question the very premise upon which universal health systems are based. Can health as a universal *good* (both as a moral value and as concrete medical services) exist in an epoch that, ideologically speaking, combines neoliberal notions of choice with capitalistic realities of deep socioeconomic inequality?

The gap between state-provisioned health services and market-driven health acquisition is inscribed in individuals' identities, granting of greater or inferior value to those individuals as moral subjects. Although many have researched how intersectional inequalities (socioeconomic, race, gender, etc.) become embodied through unequal health-care provisioning, my research also expands in another direction: I attend to how unequal access to biological services reinscribes inequalities that are then incorporated into identities.

Destination Birth—Time and Space Travel

Over the course of my research, I became increasingly concerned with the privilege and power enjoyed by foreigners living in Mexico. Many of these foreigners have resided in Mexico for many years, and some eventually gain dual citizenship. Thus, whereas professional midwives with foreign origins and transnational trajectories consider themselves *mexicanas*, their counterparts who have lived out their entire lives in Mexico continually label them as foreigners, despite their years of residence within Mexico. This insistence on signaling difference may result from resentment at the perceived ease with which foreign midwives leverage cultural capital emanating from their "Americanness," "Europeanness," and transnationalism to acquire economic resources and positions of power.

Sagrario remarked about how her former apprentice's Spanish origin has resulted in greater privilege, culminating in a directive position within the Mexican Midwifery Association. Curious about this comment, I traveled to Chiapas in June 2013 in search of Montserrat Venegas, Sagrario's former apprentice. When I walked into her alternative-birth center, my attention was drawn to all the alternative treatments, therapies, and supplements for sale in the reception area and the beautiful colors and artwork on the walls. I noticed a poster for a belly-painting workshop for pregnant mothers. The center's New Age approach to humanized birth commodifies and juxtaposes homeopathic remedies, with workshops on the midwife's "magic," and groups that celebrate women's bodies and maternity.

Montserrat guided me into a side room where we could have an intimate conversation. With her long, dark-blonde hair and bright blue eyes, she is a striking woman. She began to tell me her story: Montserrat, a native of Madrid, lived in Spain from the time of her birth until she went to the United States for college. As an undergraduate, she majored in anthropology, and subsequently she earned a master's degree in public health. She began informal midwifery training at a clinic in Guatemala before apprenticing at CASA with the internist and professional midwives. Then Montserrat went to New Orleans, where she participated in home births with "urban hippies" and "rural Christians."

It is worth mentioning that "urban hippies" and "rural Christians" are two very distinct groups originating in the United States that, despite their shared enthusiasm for humanized birth, do not overlap in the least. Furthermore, although some humanized-birth proponents in Mexico would not take offense at being described as "urban hippies" and even use "hippie" as a term to describe themselves, it is important to point out that these American categories do not map directly onto humanized birth in Mexico. That is to say, Christian practices and what it means to be a "hippie" have different roots in the United States than they do in Mexico.

At the time of the interview, Montserrat was working with the Red Cross and running her own alternative-birth center in Chiapas. Her international training evidences her heightened mobility and is a source of accrued cultural capital. As a transnational figure, she represents a conduit for Mexican clients to European and North American spaces where "whiter" pregnant women are the recipients of similar professional midwifery practices. In this way, Montserrat connects her clients to a transnational community of global professional couples who seek unity through consumption of birthing methods understood as modern because of their traditionality.

Montserrat expressed to me how exasperated she feels by contradictions in the Mexican health system and obstacles she has faced as a result of her transnational training. She studied midwifery online and is a certified nurse midwife; however, the International Confederation of Midwives does not recognize her certification, and she is not licensed to practice midwifery in Mexico. Although she is not certified or licensed, her alternative-birth center was granted a Health Establishment Code by the Mexican government, allowing her to sign and complete birth certificates. However, professional Mexican midwives who are certified and licensed do not have access to such a code. Also, indigenous women can be certified as "traditional midwives" if they demonstrate specific competencies. Yet when Montserrat approached government officials requesting to be certified as a traditional midwife, she was rejected on the basis of her race— only indigenous women can be traditional midwives, she was told. Montserrat realized that "indigeneity" is collapsed with "traditionality" in the figure of the traditional midwife, thus disabling her from obtaining government permission to practice midwifery under the rubric of "tradition-ality" in Mexico. Although Montserrat strives to make claims to "tradi-tionality," she is racially identified in a way that precludes her from being recognized as a traditional midwife. This disjuncture points to the syn-cretic nature of intersectional racialization processes—Montserrat's de-sire to be included as a *partera Mexicana* (a Mexican midwife) is overshad-owed by the European identity that others locate within her.

I asked Montserrat what the difference is between professional and traditional midwives. "I [practice midwifery] in a Western way," she an-swered. Montserrat's assertion that "the precedent depends on where you were born," emphasizes how race, class, education, and the color of one's passport (and whether one has a passport at all) are collapsed into a multi-variate social gradient that differentiates some birth attendants from oth-ers. However, Montserrat's attention to differences in origin between tra-ditional and professional midwives does not extend to a critical reflection on the socioeconomic and racial grades among professional midwives (see Nestel 2006). For example, when Flor, a CASA-trained professional mid-wife, was pregnant with her first child, she began looking for a profes-sional midwife to attend her birth. Flor considered Montserrat, but as a Mexican woman and the wife of a carpenter, there was no way she could pay the 18,000 pesos (about US$1,440) Montserrat charges.

On the topic of traditional midwives, Montserrat pointed to how these midwives possess varying levels of skill and experience. "The problem with traditional midwifery is that all traditional midwives are thrown in the same boat." As a result, skilled midwives who have accrued lots of ex-perience safely attending births but lack formal academic training are placed under the same rubric by government programs and hospital phy-sicians with midwives who do not know how to safely manage drugs, lead-ing to the overuse of oxytocin injections, the untimely transfer of dystocic mothers to hospitals, and infant deaths.

Montserrat offered Yanira as an example of a very capable and knowl-edgeable traditional midwife who is well known in Mexican humanized-birth circles and who regularly attends international midwifery confer-ences. "Yanira is a traditional midwife, but she could definitely pass a [professional midwifery] certification exam. However, one of the things the Mexican Midwifery Association decided is that professional midwives and traditional midwives cannot be treated the same way." Montserrat's comments opened a space for me to ask probing questions about poten-tial "neocoloniality" (harking back to Sagrario's observation) embedded within the Mexican Midwifery Association's organizational structure. The

Midwifery Association, led by an obstetric nurse who apprenticed with Yanira, has stated that traditional midwives cannot be inducted into its professional guild until they have successfully completed an accredited course of academic study, irrespective of empirical experience. The association's inclusion of birth attendants who lack licensure, recognition from the International Confederation of Midwives, and in the case of the association's president, any academic study of midwifery is a contradiction that bolsters Montserrat's claim that "traditional" and "professional" are respectively collapsed onto indigeneity and whiteness in ways that reinscribe inequality.

A deeply self-reflexive person, Montserrat has struggled to define and negotiate her place along this disparate racial spectrum. As the founder of an alternative-birth center, Montserrat worked in a small indigenous village for five years training traditional midwives. However, after five years she decided to evaluate her own "savior syndrome" and to discontinue her involvement in the village in favor of focusing all of her energies on prenatal education and private midwifery care in the urban center. She said, "Who am I? I have never lived in a [village]." She expressed her anxiety about NGOs that work in villages because, from her perspective, their interactions with villagers represent "a type of colonialism." She admitted to me that the language barrier between her and "non-Spanish speakers" also led her to rethink her role as a leader of midwifery training workshops. (Interestingly, Montserrat signals indigenous midwives' inability to speak Spanish instead of her inability to speak indigenous languages [see Molina 2006].) Over the course of my ethnographic research, I found that Montserrat's experience is not unique. As my fieldwork progressed, humanized birth became a critical lens for evaluating the challenges to achieving "interculturality" in Mexico, despite its ubiquitous incorporation in public health and development rhetoric.

One such challenge is economic capital. Montserrat explained to me that in Mexico, there are a lot of "hippie doulas"—"all those women who drink their menstrual blood"—who could better serve pregnant women as professional midwives; but in Mexico, you have to have money to become a professional midwife. This is especially true since a lot of upper-class Mexican women who aspire to professional midwifery attend midwifery school in El Paso, Texas, thus forgoing licensure in Mexico (Paula is one example).

Furthermore, she cast professional midwives as feminist agents of change. She opined that professional midwives in Mexico must be independent and rebellious. "We couldn't care less about the Secretariat of

Health's norms." According to Montserrat, those who are not sufficiently independent and rebellious disappear from professional midwifery, including those who have completed a full course of academic study such as the one offered at CASA—they get married and become homemakers, or they become nurses or physicians, or they do other things. While listening to her speak, I recognized that the "independent" and "rebellious" qualities she was describing are not simply characteristics of individuals but also a luxury afforded to those with racial and economic privilege. She concluded by saying, "[B]eing a professional midwife is a hard job." I agree, but I repetitively observed over the course of my fieldwork that professional midwifery is a "hard job" delimited by racializing logics of inclusion/exclusion.

My research analyzes how the remaking anew of tradition—the return to "traditional" birthing arts (home birth, midwife-assisted birth, water birth, "natural" birth)—has resulted in the commodification of indigenous culture and the re-inscription of racial inequalities. At the same time, this movement has also led to the inadvertent reconfiguring of parent-child bonds in ways that again place the burden of correctly producing future bioconsumers on women's shoulders, despite feminist rhetoric about women's liberation from (masculine) biomedical hegemony. I focus on the extremes of contemporary Mexican society—disenfranchised indigenous families and members of the global meritocracy. On the one hand, indigenous recipients of conditional cash transfers must demonstrate obedience to multiple government mandates. For them, full biological citizenship is always just out of reach. On the other hand, the privileged do not position themselves as citizens through claims to public resources; instead, they accumulate cultural capital through privatized services. Through an examination of intersectional racialization processes and patterns of bioconsumption, my ethnography unfolds at the edges of citizenship, thus making a case for the consideration of the bioconsumer. For these individuals, market-based consumption of medical services plays a formative role in how their identities are syncretically portrayed and perceived. The main stakes of bioconsumption are the presentation of self and accrual of cultural capital.

Moreover, I demonstrate how what is under negotiation in the alternative-birth movement is the social-moral body onto which identities get mapped. Close ethnographic study reveals how the so-called humanization of birth and the reduction of maternal and infant mortality are distant projects that are collapsed onto one another and produce an emerging ideology of "good parenthood." In this ideology, children represent parents' stake in the contemporary global meritocracy. This work therefore uncovers how traditional ways of birthing are being destroyed and reinvented through intersectional privilege, which is based on a model of neoliberal consumption that simultaneously promotes "humanity" and reinforces inequality by infusing transnational movements with reified understandings of gender, class, and race. I thus consider Mexican traditional midwifery a unique lens for examining how indigeneity becomes an object of consumption via ethnomedical piracy within a transnational racialized economy.

I use ethnographic evidence to demonstrate how inclusion in global meritocracies is mediated by intersectional racialization processes, resulting in claims to cultural capital and "social whitening" on a global stage. I describe how colonial legacies continue to shape identity formation and point to how intersectional identities are relationally constructed and negotiated, and operationalized transnationally with important political and economic effects. Nonindigenous individuals seek inclusion in global "white" communities oriented around commodified forms that conflate "indigeneity" with "traditionality" and "nature"; however, these communities do not unseat deep social inequalities between nonindigenous and indigenous people. More specifically, parents and families form groups oriented around a particular type of birth—their participation in these groups, which often reiterate discourse originating in the Global North and connect them to a transnational movement, is an expression of how patterns of consumption and "social whitening" operate in tandem. Thus, strategies developed in the Global North for the humanization of birth and the reduction of maternal and infant mortality are inadvertently reproducing processes of gendered racialization and reinscribing inequality between global "whites" and indigenous people. My work underlines how neoliberal consumption in the twenty-first century simultaneously promotes "humanity" *and* reinforces inequality by infusing transnational movements with reified logics of intersectional racialization.

In writing this book, I have tried to make the following interventions:

First, I have described intersectional racialization processes while critiquing the ways in which the global alternative-birth movement inadvertently appropriates and commodifies indigenous culture. When "indigeneity" is invoked in the realm of so-called humanized birth, the object is fetishized, separated entirely from its cultural, socioeconomic, and geographical context, and repackaged for mass consumption. Instead of directing attention to the body-turned-merchandise (e.g., organ trafficking and surrogacy, see Scheper-Hughes and Wacquant 2006), I used the example of midwifery in Mexico to examine racialized identities-turned-merchandise, with real effects for the bodies of women. Building upon studies that explore the political economy of the body under contemporary global capitalism, I employed a transnational context to analyze the political economy of identities vis-à-vis the body.

Second, I have complicated some of the notions of feminist liberation by asking how humanized birth may be the first step within a new intersectionally racialized regime of pressures and "requirements" presented by modern-day "good parenting." I have resisted viewing children only as commodities; however, I do argue that children represent parents' stake in our contemporary meritocracy—a system that naturalizes extreme inequality by allowing us to believe in democratic structures and the idea that education and proper preparation will open doors for children to a brilliant future. Also, I have suggested that the pressure of meritocracy pushes back into the womb. The difference between a privatized and public childhood begins in vitro with prenatal care.[1]

Third, I have examined the disparate and unequal distribution of "traditional" and ethnomedical forms of "natural" birth among racially stratified social collectivities. This book has examined the mobility of humanized-birth practitioners and participants who travel across borders to contribute to ideology and practices being produced transnationally, while comparatively immobile women are socially situated in ways that preclude their participation in medical migrations (see Roberts and Scheper-Hughes 2011). I have provided detailed ethnographic examples of how humanized birth is reshaped and reconstituted in sites that bear stark contrast to the social and geographic locations where the humanized-birth model was originally produced.

Finally, I have disrupted notions of citizenship-making by placing under the same lens those for whom citizenship is always just out of reach and those for whom citizenship is not a primary concern. The latter group's privileged access to privatized markets allows for a transnational existence. Given these examples, how might we rethink the relationship between neoliberal citizenship and consumerism? This ethnography contributes to emerging literature that rethinks states as the consolidation of territory and government, thus opening up other ways of conceptualizing polity and geography. In doing so, this book challenges Foucault's 1978 framing of biopolitics. I have used the topic of birth to provide ethnographic evidence of how biopower is not only imposed by states upon citizen-subjects, but also by powerful, extragovernmental, social and economic forces operating in the context of neoliberalism, thus resulting in real material consequences and shaping health outcomes.

This book is not a celebration of humanized birth. However, the humanization of birth is a valuable project. I do not want my work to undermine the many important efforts to de-medicalize women's birthing experiences and reduce the effects of obstetric violence. Nor do I wish to minimize the amount of love and care the parents I describe have for their children. The women whom I interviewed participate in humanized birth because they are committed to giving their children the best opportunities in life, starting with how they are born. Although I strongly agree with the de-medicalization of birth, this book does not focus on crafting a normative argument that assigns value judgments to different birthing practices. Rather, I am engaging in an analytic endeavor that uses intersectional racialization processes unfolding through the humanized-birth movement as a lens for examining pressing anthropological issues: the commodification of culture, unintended effects of feminist liberation, and the limits of citizenship in our neoliberal world.

Including full-time fieldwork and teaching and research engagements in the Mexican academy, I spent three years and seven months in Mexico, during which time I became very close to a number of informants and colleagues. I consider some of my former informants to be good friends and have maintained contact, drawing from their "organic intellectualism" (see Gramsci 1989 [1971]) when analyzing the wealth of ethnographic material I accumulated. Since concluding fieldwork, I have included informants-turned-friends in important life events such as my wedding. Likewise, the continuity of my professional engagements with Mexican colleagues post-research has resulted in bilingual and Spanish-language publications in Mexican journals, co-authorship of an English-language article, a temporary teaching appointment at UNAM, and collaborative conference presentations in the United States and Latin America. These relationships have been formative on both personal and intellectual levels, and the lessons I have learned are woven into the fabric of my analysis.

Disrupting Notions of Time and Progress: Binational, Bilingual, Bilateral Discourse

Reproduction and reproductive technologies form a crucial site for examining how people identify and represent themselves as "modern" individuals.[2] My work inverts the relationship between birth and "modernity" that is expressed in Cecilia Van Hollen's 2003 study of lower-class women's childbirth experiences and decision-making processes in South India. Furthermore, "the modern" is always evolving, yet it is always relationally defined by what is considered "traditional," and whether "tradition" is assigned a negative connotation or is romanticized and exalted (see Bauman and Briggs 2003).

In this book, I have tried to push beyond the false "modernity"-"traditionality" dichotomy to ask what can be learned from examining *emergent* traditionalities. That is to say, the book asks how couples identify themselves as modern subjects through a "return" to "traditional" ways of birthing, thus disrupting the Euro-American ontologies of time. What is revealed about the reproduction of social inequity when "traditional" methods of human reproduction are used to question the linearity of progress and the binary nature of modernity-traditionality? Instead of thinking about time in terms of rupture, this book asks: What can be gleaned from an ethnographic analysis of instances where the chronology appears to be reversed, and through a binational reading of anthropological literature (for example, considering Néstor Garcia Canclini's work in conjunction with that of US anthropologists)?

My research has been a double engagement: I performed ethnography in Mexico, and, as a visiting scholar at the Center for Superior Research and Studies in Social Anthropology (CIESAS) and professor at the National Autonomous University of Mexico (UNAM), I engaged in theoretical and methodological debates occurring in Mexico. One goal of my research is to transform how US academics think about gendered racialization, citizenship, and consumption through dialogue with Mexico, while considering how exportation of theory from the Global North to Latin America results in ideas being fractured, recast, and made more complex by Latin American theorists. Mexico has a critical scholarly tradition and is an ideal place to do transformative research, because of the insights of social-medicine scholars such as Asa Cristina Laurell,[3] critical epidemiologists such as Jaime Breilh,[4] and, of course, anthropologists Eduardo L. Menéndez[5] and Néstor García Canclini.[6] I have attempted to construct an interdisciplinary conversation between scholarship in the North and scholarship in Mexico, thus producing a mutual dialogue instead of an Anglocentric reading of theory.

Bilateral discursive engagement helps to conscientiously dismantle colonial legacies embedded in US academia. Also, unidirectional flow of frames of reference from the North to Mexico has had a profound impact on public-health policy in Mexico (see Menéndez 2009). By engaging with frames of reference from both North and South, US health scientists can begin to apply Mexican theory to Mexican policy. This type of dialogue across borders not only helps to dismantle the discursive structure through which health sciences in the North position themselves as the primary or exclusive place to cite theory, but it points to the richness of different academic disciplines around the world, and the immense knowledge and diversity of perspectives that can be gleaned and produced by participating in a truly transnational dialogue about theory. As a dual US-Mexico citizen, an ethnographer with significant research experience in Mexico, and an interdisciplinary scholar trained in the United States and engaged in theory on both sides of the border, I aim to enact "border thinking" (see Mignolo 2000) to increase dialogue among global anthropologies.

In this book's final refrain, I have drawn from binational discourse (the travel of theoretical concepts and frames of reference across national, linguistic, and academic boundaries [both apparent and obscure]) in order to analyze the time travel (between "traditional" and "modern" modes) and space travel (across Mexican states, and from the Global North to the Global South) that racialized parents and birth attendants undertake, and to observe how this physical mobility translates into social mobility in neoliberal meritocracies through incipient notions of moral superiority.

Time Travel: "Traditional Birth" in the New Age Marketplace

In this book, I have argued that what humanized-birth proponents describe as an international feminist liberation for educated women is based on the exploitation of cultural-intellectual property rights of traditional midwives and the reproduction of inequality in Mexico. Thus, my work not only uncovers the clash between commodified New Age forms and traditional practices but also highlights how intersecting forms of social inequality are actually reinforced and reinscribed by New Age ideologies that are purportedly value-inclusive and promote "humanity." I am concerned with how desire among the "global professional class" (see Sharpe 2003) for "going back to nature" and "traditional ways of birthing" reinforces socioeconomic stratification and processes of racialization in the name of humanization and commodifies culture under the guise of rejecting consumption.

In the context of traditional midwifery in Mexico, traditional midwives are excluded from practicing in hospitals. Some regions do offer certification for traditional midwives, but the exam-based evaluations pose a virtually impossible obstacle for traditional midwives with limited formal schooling. As Alyshia Gálvez describes (see Gálvez 2011:75), traditional midwives face legal problems if they practice without certification, and as a result, many have been forced to cease practicing. Whereas traditional midwives are largely excluded as participants in the commodity chain, their image is usurped, commodified, overlaid on "traditional" services and goods, and sold. My argument is not about the "large-scaling" of traditional midwifery—rather, I am diagnosing the (false) appropriation of traditional midwifery, the commodification of indigeneity, and the exclusion of traditional indigenous midwives.

In Mexico, tradition is remade "anew" through New Age iterations of humanized birth. In addition, as humanized-birth practitioners and traditional-birth attendants come into contact during training workshops, conferences, and fairs, a reordering of "tradition" and "progress" is challenging Euro-American ontologies of time. Although this has led to a change in how indigeneity is imagined and desired by nonindigenous individuals, it has translated into material differences for only a few specific indigenous participants and has failed to disrupt the undergirding racial hierarchies rooted in colonial legacies.

Examples of this complex relationship between emergent traditionalities and the commodification of indigeneity under the New Age paradigm are many. In Guerrero, Dr. Gilberto Aguilar, a health official within the state-level Secretariat of Health, told me that his office aspires to be the "pioneers" of vertical-birth positions in Mexico. For him, going back to birth postures regularly assumed by women before the biomedical naturalization of the lithotomy position (lying on one's back, feet in stirrups) is a strategic way for the state of Guerrero, a state among the poorest nationwide with respect to health indicators, to identify itself as a leader in modernity and progress through corporal techniques that have been "scientifically proven in the First World." In the context of de-medicalization, modernity is aligned with "ancestral knowledge."

Meanwhile, for Doña Eugenia's indigenous clients, modernity is sought through medicalization and pharmaceuticalization. These women avoid interacting with hospital staff because of previous experiences of racial discrimination and seek out Doña Eugenia's services over other local traditional midwives because of her skillful placement of an IV drip during the labor process, her administration of an intravenous vitamin solution during the recovery period, and her extensive in-home pharmacy of pills promising quicker results than traditional herbal remedies (see Friedlander 1975).

Doña Eugenia also offers herbal treatments, but even these services are

Figure 6.1. Doña Eugenia preparing an IV to administer postnatal vitamin solution

sufficiently "modern" since she does not rely solely on traditional knowledge passed down through the generations; rather, she studies texts produced by the University of Chapingo that catalog the effectiveness of herbs based on clinical and laboratory studies. In doing so, Doña Eugenia is drawing from academic expertise produced at an institution that groups traditional and alternative medicines in New Age fashion: herbalism, the therapeutic uses of *temascal,* and healing massage are taught alongside African traditional medicine, Chinese medicine and acupuncture, Ayurvedic medicine, biomagnetism, and homeopathy. Thus, for Doña Eugenia's clients, modernity is achieved through being cared for as modern beings.

The complex and, at times, contradictory perspectives of Dr. Aguilar and Doña Eugenia's clients are not unique by any means. A prominent humanized obstetrician in Guadalajara and a handful of his clients are featured in a French documentary on birth practices around the world. For this obstetrician, humanized birth is part of a greater movement toward natural and ecological living. He not only wants to help women become more in tune with their bodies, but he himself wants to become more in tune with the earth through sustainable farming and raising livestock. Nearby, a Colombian nurse-turned-midwife uses "traditional" Mexican rituals, *temascal,* dance circles, and herbs with her transnational clients. In Tepoztlán, Yanira[7] combines acupuncture with the traditional midwifery techniques that piqued the interest of American filmmakers who documented her work. A transnational organization in Monterrey, Nuevo León, offers transcendental yoga, chiropractic treatments, and humanized-birth services alongside "ancestral" baking classes. In a private Mexico City hospital dedicated to "natural" healing and minimal intervention, the highest technology from around the world is combined with a dedication to organic living.

My perspective on the rupture and reordering of existing Euro-American ontologies of time responds to phenomena similar to those observed by Robbie Davis-Floyd in her discussion of "postmodern" midwifery, but my interpretation bares stark contrast. For Davis-Floyd, "postmodern" midwifery is a productive combination of elements from traditional midwifery and modern-day obstetrics (see Davis-Floyd 2007). That is, the "postmodern midwife" merges techniques from past and present in a way that benefits birthing mothers. Whereas Davis-Floyd views the interpenetration of traditionality and modernity as having a positive impact on women's births, my book reframes the question entirely. I am less concerned with making value judgments about humanized birth as a potential paradigm shift in obstetrics and more concerned with the racialization, politics of portrayal, and socioeconomic inequalities that it often buttresses and masks. I am not disputing that the humanization of birth and reduction of obstetric violence are valuable projects, but I ask, in practice, who have these projects benefited?

Although the humanized-birth movement has facilitated access to demedicalized birth in the private sector for the global professional class, traditional midwives face government-sanctioned limitations on their work. The current nationwide health policy dictates that all births take place in hospital settings; however, I discovered a great deal of regional variability between policy and practice. In some places, indigenous midwives and mothers use subversive strategies to seek the midwife-attended births they desire. In other places, indigenous women seek "modernity" through biomedical births and are actively turning away from traditional midwifery (see Van Hollen 2003 and Smith-Oka 2013). In still other places, traditional midwives have transitioned to the role of contraception advocates in order to prevent being held criminally accountable for maternal mortality but nonetheless continue to be blamed for negative birth outcomes. In other regions, traditional midwifery is framed by NGO workers and members of the community as a response to inadequate health infrastructure in the state. Elsewhere, midwives have ceded births to hospital staff but regularly provide prenatal care and provide mothers with guidance that often takes precedence when these women make their reproductive decisions.

In Veracruz, midwives contend that the distance to the nearest hospital from their rural communities, combined with irregular transportation, makes it impossible for many births to be attended in hospitals, resulting in their moral obligation to attend births when they are already unfolding. However, their argument is met with further, unwritten measures attempting to curtail the practice of traditional midwifery. At a training workshop, I listened as traditional midwives complained to the regional hospital director about difficulties obtaining birth certificates for the babies they had delivered. Some were even being charged a fee by corrupt hospital administrators for birth certificates that are officially free of charge.

Despite attempted censure of traditional midwifery, in some municipalities across Veracruz, midwives are interpellated by government officials to perform unpaid duties as community health workers and contraception advocates (see Pigg 1997, 2001). One traditional midwife maintains a positive relationship with the medical intern in her village by submitting to his "supervision." Although he is still a student and she has attended thousands of births, she turns in a weekly report tallying the number of home visits she has performed, how many hospital references she has made, and how many women she has convinced to use contraceptive methods. I witnessed noticeable absences in her report—that is, she prepares herbal remedies and attends births for her fellow villagers, but these midwifery activities are not included in the report. Nonetheless, it is worthwhile for her to continue to deliver her weekly report to the medical intern because, in exchange for her submission to his "supervision," he turns a blind eye to her practice of midwifery. At the same time, her ongoing provisioning of midwifery minimizes his need to intervene in obstetric and gynecological cases, freeing him from potential accusations of molesting the village women and violent backlash were he to incur a negative birth outcome. Thus, although their performative relationship seems characterized by submission to biomedical authority, the midwife and the intern are complicit partners—he silently supports her as she fulfills her role in the community, and she frees him from his anxiety-provoking obligation to intervene.

The way the indigenous bodies of Oportunidades-receiving women are racialized is not dissimilar to what Bridges observed during her 2011 ethnography of Medicaid-insured women in New York City. Their situation is also strikingly similar to John O'Neil and Patricia Leyland Kaufert's 1995 description of the racialization of Inuit women's physiology and their births. Oportunidades mandates systematized intrusion into women's private lives, thus producing pregnancy as a gateway for state regulation of poor women. Furthermore, the bodies of Oportunidades enrollees are racialized when they are cast as "unruly" and "high risk," thus meriting heightened medicalization. Among impoverished indigenous women in Mexico, "racial folklore," deracialized racial discourse, and racism among physicians increase health disparities.

The official story in the High Mountains of Veracruz is that the women in this community are giving birth "alone" in their homes because their indigenous physiology and broader hips lead to speedy births that make it impossible for them to arrive on time. In this way, Nahua women recruit "racial folklore" and use it to serve their interests. This type of community-wide secrecy is not unique to Veracruz. I interviewed traditional midwives and indigenous mothers in the mountains of Guerrero and though traditional midwives tell officials they are not attending births in that region, it is not uncommon for women to give birth "alone." One mother told me that she gave birth "alone" to eleven children, and each time, the birth was so swift that she could not make it to the hospital.

In Oaxaca, the threat of financial loss has not been sufficient to ensure that women attend all their prenatal visits, so the Secretariat of Health has instituted an "Obstetric Godmothers Program" (Programa de Madrinas Obstétricas), thus adding a financial incentive for female members of the community to ensure that their pregnant neighbors attend all required prenatal consults. After her contract ended at the Center for Gender Equity and Reproductive Health, Sagrario accepted a position within the Guerrero Secretariat of Health. From her post, she proposed that instead of paying stipends to lay women to ensure that pregnant women comply with biomedical mandates as in the neighboring state of Oaxaca, traditional midwives in Guerrero who pass a certification process should be paid monthly stipends for their midwifery work. Shortly thereafter, Sagrario began focusing her energies on the freshly inaugurated professional midwifery school in Tlapa, Guerrero, leading her away from advocacy for the practice of traditional midwifery. Since the conclusion of my fieldwork, another professional midwifery school modeled after CASA has opened in the state of Oaxaca, thereby strengthening the strategy of professional midwifery in the region.

In Chiapas, traditional midwives spoke openly to me about their practice of midwifery, and mothers were forthcoming about choosing to have a traditional midwife attend their births instead of trekking to a distant hospital that is often overcrowded, understaffed, and lacking medical supplies. One mother told me that even though the Oportunidades program requires her to go to prenatal consults, this has no effect on the prenatal care she receives from the midwife she trusts. While she relies on the knowledge of the midwife to make decisions about her pregnancy, physicians at the government clinic remain totally unaware that she is receiving ongoing midwifery care. Concurrent prenatal care with traditional midwives is a common omission in clinical settings. In Chiapas, traditional midwives do not act as hospital referralists at the service of the state; however, their active role is not often officially acknowledged. The ambivalent relationship between traditional midwives and clinical care providers is mediated by Global Pediatric Alliance, an NGO based in San Francisco, California. Global Pediatric Alliance's binational team negotiates with government leaders on behalf of traditional midwives.

In Quintana Roo, virtually all births take place in hospital settings, very few traditional midwives continue to attend births, and the population adheres to the national policy. Traditional midwives in Quintana Roo are frequent recipients of workshops, credentials, and certificates, but one midwife complained to me that the result of all of this "training" has been their conversion into contraception *promotoras* (health promoters). She commented, "We are the social workers outside of the hospital. There are no rights for *indígenas*." She complained that despite generalized compliance with government mandates and attendance at relentless social-worker-led training sessions, traditional midwives are still the scapegoats for maternal mortality in the state. In the process, multiple measures of inequality and related risk factors for maternal mortality are obscured.

Throughout my ethnographic fieldwork, I noticed that the regional variability of restrictions placed upon traditional midwifery practice stems from content differences among the training workshops that traditional midwives receive. In states like Veracruz, Guerrero, and Quintana Roo, traditional midwives are instructed to refer birthing mothers to the nearest hospital, but in the Huasteca region of San Luis Potosí state, traditional midwives are "medicalized," instructed not to use herbal remedies, and taught to perform an episiotomy during all of the births they attend.

Space Travel: Transnationalism in the Humanized-Birth Movement

Humanized birth in Mexico is the result of the transnational flow of ideas, people, and practices. But to what degree are comparisons of professional midwifery and alternative birth in Mexico and in the developed world meaningful and informative? Given that such comparisons can be made, what are they informative about? In Chiapas, I interviewed Ximena González, the local director of Global Pediatric Alliance. In her opinion, when people use Chilean professional midwives as an example of how professional midwifery can be transformative for women's health through marked reduction in maternal and infant health problems, their argument does not take into account the political, economic, and social realities of Mexico. According to Ximena, it is impossible to compare the successful impact of professional midwifery in Chile on maternal and infant health with how professional midwifery is unfolding in Mexico because of their distinct contexts.

I agree with Ximena in that strategies for ameliorating negative health outcomes in one nation will not produce the same results in another nation if they are applied wholesale—for professional midwifery to result in a similar reduction in maternal mortality in Mexico, a number of adaptations accounting for georacial and socioeconomic differences must be made to the Chilean model. However, I am more concerned with asking why these comparisons are being made. Such comparisons are born of lingering and consequential aspirations of modernity and "whiteness," and a desire to be aligned with whiter, more developed countries.

During that same trip, I visited an organization of traditional indigenous medicine doctors and midwives, where I interviewed the director and several members of the staff. At the time of my visit, some traditional midwives from the association were on a trip to Germany, where they had been invited by a group of obstetricians and professional midwives to appear at a conference. The organization has very limited funding, and its members' lives are marked by poverty. In this book, I have explored how the image of indigeneity is fetishized in international forums and have argued that in many cases, this celebration of "ancestral knowledge" and "humanization" is ironically and, at times, unwittingly rooted in notions of racial hierarchy that in effect reify and reinscribe race-based inequality. Through ethnographic examples, I have suggested that this decontextualization and appropriation of indigenous peoples' images is articulated in multiple and complex ways: some indigenous individuals feel objectified; others engage with transnational politics of representation, using their indigeneity as a resource through which to achieve various sorts of recognition that are meaningful to them, despite continued economic scarcity; and still others leverage their identities with lucrative results, leading to violent backlash from their communities.

In essence, I point to the simultaneous fetishization of "indigeneity" and silencing/surveilling of indigenous people and their practices; however, I also emphasize the agency and dynamism with which indigenous people engage the commodification of their culture. In doing so, I draw attention to a mix of exploitation and entrepreneurship that throws into question dichotomous notions of victor and victim. When thinking about ethnomedical tourism, I am simultaneously pointing to how the commodification of "indigeneity" collapses multiple ways of being indigenous and repackages them for mass consumption, and also how tourism could potentially revitalize and invigorate individuals' pride in their culture.

Beyond Citizenship: Moral Superiority in Neoliberal Meritocracies

This has been a story about travelers and non-travelers. I have developed the parenthetical concept of (im)mobility to signal how mobility can result in immobility, and conversely, how immobility can produce mobility (i.e., Adeli and Yanira, respectively). Beyond that, I have examined often concomitant relationships between physical and social mobility. Where others have used a human rights framework to write about mobility as a privilege for tourists and expatriates on the one hand, and a stigma for undocumented migrants on the other (see Andersson 2014), I have placed individuals with disparate degrees of mobility (along with divergent socioeconomic and georacial positionalities) under the same lens to problematize the appropriateness of citizenship as an analytic in globalized neoliberal contexts. My ethnographic research unfolded within a context of privatization of (ethno)medical services, leading me to observe the decentering of citizenship as the most appropriate category for analysis. At stake is the relationship between states and individuals who, by reconstituting citizen and consumer subjectivities, are challenging anthropological notions of how biopower operates.

My ethnographic observations of humanized birth across Mexico provided many similarities to Roberts' description of cesarean section in Ecuador. Although these birthing methods are seemingly "opposite," they are imbued with synonymous meanings in their respective contexts. Ecuadorian women pay to have their bodies cut because this transforms them into more desirable, whiter beings. Women are not seeking citizenship, since in Ecuador, citizenship in the medical realm is denigrated. Instead, the scar evidences the woman's ability to stand apart from the governed masses who need to make citizenship claims to state institutions for social services (on surveillance, see Gordon 1988 and Foucault 1990 [1978]). These scars enact a racialized relationship to the nation and effectively whiten women, as browner bodies are cast as able to withstand vaginal birth within public maternity care. As an intersectional scholar, my reading of Roberts' work is that cesarean scars also mark mothers seeking *privatized* care as *women*. That is, the cesarean scar serves as an embodied intersection of superior race, higher class, and feminized gender. Building upon Roberts' work, I have considered the role of citizenship in relation to transnational communities of bioconsumption, and have observed how, in lieu of a physical scar marking women's bodies, cultural capital gleaned from practicing a certain type of birth is mapped onto moral bodies.

My perspective draws from and simultaneously resists both Rose and Novas' interpretation of Petryna's biological citizenship and García Canclini's consumer citizenship. Nikolas Rose and Carlos Novas (2008) broaden Petryna's notion of biological citizenship by pointing to new forms of identity and morality created along with novel transnational citizenship projects. Similarly, I point to the transnational moral communities to which parents in the Global South seek membership, inclusion, and belonging. In the same vein as Rose and Novas, I assert that what is at stake is not necessarily material, economic, or medical resources, but, rather, claims to cultural capital through production of new identities and novel moral scales. Individuals who identify with the humanized-birth movement and practice natural, home and/or water birth, skin-to-skin contact with the newborn, and extended breastfeeding consider themselves better parents and affirm their children are more emotionally balanced, self-assured, and intelligent. However, I resist Rose and Novas' suggestions regarding the partial delinking of citizenship and nation since broadening the notion of citizenship to include transnational social networks runs the risk of stripping citizenship of its essential meaning and depleting its analytical usefulness.

By bringing Latin American (and especially Mexican) scholarship to bear on the concept of biological citizenship, I draw attention to the roles consumerism, socioeconomic class, and representations originating in the Global North play in the construction of global, biological, consumption-oriented communities. Néstor García Canclini argues that while citizenship used to signify equality of abstract rights and collective participation in public democratic spaces, nowadays questions of belonging, information, and representation are answered in the realm of private consumption and mass media—effectively rendering citizens of the eighteenth century into consumers of the twentieth (or twenty-first) century. Identity is now configured by consumption—how much one possesses and is capable of appropriating. Thus, according to García Canclini, the neoliberal conception of globalization reserves the right of being a citizen for elites.

García Canclini strongly implicates the United States in the global conversion to consumer citizenship. He suggests international uniformity, imposed by neoliberal planning "far away" (often originating in North America), has led to individuals feeling the only things accessible to them are goods and messages arriving to their homes, to use "as they see fit." The tastes and consumption patterns of audiences are often scripted in the United States—so much so that García Canclini calls identities "multimedia spectacles" and suggests Latin America and Europe are "suburbs" of Hollywood. In contrast to García Canclini's perspective on the US presence in Latin America, I point to the multiple imbrications of the Global North and global "whites" in shaping what is considered progressive and desirable in Mexico.

From my perspective, the fact that so much of contemporary social life is ordered by neoliberal patterns of consumption problematizes citizenship as an adequate explanatory concept for how individuals negotiate both transnational and locally situated inequalities in their everyday lives. During ethnographic research, I observed how bioconsumer citizens seek *inclusion* in global biological and consumerism-oriented communities rather than rights and resources from a particular nation or state.

At the same time, I resist a simple switch from the citizenship modality to the consumer modality because doing so would be overly reductive. Instead of discarding the concept of citizenship, I have tried to explore its limits and determine how and for whom it operates in our globalized world. Furthermore, I am not seeking out the limits of citizenship for its own sake. My conceptual project is not a border mapping of where the edge of citizenship and the frontier of consumption meet, but rather an examination of the productive elements of this friction. That is, what do the limits of citizenship and the increasing terrains engulfed by bioconsumption signal about shifts in the societal fabric and underlying values and aspirations? What do novel ways of constructing identity vis-à-vis the body indicate about desires to access transnational social networks through the global marketplace?

The humanized-birth proponents' project—to enact a feminized, moralized, "purified" motherhood—is a critique of García Canclini's description of consumption since it unfolds around a *moral* fluorescence and through *moral* spaces that allow ideologies to flow "freely." The goal of these aspirational mothers is not to have the most, but to be the best (see Currid-

Halkett 2017). It is not that the pathway to citizenship in neoliberal socie-
ties is through consumption (as García Canclini 2001 [1995] argues); rather,
cultural capital is earned by parents who set themselves apart as morally
superior in neoliberal meritocracies. However, my ethnographic analysis of
meritocratic aspirations has revealed a series of contradictions. I observed
neoliberal parenting in action, and the many ways neoliberal ideology re-
produces classism, gender inequality, and mother-blaming even as it casts
parents as expert consumers with many options from which to choose.

Final Notes on Travel: Reflections for Future Work

I conclude this book with reflections on how the lens of intersectional racialization processes—along with my perspectives on (im)mobility and
bioconsumption—can be leveraged to diagnose other manifestations
of social transition in different contexts. In this book I have provided a
framework for mapping physical mobility onto social mobility. I link
these (im)mobilities among the "global professional class" (Kapoor 2004)
to the partial decentering of the coinstantiation of territory and government. This rethinking of the relationship between polity and geography,
in turn, reframes anthropological notions of biopolitics since biopower is
not only exerted by governments upon citizen-subjects, but also by transnational social collectivities. In so doing, the utility of citizenship as a category for explaining how individuals gain entrance, access resources, and
construct identities is thrown into critical relief, thus opening up a way
to think about the productive ferments at the edge of citizenship and the
frontier of bioconsumption. This conceptual journey allows for the unrav-
eling of value-laden and morally infused threads in the globalized neoliberal fabric.

Examples abound. What do the medical migration patterns of Winter Texans to clinics in Northern Mexico reveal? What about medical migration in the reverse direction by Northern Mexicans to clinics in the
"Global North" just five miles beyond the US-Mexico border? What of the
(ethno)medical longings for traditional Chinese medicine in Chinatowns
throughout "the West" and even in Latin America? What are the social motivations behind the commodification of other (ethno)medical practices,
for example, New Age iterations of Ayurveda? What is uncovered by the
intersection of "indigenous" medicine and tourism in different contexts
around the globe, for example, shaman tourism, and ayahuasca retreats?
In which ways might the booming cosmetic-surgery industry in countries

such as Thailand reinscribe existing social inequality? What is the texture of relationships between hopeful parents from the Global North and the surrogates they employ in the Global South, and to what degree do these socioeconomically discordant relationships provide a framework for identity formation? How are the personal aspirations of those who are never quite citizens altered by the knowledge that one of their kidneys is living out life (sans the totality of the person it originated from) in a body marked by privilege?

These are only a small portion of the questions that can be investigated through the conceptual lens of intersectional racialization processes, and all have broader impacts beyond the academy. For example, what are the implications for global health policy? Furthermore, these are all potential examples of how (im)mobility and bioconsumption are, in themselves, intersectional racialization processes. This book is only the beginning of the story.

Notes

Introduction

1. This figure is taken from the Mexican Institute of Social Security (IMSS) website (imss.gob.mx) and its publication "Guía de Práctica Clínica: Vigilancia y manejo de parto. Evidencias y Recomendaciones. Catalogo Maestro de Guías de Práctica Clínica: IMSS-052–08."

2. Cinthya Sánchez, "En México, uno de cada dos niños hoy nace por cesárea," archivo.eluniversal.com.mx/cultura/63403.html, July 18, 2010, accessed September 21, 2014.

3. At the time of my writing, agreements are being drafted between the Center for the Adolescents of San Miguel de Allende (CASA) and officials in Veracruz and Chiapas proposing the opening of new professional midwifery schools modeled after, and administrated by, CASA. In 2016, a professional midwifery school modeled after and partially funded by CASA opened in the State of Guerrero. Also, in 2012 a state-funded professional midwifery school opened in Guerrero. The Guerrero school graduated its first cohort in June 2015.

4. See Marcus 1995, Menéndez 1996, Rapp 2000, and Wilson 2004.

5. Combining informal interviews, in-depth interviews, and people I have observed, there are 2,069 subjects included in this study, 967 of whom were observed in large group settings (training workshops, "pláticas," conferences, institutional meetings, etc.) and 1,094 of whom I observed on a more individual or family-level basis. Within my study are 111 professional midwives, 166 physicians, 288 traditional midwives, 65 nurses, 14 NGO administrators, 17 Secretary of Health administrators, 18 hospital administrators, 8 doulas, 5 promotores de salud (health promoters/community health workers), 12 prenatal educators, 7 medical school professors, 22 professional midwifery school instructors, 9 medical anthropologists, 11 people within the field of public health/public policy, 125 mothers (33 in the postpartum period, 17 in active labor, 7 births), 31 fathers, and 19 pregnant women. Geographically, I have observed 306 subjects in Guanajuato, 137 in Guerrero, 247 in Jalisco, 68 in the Federal District, 296 in San Luis Potosí, 700 in Veracruz, 85 in Chiapas, 72 in Oaxaca, 103 in Quintana Roo, 8 in Michoacán, 18 in Nuevo León, 7 in California (people who also work in Mexico), 3 in Mexico and the United States, 20 in multiple Mexican states, and 40 dispersed elsewhere.

6. See, for example, Davis-Floyd 2009, Katz Rothman 2007, MacDonald 2008, and Simonds 2007.

7. See Glenn 2002, Roberts 1997, Grzanka 2014, Crenshaw 2014, and Haraway 2014.

8. See "A Cosmopolitanism of Connections" (2010) by Craig Calhoun, and *Cosmopolitan Conceptions: IVF Sojourns in Global Dubai* (2015) by Marcia C. Inhorn. A useful source when thinking about how our lives and bodies are shaped by market forces is Joseph Dumit's *Drugs for Life: How Pharmaceutical Companies Define Our Health.*

9. Drawing from anthropologists Zuanilda Mendoza González (2010–2011), Setha Low and Denise Lawrence-Zúñiga (2002), Nancy Munn (1996), Miles Richardson (1982), and Marc Augé (1995); sociologist Zygmunt Bauman (1993) and John Urry (2007); geographers Liz Bondi, Mick Smith, and Joyce Davidson (2005), and Yi-Fu Tuan (2001); novelist Jamaica Kinkaid (2000); public-health scholar Ana Langer and psychologist Kathryn Tolbert (Langer and Tolbert 1996); and media analyst Joost Van Loon (2005), among others.

10. See, for example, Kim Tallbear's *Native American DNA: Tribal Belonging and the False Promise of Genetic Science;* Jenny Reardon's *Race to the Finish: Identity and Governance in the Age of Genomics;* Inhorn's *Cosmopolitan Conceptions;* and Sahra Gibbon, Mónica Sans, and Ricardo Ventura Santos' *Racial Identities, Genetic Ancestry, and Health in South America: Argentina, Brazil, Colombia, and Uruguay.*

11. See Roberts 2012a and 2012b, Montoya 2011, and de la Cadena 2000.

12. For example, Sesia 2007, and Pigg 1997, 2001.

13. See Lakoff 2005; Tsing 2000, 2005; Hannerz 1996; Kearney 1996; Appadurai 1996; and Ong 1999, 2003; Mignolo 2000.

Chapter 1: Commodifying Indigeneity

1. My translation, nanahtli.wordpress.com.

2. As of this writing, I have prepared an article that analyzes the social mechanisms undergirding corruption in the Mexican health care system. The article is tentatively titled "Blind Spot: Biopower, Public Secrecy, and Syndemic Vulnerability in Mexican Health Care Corruption."

3. See en.wikipedia.org/wiki/Capulálpam_de_M%C3%A9ndez. Alyshia Gálvez includes a photo of the center's *temascal* in her 2011 book, *Patient Citizens, Immigrant Mothers* (see p. 62). Capulálpam is a part of the Ixtlán de Juárez region, where Gálvez carried out a portion of her ethnographic research (see Gálvez 2011:14).

Chapter 2: Humanized Birth

1. Information in this paragraph was taken from a PowerPoint presentation Dr. Almaguer posted online: "Modelo de Atención Intercultural a las Mujeres en el Embarazo, Parto y Puerperio, con Perspectiva de Género," *gob.mx/cms/uploads /attachment/file/29343/GuiaImplantacionModeloParto.pdf.*

2. Personal communication with Sharon Bissell Sotelo, the director of the MacArthur Foundation's Mexico Office on September 6, 2013.

3. See the IMSS website (imss.gob.mx) and its publication "Guía de Práctica Clínica: Vigilancia y manejo de parto. Evidencias y Recomendaciones: Catalogo Maestro de Guías de Práctica Clínica" (IMSS-052-08). Also see Sánchez, "En México, uno de cada dos niños hoy nace por cesárea," archivo.eluniversal.com.mx /cultura/63403.html.

4. In this section, I highlight examples drawn from my own Facebook news-feed. Connecting with informants-turned-friends through Facebook and being exposed to their posts helped me to better understand the contours of the humanized-birth movement and its expectations. I obtained consent from all my informants for participant-observation and in-depth interviews; however, I did not subsequently request specific consent regarding social-media posts. Since social-media users routinely re-post others' posts, causing certain threads to "go viral," and since the viewer may only have access to the most recent (re)post because of privacy settings, it can be difficult to trace comments, images, and ideas back to their original author. Instead, I decided to de-identify all of the social-media examples in this chapter to the extent possible.

5. Described in further detail in Chapter 6.

6. See Melton 1990, Heelas 1996, Hanegraaff 2001, and Champion 1995.

7. For examples of the effects of New Age practices on the contemporary construction of identities, see Galinier 2008, Sarrazin 2008, and de la Peña 2002.

Chapter 3: Intersectionality

1. See, for example, Tallbear's *Native American DNA*, Reardon's *Race to the Finish*, Inhorn's *Cosmopolitan Conceptions*, and Gibbon, Sans, and Ventura Santos' *Racial Identities*.

2. Personal communication in March 2011 with Sagrario, general director of CASA at the time.

3. Personal correspondence with Sagrario, September 2011. At that point, Sagrario was the adviser for Mexico's National Center for Gender Equity and Reproductive Health, a sub-bureau of the Ministry of Health.

4. Armen Keteyian, "Mexican Murder Mystery: Three Americans Dead in Last Three Weeks," *CBS News*, February 15, 2011, April 2, 2011, cbsnews.com/8301-31727 _162-20032001-10391695.html.

5. See thestar.com/news/crime/2013/09/27/mexican_police_suspect_robbery _was_motive_in_brutal_beating_that_killed_canadian_artist.html.

Chapter 4: A Cartography of "Race" and Obstetric Violence

1. See Roberts 2015, Fraser 1995, Goldade 2007, Morgan and Roberts 2012, and Pashigian 2009.

2. See Douglass 2005, Horn 1994, Nouzeilles 2003, and Stepan 1991.

3. See Breilh 2003, 2008b; Laurell 1997, 2013; Laurell and López Arellano 1996; Waitzkin and Iriart 2000; and Waitzkin 2011.

4. See Pitt-Rivers 1973, Wade 1993, de la Cadena 1995, and Colloredo-Mansfeld 1998.

5. See de la Cadena 2000, Leinaweaver 2008, Hordge-Freeman 2015, Orlove 1998, and Smith 1996.

6. See Clark 1998 and Ewig 2010.

7. For more examples of how the Mexican government subjugates indigenous women and how, in turn, these women exercise subversive agency, see Chapter 1.

8. See, for example, L. M. Neufeld, "The Oportunidades Program and Child Growth: Mexico Perspectives," in V. R. Preedy, ed., *Handbook of Growth and Growth Monitoring in Health and Disease*, 1659–1671, link.springer.com/chapter/10.1007/978-1-4419-1795-9_100.

Conclusion

1. On the privatization of childhood and neoliberal parenting, see Lareau's *Unequal Childhoods: Class, Race, and Family Life*; Charis Thompson's "Three Times a Woman" and *Making Parents: The Ontological Choreography of Reproductive Technologies*; and Folbre's *Greed, Lust, and Gender: A History of Economic Ideas*.

2. See, for example, Rapp 2000, Roberts 2006, Martin 2001, and Van Hollen 2003.

3. See Laurell 1997; and Laurell and López Arellano 1996.

4. Although Breilh completed graduate studies in Mexico, he has returned to his natal country of Ecuador, where he teaches at la Universidad Andina Simón Bolivar. See Breilh 1998, 2003, and 2008a.

5. See Menéndez 1983, 1996, 2009, 2010.

6. García Canclini is originally from Argentina and is a professor at la Universidad Autónoma de México–Xochimilco. See García Canclini 2001, 2009.

7. Introduced at the beginning of the book.

Bibliography

Adams, Vincanne. 2016. *Metrics: What Counts in Global Health.* Durham, N.C.: Duke University Press.

Aguilar Ros, Alejandra. 2008. "Danzando a Apaxuki: La Semana Santa en San Andrés Cohamiata desde los mestizos visitantes." In *Raíces en movimiento: Prácticas religiosas tradicionales en contextos translocales,* ed. Kali Argyriadis, Renée de la Torre, Cristina Gutiérrez Zúñiga, and Alejandra Aguilar Ros, 159–192. Guadalajara, Mexico: El Colegio de Jalisco/CEMCA/CIESAS/IRD/ITESO.

Andersson, Ruben. 2014. *Illegality, Inc.: Clandestine Migration and the Business of Bordering Europe.* Berkeley: University of California Press.

Appadurai, Arjun. 1996. *Modernity at Large: Cultural Dimensions of Globalization.* Minneapolis: University of Minnesota Press.

Augé, Marc. 1995. *Non-Places: Introduction to an Anthropology of Supermodernity.* London: Verso.

Bashkow, Ira. 2006. *The Meaning of Whitemen: Race and Modernity in the Orokaiva Cultural World.* Chicago: University of Chicago Press.

Bauman, Richard, and Charles L. Briggs. 2003. *Voices of Modernity: Languages, Ideologies, and the Politics of Inequality.* Cambridge, UK: Cambridge University Press.

Bauman, Zygmunt. 1993. *Postmodern Ethics.* Oxford: Blackwell Publishers.

Berry, Nicole S. 2013 [2010]. *Unsafe Motherhood: Mayan Maternal Mortality and Subjectivity in Post-War Guatemala.* New York: Berghahn Books.

Biehl, João, and Torben Eskerod. 2007. *Will to Live: AIDS Therapies and the Politics of Survival.* Princeton: Princeton University Press.

Billig, Michael. 1999. "Commodity Fetishism and Repression: Reflections on Marx, Freud and the Psychology of Consumer Capitalism." *Theory and Psychology* 9, no. 3:313–329.

Bondi, Liz, Mick Smith, and Joyce Davidson. 2005. *Emotional Geographies.* Aldershot, U.K.: Ashgate.

Bourdieu, Pierre. 1984. *Distinction: A Social Critique of the Judgement of Taste.* Cambridge: Harvard University Press.

Brandes, Stanley H. 2006. *Skulls to the Living, Bread to the Dead: The Day of the Dead in Mexico and Beyond.* Malden, Mass.: Blackwell Publishers.

Breilh, Jaime. 1998. "La sociedad, el debate de la modernidad y la nueva epidemiología." *Revista Brasileira de Epidemiologia* 1, no. 3:207–233.

————. 2003. *Epidemiología crítica: Ciencia emancipadora e interculturalidad.* Buenos Aires, Argentina: Lugar Editorial.

————. 2008a. "Latin American Critical ('Social') Epidemiology: New Settings for an Old Dream." *International Journal of Epidemiology* 37:745–750.

————. 2008b. "Una perspectiva emancipadora de la investigación e incidencia basada en la determinación social de la salud." In *Taller Latinoamericano sobre Determinantes Sociales de la Salud: documento para la discusión,* 14–29. Mexico City: ALAMES.

Bridges, Khiara M. 2011. *Reproducing Race: An Ethnography of Pregnancy as a Site of Racialization.* Berkeley: University of California Press.

Briggs, Charles, and Clara Mantini-Briggs. 2003. *Stories in the Time of Cholera: Racial Profiling During a Medical Nightmare.* Berkeley: University of California Press.

Brooks, David. 2000. *Bobos in Paradise: The New Upper Class and How They Got There.* New York: Simon and Schuster Paperbacks.

Brubaker, Sarah J., and Heather E. Dillaway. 2009. "Medicalization, Natural Childbirth and Birthing Experiences." *Sociology Compass* 3, no. 1:31–48.

Buzinde, Christine N., and Careen Yarnal. 2012. "Therapeutic Landscapes and Postcolonial Theory: A Theoretical Approach to Medical Tourism." *Social Science and Medicine* 74, no. 5:783–787.

Cabral Soto, Javier, with Ángel Flores Alvarado, María del Carmen Baltazar Rivas, Fabiola García Vargas, María Concepción Orozco Meinecke, and Carlos Brambila Paz. 2000. *Salud sexual y reproductive en jovenes indígenas de las principales etnias de México.* Mexico City: Instituto Mexicano de Seguro Social.

Calhoun, Craig. 2010. "A Cosmopolitanism of Connections." In *The Cosmopolitan Idea,* ed. Hillary Ballon, Chap. 1. New York: New York University Abu Dhabi.

Carrillo, Ana. 2002. "Physicians 'Who Know' and Midwives 'Who Need to Learn.'" In *Midwives in Mexico: Continuity, Controversy and Change,* ed. Robbie Davis-Floyd, Marcia Good-Maust, and Miguel Gúemez Piñeda. Austin: University of Texas Press.

Champion, Françoise. 1995. "Persona religiosa fluctuante, electicismos y sincretismos." In *El hecho religioso. Enciclopedia de las grandes religiones,* ed. Jean Delumeau, 705–737. Madrid: Alianza Editorial.

Chow, Rey. 2002. *The Protestant Ethnic and the Spirit of Capitalism.* New York: Columbia University Press.

Clark, Kim A. 1998. "Race, 'Culture,' and Mestizaje: The Statistical Construction of the Ecuadorian Nation, 1930–1950." *Journal of Historical Sociology* 11, no. 2: 185–211.

Clifford, James. 2001. "Indigenous Articulations." *Contemporary Pacific* 13, no. 2: 468–490.

————. 2013. *Returns: Becoming Indigenous in the Twenty-First Century.* Boston: Harvard University Press.

Cohen, Cathy J. 1997. "Punks, Bulldaggers, and Welfare Queens: The Radical Potential of Queer Politics." *GLQ* 3:437–465.

Colen, Shellee. 1995. "Like a Mother to Them: Stratified Reproduction and West Indian Childcare Workers and Employers in New York." In *Conceiving the New World Order: The Global Politics of Reproduction*, ed. Faye D. Ginsburg and Rayna R. Rapp, 78–102. Berkeley: University of California Press.

Colloredo-Mansfeld, Rudi. 1998. "'Dirty Indians': Radical Indigenas and the Political Economy of Social Difference in Modern Ecuador." *Bulletin of Latin American Research* 17, no. 2:185–205.

Comaroff, John L., and Jean Comaroff. 2009. *Ethnicity, Inc.* Chicago: University of Chicago Press.

Crenshaw, Kimberlé Williams. 2014. "The Structural and Political Dimensions of Intersectional Oppression." In *Intersectionality: A Foundations and Frontiers Reader*, ed. Patrick R. Grzanka, 16–21. Boulder: Westview Press.

Crenshaw, Kimberlé, Neil Gotanda, Gary Peller, and Kendall Thomas, eds. 1995. *Critical Race Theory: The Key Writings That Formed the Movement*. New York: New Press.

Crossley, Michele L. 2007. "Childbirth, Complications, and the Illusion of 'Choice': A Case Study." *Feminism Psychology* 17, no. 4:543–563.

Currid-Halkett, Elizabeth. 2017. *The Sum of Small Things: A Theory of the Aspirational Class*. Princeton: Princeton University Press.

Davis-Floyd, Robbie. 2001. "La Partera Profesional: Articulating Identity and Cultural Space for a New Kind of Midwife in Mexico." *Medical Anthropology* 20, no. 2–3:185–243.

———. 2004 [1992]. *Birth as an American Rite of Passage*. Berkeley: University of California Press.

———. 2007. "Daughter of Time: The Postmodern Midwife." *Revista da Escola de Enfermagem da Universidade de São Paulo* 41, no. 4:705–710.

Davis-Floyd, Robbie, with Leslie Barclay, Jan Tritten, and Betty-Anne Daviss. 2009. *Birth Models That Work*. Berkeley: University of California Press.

De Genova, Nicholas. 2005. *Working the Boundaries: Race, Space, and "Illegality" in Mexican Chicago*. Durham, N.C.: Duke University Press.

De la Cadena, Marisol. 1995. "'Women Are More Indian': Ethnicity and Gender in a Community Near Cuzco." In *Ethnicity, Markets, and Migration in the Andes: At the Crossroads of History and Anthropology*, ed. Brooke Larson, Olivia Harris, and Enrique Tandeter, 329–348. Durham, N.C.: Duke University Press.

———. 2000. *Indigenous Mestizos: The Politics of Race and Culture in Cuzco, Peru, 1919–1991*. Durham, N.C.: Duke University Press.

———. 2015. *Earth Beings: Ecologies of Practice Across Andean Worlds*. Durham, N.C.: Duke University Press.

De la Peña, Francisco. 2002. *Los hijos del sexto sol*. Mexico City: Instituto Nacional de Antropología e Historía.

De la Torre, Renée, Cristina Gutiérrez Zúñiga, and Nahayeilli Juárez Huet. 2013. *Variaciones y apropaciones latinoamericanas del New Age*. Mexico City: Publicaciones de Casa Chata.

Deomampo, Daisy. 2013. "Gendered Geographies of Reproductive Tourism." *Gender and Society* 27, no. 4:514–537.

———. 2016. *Transnational Reproduction: Race, Kinship, and Commercial Surrogacy in India*. New York: New York University Press.

De Zavala, L. 1976. *Obras: Viaje a los Estados Unidos del Norte de America.* Mexico City: Editorial Porrura.

Douglass, Carrie B. 2005. *Barren States: The Population "Implosion" in Europe.* Oxford: Berg Publishers.

Dumit, Joseph. 2012. *Drugs for Life: How Pharmaceutical Companies Define Our Health.* Durham, N.C.: Duke University Press.

Ewig, Christina. 2010. *Second-Wave Neoliberalism: Gender, Race, and Health Sector Reform in Peru.* University Park: Pennsylvania State University Press.

Fadiman, Anne. 1997. *The Spirit Catches You and You Fall Down.* New York: Farrar, Straus and Giroux.

Fanon, Frantz. 2008 [1952]. *Black Skin, White Masks.* New York: Grove Press.

Fassin, Didier. 2010. "Inequality of Life." In *In the Name of Humanity,* ed. Miriam Ticktin and Ilana Feldman, 238–255. Durham, N.C.: Duke University Press.

———. 2012. *Humanitarian Reason: A Moral History of the Present.* Berkeley: University of California Press.

Fitzgerald, David. 2009. *A Nation of Emigrants: How Mexico Manages Its Migration.* Berkeley: University of California Press.

Folbre, Nancy. 2010. *Greed, Lust, and Gender: A History of Economic Ideas.* Oxford: Oxford University Press.

Foucault, Michel. 1973. *The Birth of the Clinic: An Archaeology of Medical Perception.* New York: Pantheon.

———. 1988. "Technologies of the Self." In *Technologies of the Self: A Seminar with Michel Foucault,* ed. L. H. Martin, 16–49. London: Tavistock.

———. 1990 [1978]. *The History of Sexuality.* United Kingdom: Vintage.

Fraser, Gertrude J. 1995. "Modern Bodies, Modern Minds: Midwifery and Reproductive Change in an African American Community." In *Conceiving the New World Order: The Global Politics of Reproduction,* ed. Faye D. Ginsburg and Rayna Rapp, 42–58. Berkeley: University of California Press.

Friedlander, Judith. 1975. *Being Indian in Hueyapan: A Study of Forced Identity in Contemporary Mexico.* New York: St. Martin's Press.

Galinier, Jacques. 2008. "Indio de estado versus indio nacional en la Mesoamérica moderna." In *Raíces en movimiento. Prácticas religiosas tradicionales en contextos translocales,* ed. Kali Argyriadis, Renée de la Torre, Cristina Gutiérrez Zúñiga, and Alejandra Aguilar Ros, 45–72. Guadalajara, Mexico: El Colegio de Jalisco/CEMCA/CIESAS/IRD/ITESO.

Gálvez, Alyshia. 2011. *Patient Citizens, Immigrant Mothers: Mexican Women, Public Prenatal Care, and the Birth-Weight Paradox.* New Brunswick, N.J.: Rutgers University Press.

García Canclini, Néstor. 2001 [1995]. *Consumidores y ciudadanos: Conflictos multiculturales de la globalización.* Mexico City: Grijalbo.

———. 2009 [1990]. *Culturas híbridas: Estrategias para entrar y salir de la modernidad.* Mexico City: Grijalbo.

Gibbon, Sahra, with Mónica Sans and Ricardo Ventura-Santos, eds. 2011. *Racial Identities, Genetic Ancestry, and Health in South America: Argentina, Brazil, Colombia, and Uruguay.* New York: Palgrave Macmillan.

Glenn, Evelyn Nakano. 2002. *Unequal Freedom: How Race and Gender Shaped American Citizenship and Labor.* Boston: Harvard University Press.

Goffman, Erving. 1959. *The Presentation of Self in Everyday Life.* Garden City, N.Y.: Doubleday.

Goldade, Kate. 2007. "Reproduccón transnacional: La salud reproductive, las limitaciones y las contradicciones para las migrantes laborales nicaragüenses en Costa Rica." In *El mito roto: Inmigración y emigración en Costa Rica,* ed. C. S. García, 233–260. San José: UCR Press.

Gordon, Deborah. 1988. "Tenacious Assumption in Western Medicine." In *Biomedicine Examined: Culture, Illness, and Healing,* ed. Margaret Lock and Deborah Gordon, 19–56. Dordrecht: Kluwer Academic.

Gramsci, Antonio. 1989 [1971]. *Selections from the Prison Notebooks.* New York: International Publishers.

Grzanka, Patrick R., ed. 2014. *Intersectionality: A Foundations and Frontiers Reader.* Boulder: Westview Press.

Gutmann, Matthew. 2002. *The Romance of Democracy: Compliant Defiance in Contemporary México.* Berkeley: University of California Press.

Hanegraaff, Wouter. 2001. "Prospects for the Globalization of New Age: Spiritual Imperialism Versus Cultural Diversity." In *New Age Religion and Globalization,* ed. M. Rothstein,15–30. Aarhus: Aarhus University Press.

Hannerz, Ulf. 1996. *Transnational Connections.* New York: Routledge.

Haraway, Donna. 1989. *Primate Visions: Gender, Race, and Nature in the World of Modern Science.* New York: Routledge.

———. 1991. *Simians, Cyborgs, and Women: The Reinvention of Nature.* New York: Routledge.

———. 2014. "Situated Knowledges and the Persistence of Vision." In *Intersectionality: A Foundations and Frontiers Reader,* ed. Patrick R. Grzanka, 41–47. Boulder: Westview Press.

Hartigan, John. 2010. *What Can You Say: America's National Conversation on Race.* Stanford: Stanford University Press.

Heelas, Paul. 1996. *The New Age Movement: The Celebration of the Self and the Sacralization of Modernity.* Oxford: Blackwell Publishers.

Hegel, G. W. F. 1977. *Phenomenology of Spirit.* Translated by A. V. Miller. Oxford: Oxford University Press.

Hendrickson, Carol Elaine. 1995. *Weaving Identities: Construction of Dress and Self in a Highland Guatemala Town.* Austin: University of Texas Press.

Hochschild, Arlie. 2012. *The Managed Heart: Commercialization of Human Feeling.* Berkeley: University of California Press.

Holmes, Seth. 2013. *Fresh Fruit, Broken Bodies: Migrant Farmworkers in the United States.* Berkeley: University of California Press.

Holston, James. 2009 [2007]. *Insurgent Citizenship: Disjunctions of Democracy and Modernity in Brazil.* Princeton: Princeton University Press.

Hordge-Freeman, Elizabeth. 2015. *The Color of Love: Racial Features, Stigma and Socialization in Black Brazilian Families.* Austin: University of Texas Press.

Horn, David. 1994. *Social Bodies: Science, Reproduction, and Italian Modernity.* Princeton: Princeton University Press.

Howes-Mischel, Rebecca. 2009. "Regimes of Responsible Pregnancy Management: Creating Reproductive Subjects in Oaxaca, Mexico." *Anthropology News* (February):16–17.

Ikemoto, Lisa. 2009. "Reproductive Tourism: Equality Concerns in the Global Market for Fertility Services." *Law and Inequality: A Journal of Theory and Practice* 27, no. 2:277–309.

Inhorn, Marcia Claire. 2015. *Cosmopolitan Conceptions: IVF Sojourns in Global Dubai.* Durham, N.C.: Duke University Press.

Jordanova, Ludmilla. 1995. "Interrogating the Concept of Reproduction in the Eighteenth Century." In *Conceiving the New World Order: The Global Politics of Reproduction,* ed. Faye D. Ginsburg and Rayna Rapp, 369–386. Berkeley: University of California Press.

Kapoor, Ilan. 2004. "Hyper-Self-Reflexive Development? Spivak on Representing the Third World 'Other.'" *Third World Quarterly* 4:627–647.

Katz Rothman, Barbara. 2007. "A Lifetime's Labor: Women and Power in the Birthplace." In *Laboring On: Birth in Transition in the United States,* ed. Wendy Simonds, Barbara Katz Rothman, and Bari Meltzer Norman, xi–xxii. New York: Routledge.

Kaufert, Patricia Leyland, and John D. O'Neil. 1995. "Irniktakpunga!: Sex Determination and the Inuit Struggle for Birthing Rights in Northern Canada." In *Conceiving the New World Order: The Global Politics of Reproduction,* ed. Faye D. Ginsburg and Rayna R. Rapp, 59–73.

Kearney, Michael. 1996. *Reconceptualizing the Peasantry: Anthropology in Global Perspective.* Boulder: Westview Press.

Kincaid, Jamaica. 2000. *A Small Place.* New York: Farrar, Straus and Giroux.

Lakoff, Andrew. 2005. *Pharmaceutical Reason: Knowledge and Value in Global Psychiatry.* Cambridge, U.K.: Cambridge University Press.

Lancaster, Roger N. 1992. *Life Is Hard: Machismo, Danger, and the Intimacy of Power in Nicaragua.* Berkeley: University of California Press.

Langer, Ana, and Kathryn Tolbert. 1996. *Mujer: Sexualidad y salud reproductive en México.* Mexico City: EDAMEX, S.A. de C.V., and The Population Council.

Lareau, Annette. 2003. *Unequal Childhoods: Class, Race, and Family Life.* Berkeley: University of California Press.

Larsen, Jonas, John Urry, and Kay Axhausen. 2008. *Mobilities, Networks, Geographies.* Hampshire, U.K. and Burlington, Vt.: Ashgate.

Larson, Brooke. 2004. *Trials of Nation Making: Liberalism, Race, and Ethnicity in the Andes, 1810–1910.* Cambridge, U.K.: Cambridge University Press.

Latour, Bruno. 1974. *Science in Action.* Cambridge: Harvard University Press.

Laurell, Asa Cristina. 1997. *La reforma contra la salud y la Seguridad Social: Una mirada crítica y una propuesta alternativa.* Mexico City: Friedrich Ebert Stiftung.

———. 2013. *Impacto del Seguro Popular en el sistema de salud.* Buenos Aires: CLACSO.

Laurell, Asa Cristina, and O. López Arellano. 1996. "Market Commodities and Poor Relief: The World Bank Proposal for Health." *International Journal of Health Services* 26, no. 1:1–18.

Leinaweaver, Jessaca B. 2008. *The Circulation of Children: Kinship, Adoption, and Morality in Andean Peru.* Durham, N.C.: Duke University Press.

Lomnitz Adler, C. 2005. *Death and the Idea of Mexico.* Brooklyn, N.Y.: Zone Press.

López Obrador, Andrés Manuel. 2010. *La mafia que se adueñó de México . . . y el 2012.* Mexico City: Grijalbo Mondadori S.A.

Low, Setha M., and Denise Lawrence-Zúñiga. 2002. *The Anthropology of Space and Place: A Reader.* Oxford: Blackwell Publishers.

MacDonald, Margaret. 2008. *At Work in the Field of Birth: Midwifery Narratives of Nature, Tradition, and Home.* Nashville, Tenn.: Vanderbilt University Press.

Maldonado, Andrea. 2010. "Culture: The New Drug of Choice in Mexico City." Ph.D. diss. research proposal, Department of Anthropology, Brown University.

Malkki, Liisa. 1996. "Speechless Emissaries: Refugee, Munitarianism, and Dehistoricization." *Cultural Anthropology* 11, no. 3:377–404.

———. 2010. "Children, Humanity, and the Infantilization of Peace." In *In the Name of Humanity,* ed. Miriam Ticktin and Ilana Feldman, 58–85. Durham, N.C.: Duke University Press.

Marcus, George E. 1995. "Ethnography in/of the World System: The Emergence of Multi-Sited Ethnography." *Annual Review of Anthropology* 24, no. 1:95–117.

Martin, Emily. 2001. *The Woman in the Body: A Cultural Analysis of Reproduction.* Boston: Beacon Press.

Melton, Gordon J., et al. 1990. *New Age Encyclopedia.* Detroit: Gale Research.

Mendoza González, Zuanilda. 2010–2011. "'Parir en la casa o en el hospital.' Saberes acerca del parto de mujeres triquis migrantes a la Ciudad de México." In *La Antropología médica en México (Rivista della Società Italiana di Antropologia Medica),* ed. Rosa María Osorio Carranza, 29–32, 59–81. Perugia, Italy: Fondazione Angelo Celli per una Cultura della Salute.

Menéndez, Eduardo L. 1983. *Hacia una práctica médica alternativa.* Hegemonía y autoatención (gestión) en salud, vol. 86: Cuadernos de la Casa Chata. Mexico City: Centro de Investigaciónes y Estudios Superiores en Antropología Social.

———. 1996. *De algunos alcoholismos y algunos saberes: Atención primaria y proceso de alcoholización.* Mexico City: CIESAS.

———. 2009. *De sujetos, saberes y estructuras: Introducción al enfoque relacional en el estudio de la salud colectiva.* Buenos Aires: Lugar Editorial.

———. 2010 [2002]. *La parte negada de la cultura: Relativismo, diferencias y racismo.* Argentina: Prohistoria Ediciones.

Merleau-Ponty, Maurice. 1996. *Phenomenology of Perception.* New York: Routledge.

Mignolo, Walter D. 2000. *Local Histories/Global Designs: Coloniality, Subaltern Knowledges, and Border Thinking.* Princeton: Princeton University Press.

Molina, Natalia. 2006. *Fit to Be Citizens? Public Health and Race in Los Angeles, 1879–1939.* Berkeley: University of California Press.

———. 2013. *How Race Is Made in America: Immigration, Citizenship, and the Historical Power of Racial Scripts.* Berkeley: University of California Press.

Molinié, Antoinette. 2013. "La invención del new age andino." In *Variaciones y apropaciones latinoamericanas del New Age,* ed. Renée de la Torre, Cristina Gutiérrez Zúñiga, and Nahayeilli Juárez Huet, 285–308. Mexico City: Publicaciones de Casa Chata.

Molyneux, Maxine. 2006. "Mothers at the Service of the New Poverty Agenda: Progresa/Oportunidades, Mexico's Conditional Transfer Programme." *Social Policy and Administration* 40, no. 4:425–449.

Montoya, Michael. 2011. *Marking the Mexican Diabetic: Race, Science, and the Genetics of Inequality.* Berkeley: University of California Press.

Moraga, Cherrie L. 1983. *Loving in the War Years: Lo que nunca pasó por sus labios.* Boston: South End.

Morgan, Lynn, and Elizabeth F. S. Roberts. 2012. "Reproductive Governance in Latin America." *Anthropology and Medicine* 19, no. 2:241–254.

Munn, Nancy. 1996. "Excluded Spaces: The Figure in the Australian Aboriginal Landscape." *Critical Inquiry* 22:446–465.

Nader, Laura. 1972. "Up the Anthropologist: Perspectives Gained from Studying Up." In *Reinventing Anthropology,* ed. Dell H. Hymes, 284–311. New York: Pantheon Books.

Nazar-Beutelspacher, Austreberta, Benito Salvatierra Izaba, and Emma Zapata Martelo. 2007. "Atención del parto, migración rural-urbana y políticas públicas de salud reproductive en población indígena de Chiapas." *Ra Ximhai* 3, no. 3: 763–779.

Nestel, Sheryl. 2006. *Obstructed Labour: Race and Gender in the Re-Emergence of Midwifery.* Vancouver: University of British Columbia Press.

Neufeld, L. M. 2012. "The Oportunidades Program and Child Growth: Mexico Perspectives." In *Handbook of Growth and Growth Monitoring in Health and Disease,* ed. V. R. Preedy, 1659–1671. New York: Springer.

Nouzeilles, Gabriela. 2003. "Hysteria in Turn-of-the-Century Buenos Aires." In *Disease in the History of Modern Latin America: From Malaria to AIDS,* 51–75. Durham, N.C.: Duke University Press.

Ong, Aihwa. 1999. *Flexible Citizenship: The Cultural Logics of Transnationality.* Durham, N.C.: Duke University Press.

———. 2003. *Buddha Is Hiding: Refugees, Citizenship, the New America.* Berkeley: University of California Press.

———. 2006. *Neoliberalism as Exception: Mutations of Citizenship and Sovereignty.* Durham, N.C.: Duke University Press.

Orlove, Benjamin. 1998. "Down to Earth: Race and Substance in the Andes." *Bulletin of Latin American Research* 17, no. 2:207–222.

Ortner, Sherry. 1972. "Is Female to Male as Nature Is to Culture?" *Feminist Studies* 1, no. 2:5–31.

Pashigian, Melissa. 2009. "Inappropriate Relations: The Ban on Surrogacy with In Vitro Fertilization and the Limits of State Renovation in Contemporary Vietnam." In *Assisting Reproduction, Testing Genes: Global Encounters with New Biotechnologies,* ed. D. Birenbaum-Carmeli and M. C. Inhorn, 164–188. New York: Berghahn Books.

Petryna, Adriana. 2002. *Life Exposed: Biological Citizens After Chernobyl.* Princeton: Princeton University Press.

———. 2009. *When Experiments Travel: Clinical Trials and the Global Search for Human Subjects.* Princeton: Princeton University Press.

Pigg, Stacy Leigh. 1997. "Finding, Knowing, Naming, and Training 'Traditional Birth Attendants' in Nepal." In *Childbirth and Authoritative Knowledge: Cross-Cultural Perspectives,* ed. Robbie Davis-Floyd and Carolyn F. Sargent, 233–262. Berkeley: University of California Press.

———. 2001. "Languages of Sex and AIDS in Nepal: Notes on the Social Production of Commensurability." *Cultural Anthropology* 16, no. 4:481–541.

Pitt-Rivers, Julian. 1973. "Race in Latin America: The Concept of Raza." *Archives Européennes de Sociologie* 14, no. 1:3–31.

Rabinow, Paul. 1996. *Essays on the Anthropology of Reason*. Princeton: Princeton University Press.

Rapp, Rayna. 2000. *Testing Women, Testing the Fetus: The Social Impact of Amniocentesis in America*. New York: Routledge.

Reardon, Jenny. 2004. *Race to the Finish: Identity and Governance in an Age of Genomics*. Princeton: Princeton University Press.

Richardson, Miles. 1982. "Being-in-the-Plaza Versus Being-in-the-Market: Material Culture and the Construction of Social Reality." *American Ethnologist* 9:421–436.

Ritzer, George. 2001. *Explorations in the Sociology of Consumption: Fast Food, Credit Cards, and Casinos*. London: Sage Publications.

Roberts, Dorothy. 1997. *Killing the Black Body: Race, Reproduction, and the Meaning of Liberty*. New York: Vintage Books.

Roberts, Elizabeth F. S. 2006. "God's Laboratory: Religious Rationalities and Modernity in Ecuadorian In Vitro Fertilization." *Cultural Medicine and Psychiatry* 30:507–536.

———. 2012a. *God's Laboratory: Assisted Reproduction in the Andes*. Berkeley: University of California, Press.

———. 2012b. "Scars of Nation: Surgical Penetration and the State in Ecuador" *Journal of Latin American and Caribbean Anthropology* 17, no. 2:215–237.

———. 2015. "Reproduction and Cultural Anthropology." In *International Encyclopedia of the Social and Behavioral Sciences*, ed. James D. Wright, 2nd ed., vol. 20, 450–456. Oxford: Elsevier.

Roberts, Elizabeth F. S., and Nancy Scheper-Hughes. 2011. "Introduction to Medical Migrations." *Body and Society* 17, no. 2–3:1–30. London: Sage Publications.

Rosaldo, Renato. 1989. "Imperialist Nostalgia." In "Memory and Counter-Memory," special issue, *Representations* 26:107–122.

Rose, Nikolas, and Carlos Novas. 2008 [2005]. "Biological Citizenship." In *Global Assemblages: Technology, Politics, and Ethics as Anthropological Problems*, ed. Aihwa Ong and Stephen J. Collier, 439–463. Malden, Mass.: Blackwell Publishing.

Rotman Zelizer, Viviana A. 1994. *Pricing the Priceless Child: The Changing Social Value of Children*. Princeton: Princeton University Press.

Sarrazin, Jean-Paul. 2008. "El Chamanismo es un camino. Las culturas indígenas como Fuentes de sabiduría spiritual en Bogotá." In *Raíces en movimiento. Prácticas religiosas tradicionales en contextos translocales*, ed. Kali Argyriadis, Renée de la Torre, Cristina Gutiérrez Zúñiga, and Alejandra Aguilar Ros, 329–362. Guadalajara, Mexico: El Colegio de Jalisco/CEMCA/CIESAS/IRD/ITESO.

Scheper-Hughes, Nancy. 2000. "The Global Traffic in Human Organs." *Current Anthropology* 41, no. 2:191–224. Scheper-Hughes, Nancy, and Loïc Wacquant. 2006. *Commodifying Bodies*. London: Sage.

Scheper-Hughes, Nancy, and Margaret Lock. 1987. "The Mindful Body: A Prolegomenon to Future Work in Medical Anthropology." *Medical Anthropology Quarterly* 1, no. 1:6–41.

Sesia, Paola M. 2007. "Reproductive Health and Reproductive Rights After the Cairo Consensus: Accomplishments and Shortcomings in the Establishment of Innovative Public Policies in Oaxaca." *Sexuality Research and Social Policy, Journal of N.S.R.C.* 4, no. 3:34–49.

Sharpe, Jenny. 2003. "A Conversation with Gayatri Chakravorty Spivak: Politics and the Imagination." *Journal of Women in Culture and Society* 28, no. 2:609–624.

Simonds, Wendy. 2007. "Origin Stories." In *Laboring On: Birth in Transition in the United States,* ed. Wendy Simonds, Barbara Katz Rothman, and Bari Meltzer Norman, xxiii–xlv. New York: Routledge.

Smith, Carol A. 1996. "Myths, Intellectuals, and Race/Class/Gender Distinctions in the Formation of Latin American Nations." *Journal of Latin American Anthropology* 2, no. 1:148–169.

Smith-Oka, Vania. 2013. *Shaping the Motherhood of Indigenous Mexico.* Nashville, Tenn.: Vanderbilt University Press.

Sofia, Zoë. 1984. "Exterminating Fetuses: Abortion, Disbarment, and the Sexo-Semiotics of Extra-Terrestrialism." *Diacritics* 14, no. 2:47–59.

Spivak, Gayatri Chakravorty. 1988a. "Can the Subaltern Speak?" In *Marxism and Interpretation of Culture,* ed. Cary Nelson and Lawrence Grossberg, 271–313. Chicago: University of Illinois Press.

———. 1988b. *In Other Worlds: Essays in Cultural Politics.* New York: Routledge.

———. 1999. *A Critique of Postcolonial Reason: Toward a Critique of the Vanishing Present.* Cambridge: Harvard University Press.

Spivak, Gayatri, and Sarah Harasym. 1990. *The Post-Colonial Critic: Interviews, Strategies, Dialogues.* New York: Routledge.

Stepan, Nancy. 1991. *The Hour of Eugenics: Race, Gender, and Nation in Latin America.* Ithaca: Cornell University Press.

Stoller, Paul. 1997. *Sensuous Scholarship.* Philadelphia: University of Pennsylvania Press.

Stutzman, Ronald. 1981. "El Mestizaje: An All-Inclusive Ideology." In *Cultural Transformations and Ethnicity in Modern Ecuador,* ed. N. Whitten, 45–94. Urbana: University of Illinois.

Suárez-Orozco, M., and Mariela Paéz. 2009. *Latinos: Remaking America.* Berkeley: University of California Press.

Tallbear, Kim. 2013. *Native American DNA: Tribal Belonging and the False Promise of Genetic Science.* Minneapolis: University of Minnesota Press.

Thompson, Charis. 2005. *Making Parents: The Ontological Choreography of Reproductive Technologies.* Cambridge: MIT Press.

———. 2011. "Medical Migrations Afterword: Science as a Vacation?" *Body and Society* 17, no. 2–3:205–213.

———. 2012. "Three Times a Woman: A Gendered Economy of Stem Cell Innovation." UCLA Center for the Study of Women blog, https://escholarship.org/uc/item/7oh7k694.

Tsing, Anna Lowenhaupt. 2000. "The Global Situation." *Cultural Anthropology* 15, no. 3:327–370.

———. 2005. *Friction: An Ethnography of Global Connection.* Princeton: Princeton University Press.

———. 2015. *The Mushroom at the End of the World: On the Possibility of Life in Capitalist Ruins.* Princeton: Princeton University Press.

Tuan, Yi-Fu. 2001. *Space and Place: The Perspective of Experience.* Minneapolis: University of Minnesota Press.

Unnithan-Kumar, Maya. 2004. *Reproductive Agency, Medicine and the State: Cultural Transformations in Childbearing.* New York: Berghahn Books.

Urry, John. 2007. *Mobilities*. Cambridge, U.K.: Polity Press.

Van Hollen, Cecilia. 2003. *Birth on the Threshold: Childbirth and Modernity in South India*. Berkeley: University of California Press.

Van Loon, Joost. 2005. "Epidemic Space." *Critical Public Health* 15, no. 1:39–52.

Veblen, Thorstein. 1899. *The Theory of the Leisure Class: An Economic Study in the Evolution of Institutions*. Basingstoke, U.K.: Macmillan. Available at moglen. law.columbia.edu/LCS/theoryleisureclass.pdf.

————. 2006 [1902]. *Conspicuous Consumption*. New York: Penguin.

Villet, Charles. 2011. "Hegel and Fanon on the Question of Mutual Recognition: A Comparative Analysis." *Journal of Pan African Studies* 4, no. 7:39–51.

Wacquant, Loïc. 2005. "Carnal Connections: On Embodiment, Apprenticeship, and Membership." *Qualitative Sociology* 28, no. 4:445–474.

Wade, Peter. 1993. "Race, Nature and Culture." *Man* 28, no. 1:17–34.

Waitzkin, Howard. 2011. *Medicine and Public Health at the End of Empire*. Boulder: Paradigm Publishers.

Waitzkin, Howard, and Celia Iriart. 2000. "How the United States Exports Managed Care to Third-World Countries." *Monthly Review* 52, no. 1:21–35.

Weismantel, Mary. 2001. *Cholas and Pishtacos: Stories of Race and Sex in the Andes*. Chicago: Chicago University Press.

Wilson, Ara. 2004. *The Intimate Economies of Bangkok: Tomboys, Tycoons, and Avon Ladies in the Global City*. Berkeley: University of California Press.

Index